Research Method in the Postmodern

QUALITATIVE STUDIES SERIES

General Editors: Professor Ivor F. Goodson, Warner Graduate School, University of Rochester, USA and Centre for Applied Research in Education, University of East Anglia, Norwich, UK and Professor James J. Sheurich, Department of Educational Administration, University of Texas at Austin, Austin, TX 78712, USA.

QUALITATIVE STUDIES SERIES: 3

Research Method in the Postmodern

James Joseph Scheurich

 The Falmer Press

(A member of the Taylor & Francis Group)
London • Washington, DC

UK   The Falmer Press, 1 Gunpowder Square, London, EC4A 3DE
USA   The Falmer Press, Taylor & Francis Inc., 1900 Frost Road, Suite 101,
        Bristol, PA 19007

First published in 1997

**A catalogue record for this book is available from the
British Library**

**Library of Congress Cataloging-in-Publication Data are
available on request**

ISBN 0 7507 0709 7 cased
ISBN 0 7507 0645 7 paper

Jacket design by Caroline Archer

Typeset in 10/12 pt Times by
Graphicraft Typesetters Ltd., Hong Kong

*Printed in Great Britain by Biddles Ltd., Guildford and King's Lynn
on paper which has a specified pH value on final paper
manufacture of not less than 7.5 and is therefore 'acid free'.*

Contents

Preface

The isolation of different points of emergence does not conform to the successive configurations of an identical meaning; rather, they result from substitutions, displacements, disguised conquests, and systematic reversals. If interpretation were the slow exposure of the meaning hidden in an origin, then only metaphysics could interpret the development of humanity. But if interpretation is the violent and surreptitious appropriation of a system of rules, which in itself has no essential meaning, in order to impose a direction, to bend it to a new will, to force its participation in a new game, and to subject it to secondary rules, then the development of humanity is a series of interpretations. (FOUCAULT, M. (1977) 'Nietzsche, genealogy, history' in *Language, Counter-Memory, Practice* [D.F. Bouchard, trans.], Ithaca, NY, Cornell University Press, pp. 151–2.)

Acknowledgments

I want to acknowledge the loved ones I live with — Patti, Corinna, Jasper, Roo, Sid. I want to also acknowledge the loved ones I do not live with — Bea and Jim, Tonya, Noah, Nyja, Kelsy, Toshi, Raven, Patti and Mary, Melanie and her large and small puppies, Twizzle, and Begwhin. I also want to acknowledge all my friends and colleagues — Larry, Pedro, Claudia, Kofi, Lonnie, Sarah, Charol, Julie, Jay, both Pats, Diane, Gary, Juanita, Michelle, Deborah, Gerardo, Lynn, Annie, Bob, Lisa, Doug, Anne, O.L., and others I am sure I have not remembered when I was composing this. The contributions of everyone are beyond number and definition. However, most fundamentally, as will hopefully be understood by the end of this book, it is the archaeology that writes all of us and writes this book. Somewhat like the unsigned, untitled wall drawings of the ancients or the old oral stories handed down from generation to generation, no autonomous, individual singularity wrote this book, and no other autonomous, individual singularities assisted.

Both the author and publisher would like to thank the following

Chapter 1 'Educational Reforms Can Reproduce Societal Inequalities: A Case Study', was first published in *Educational Administration Quarterly*, **27**, 3, 1991, pp. 297–320. Reprinted by permission of Stage Publications Inc.

Chapter 2 'Social Relativism: (Not Quite) a Postmodernist Epistemology', was first published in Maxcy, S. (Ed) *Postmodern School Leadership: Meeting the Crises in Educational Administration*, pp. 17–46, Praeger, an imprint of Greenwood Publishing Group Inc., Westport, CT. Reprinted with permission.

Chapter 3 'Interviewing', appeared in *International Journal of Qualitative Studies in Education*, **8**, 3, pp. 239–52, 1995.

Chapter 4 'Validity', appeared in *International Journal of Qualitative Studies in Education*, **9**, 1, pp. 49–60, 1996.

Chapter 5 'Policy Archaeology', appeared in *Journal of Education Policy*, **9**, 4, pp. 297–316, 1994.

Chapter 6 'Toward a White Discourse on White Racism', was first published in *Educational Researcher*, **22**, 8, pp. 5–19, 1993. Copyright (1993) by the American Educational Research Association. Reproduced by permission of the publisher.

Chapter 7 'Coloring Epistemologies: Are our Research Epistemologies Racially Based?', *Educational Researcher*, **27**, 4, 1997. Copyright (1993) by the American Educational Research Association. Reproduced by permission of the publisher.

Introduction

An 'introduction' typically offers an overview narrative of a work and directs the reader's attention to the key issues, creating a semblance of a coherence that progresses through a story or argument. I cannot, however, provide any submission of this sort. I can offer, instead, a simulacral story, that is, a story of something that never existed. I can also offer several arguments, perhaps even a family resemblance of arguments, though some of them are unruly and contradict each other. I could imply, even subtly, that I have gained, risen, improved, grown theoretically and personally. I could suggest that I have made sharp, carefully worded, clear arguments, never violating their logical trajectories. However, none of these are suitable. Instead, I have wavered and mis-stepped; I have gone backward after I have gone forward; I have drifted sideways along a new imaginary, forgetting from where I had once thought I had started. I have fabricated personae and unities, and I have sometimes thought I knew something of which I have written. However, *caveat emptor*, all that follows is never that which it is constructed to appear, an apt description, in my opinion, of all writing.

None of these refusals, though, are meant to suggest I have no ethical, political, or spiritual commitments, as is sometimes imputed to postmodernists. Indeed, I would say that I have strong ethical, political, and spiritual commitments and that I primarily try to write out of such commitments, even though I also assume that there is much in my writing that 'I' do not control (perhaps very little or none at all), that I contradict myself or that myself is contradicted, that that which I oppose is as much inside as outside, and that my commitments themselves are more constituted by my time and place than by anything called personal choices. Nonetheless, given these, what is most disturbing to me — and it is a theme that runs throughout this book — is not just the pervasive assumption, implicit more than explicit, that the West knows best or that the West is the best, but that the Western modernist imperium is constituting our common, everyday assumptions about researchers, research, reality, epistemology, methodology, etc. What I am suggesting here is that even though we researchers think or assume we are doing good works or creating useful knowledge or helping people or critiquing the status quo or opposing injustice, we are unknowingly enacting or being enacted by 'deep' civilizational or cultural biases, biases that are damaging to other cultures and to other people who are unable to make us hear them because they do not 'speak' in our cultural 'languages'.

For example, in chapter 6 I will argue that validity, whether defined as truth or as trustworthiness, whether defined by interpretivists or by criticalists, is an enactment of a modernist bias, an exclusionary, damaging bias. In chapter 7 I will argue that our range of research epistemologies, from positivism and interpretivism to criticalism and postmodernism, are racially/culturally biased, even though researchers may have not considered this possibility. Similarly, in the final chapter I will argue that the mind frame that researchers most commonly assume and, thus, take for granted is deeply biased in ways we do not typically question, resulting in an imperial arrogance, even if unintended. It is, then, this unintended, largely consciously unknown arrogance (particularly as it affects the intersecting formations of race, gender, class, sexual orientation, and disability) within and against which I try to offer my own persistent engagement.

Why, though, do I call this latter engagement 'postmodernism?' I call it this because, in my view, postmodernism is Western civilization's best attempt to date to critique its own most fundamental assumptions, particularly those assumptions that constitute reality, subjectivity, research, and knowledge. I do not call my engagement 'poststructuralism', even though this latter label is probably more appropriate and even though I draw extensively on the French poststructuralists, because few researchers in education or the social sciences, especially in the US, have much familiarity with this term.[1] Moreover, though I have been considerably influenced by the French poststructuralists in general and Foucault in particular, I have no interest in any pretension that my (mis)reading or (mis)use of their works is one of which they would approve.

The final issue I want to make in this introduction to the introduction is that I see the university as a social space in which difficult issues — in a political or a philosophical sense — can be raised. For instance, some political perspectives, like feminism or critical theory, can easily get one fired, while there is, at least, some support for a consideration of these perspectives in some departments in some universities. Many of my colleagues understand this, but some seem not to understand that the university is also a space in which to raise difficult philosophical issues. For example, one complaint I frequently hear or read is that postmodernism is not directly useful in assisting schools or that it is difficult to access (Lather, 1986) so we ought not to focus on it or do it. While I would disagree, for instance, that it is not useful or that it is more difficult to access than highly technical discussions of statistical issues[2], I am willing to grant, for the moment, that it is often not as easy to see its usefulness as it is to see the usefulness, say, of Garcia's (1986) research on the education of bilingual children or Ladson-Billings' (1994) research on successful teachers of African-American children. However, again, I would argue that the university, including within education, is a space in which difficult philosophical issues need to be raised, issues which may not bear any immediate applications for schooling, much like basic research may not bear any immediate applied products, but these issues may challenge the most basic assumptions upon which our thought and practice is based, including those about research itself. And it is to these assumptions about research that this book is addressed.

(Mis)Reading this Book

This book is decidedly not a survey of postmodernist research methods nor a survey of research methods in the postmodernist era. It is, instead, a raggedy pastiche of essays whose orientation is postmodernist. Accordingly, while I know each reader will (mis)appropriate or (mis)read these essays in her or his own way, I want to suggest some possible (mis)readings. *One way* this book might be read is to read the chapters/essays sequentially as an intellectual or philosophical journey that starts with critical theory and then quickly proceeds into postmodernism. However, beware; while this sort of narrative is seductive to our modernist cultural inclinations, it is a simulacra, an imitation of something that never existed. That is, to read the chapters linearly as a philosophical journey is to construct a narrative that never really existed. More simply, it did not happen that way. To think that the journey happened in some way that fits a particular narrative structure that is endemic to modernism itself is to overlay a pre-set structure or pattern onto that which fits and that which does not, to commit inclusions and exclusions, though the 'control' or 'order' of the structure is ever, to some degree, incomplete, contradictory, heterological, and productive of its own subversions.

Nonetheless, this journey 'story' is there if that is what is desired. It starts with a case study, done several years ago from a critical theory perspective (which is the frame within which my professorial career started), on the effort of a school district to develop major reforms that are based on the input of 'all' stakeholders, including low SES patrons and patrons of color. The resulting decisions, contrary to the espoused efforts at inclusion, reproduce racial and class inequalities. The methodology of the study is qualitative with the data drawn from interviewing a purposive range of participants involved in the reform effort. The underlying and unexamined assumptions, though, are realist ones. For example, I assumed that I was an autonomous agent or researcher who could reasonably see and understand what was really occurring in this district's reform effort. In fact, I thought I, the critical researcher hero, was uncovering the really real that was being ignored or, worse, hidden by the 'bad guys'. What I did not understand, at the time, was that my 'I', the research, the results, the district's reform effort, and the bad guys were all being constituted by the same set of 'deep' modernist assumptions. It is not that I am now disputing the racism and classism in the district's reform effort; it is the set of assumptions that I used throughout this study that I am questioning. However, this chapter is a good example of a typical qualitative study and a good example of what I think is inadequate in research and what this book is meant to argue against.

The journey continues with the second chapter, a transitional piece in the sense that it is an incomplete effort to shift from a realist position to a postrealist one, while maintaining a criticalist orientation. In this chapter I am trying to develop an epistemology I called at the time 'social relativism', but I am mainly arguing with various neo-realist and postfoundational positions that I considered inadequate efforts to address questions and issues raised by criticalist-oriented postmodernists. However, my students often like this piece as a bridge for beginning to understand postmodernism.

In the third chapter, my shift to a postmodernist perspective has been made. This chapter is 'A postmodernist critique of research interviewing', and in it I critique the 'new' (at the time) 'postpositivist'[3] reconceptualizations of interviewing as being but another version of modernism. I do this principally through a critique of Mishler's *Research Interviewing: Context and Narrative* (1986), which I think is the best interpretivist work on interviewing. I try to show that both the typical conceptions of interviewing and the supposedly more radical ones are both still safely moored in modernist assumptions. I also show how the criticalist view of the power relationship between the interviewer and interviewee is similarly moored. Throughout this chapter, my basic points are that language itself is deeply indeterminant, that the subjectivity of the interviewer and interviewee is deeply indeterminate, that the interaction between the two is indeterminate, and that the power between the two cannot be simplistically reduced to the dominance of the interviewer and the compliance or resistance of the interviewee. However, there are at least two assumptions I would no longer agree with: first, as indeterminant and unconsciously driven as subjectivity is portrayed here, I have still left it basically in place as a singularity. In addition, I have implied that outside the imposed order lies a wild, disobedient disorder or a kind of rebellious, froward freedom (a common position among many postmodernists, though I would say it is get another modernist leftover). Neither of these would I now support.

The fourth chapter addresses validity, the positivist ghost that continues to haunt virtually all discussions of research, whether conventional or radical. In this chapter, entitled 'The masks of validity: A deconstructive investigation', I try to show that all of the 'new', supposedly radical, types of validity, from Lincoln and Guba's (1985) and Mishler's (1986) interpretivist or constructivist types of validity to Lather's (1986) criticalist-based catalytic validity, are, again, reproductions of modernism. I end with a discussion of some alternative imaginaries of validity, though I sceptically follow with: 'I am troubled by the anonymous imperial violence that slips quietly and invisibly into our (my) best intentions and practices, and even, into our (my) tranformational yearnings. I fear our restless civilizational immodesty; I fear the arrogance we enact "unknowingly"' — that theme I mentioned earlier that pervades much of my work. However, I, again, assume, subtextually, as frequently did Foucault, that there is some kind of wild Other space that has neither been incorporated into the Same nor is a function of the latter. Today, I would say, spinning off of Bhabha (1985), that both the Same and the Other, the included and the excluded, are archaeologically constituted, and that there are no archaeology-free badlands (a view which will be discussed in the final chapter).

In the fifth chapter, entitled 'Policy archaeology: A new policy studies methodology', I lay out what I think a postmodernist approach to policy research might look like. Drawing extensively on Foucault's early, archaeological work (1972, 1973, 1979 and 1988) and converting it to my own intentions and desires, I try to show how one might use a poststructuralist perspective to think through to a research method. However, Yvonna Lincoln, in a personal conversation, has told me that this chapter is basically a constructivist one. I do not disagree with her; poststructuralism is thoroughly constructivist. However, it is a constructivism that explicitly and radically engages the foundational assumptions of modernity, which most constructivism does not do. Furthermore, this chapter represents a significant shift for me; I begin to work extensively with my reconstruction of Foucault's notion of archaeology, a reconstruction that gets extended in the final chapter.

The sixth and seventh chapters are examples of the application of archaeology to racial issues. The sixth chapter, 'Toward a white discourse on white racism', though, is primarily useful as an early effort in this regard. I did not ostensibly write this one out of an archaeological perspective, but in retrospect I can 'see' some of the outlines of my later archaeological orientation. For example, in this chapter it is evident that I am strongly suggesting that a white person is significantly constituted by her/his racial positionality and that there is no real escape, critical or otherwise, from that positionality (see chapter 8 for more on this). I argue that while this is not hopeless, there is also no racism-free or utopian space available, a contention that riled several white professors who seemed to feel that their anti-racism and their anti-racist activism allowed them to claim a different positionality. Nonetheless, this chapter is a still a far cry from truly being archaeological, a limitation that the following chapter does not have.

The seventh chapter, 'Coloring epistemology: Are our research epistemologies racially biased?', is thoroughly archaeological; however, since it is written to communicate to a broader audience, the archaeological perspective is more implicit than explicit. What I am arguing here is that racism in research (and by strong implication racism in general) is not most fundamentally individual, institutional, or societal, but basically is what I label civilizational (the latter is a stand-in term for 'archaeological'). White supremacy is built in or embedded at the deepest level of Western modernism, at the deepest levels of our primary assumptions, including those from which the very idea of research is derived; white supremacy is interlaced within the rules, the assumptions, that constitute all of our most fundamental categories — the individual, truth, knowledge, research, reality, reason, etc. Consequently, the sixth and seventh chapters can be seen, respectively, as an early exploration of an archaeological view and then a later, more fully developed one. However, neither of these chapters nor the fifth one extends an archaeological view as far as I do in the final chapter.

The eighth and final chapter, then, is an initial, somewhat unpolished exploration of a postrealist position that radically challenges modernist subjectivity, reason, and 'the real'. In this chapter, I offer an archaeological perspective that has no use for individual subjectivity, that characterizes reason as a historicized archaeological production, and that argues that the real is just another category in the archaeological array, though certainly a 'deep' and important one. I start with a discussion of realism, which I think is an apt label for the philosophical frame that underlies most research, from positivist and interpretivist research to constructivist and criticalist research. However, I mostly focus on pushing my view of archaeology in 'Policy archaeology' toward a more radical reconstruction of subjectivity, reason, and the real. In addition, I try to connect all of this to research.

A second way to read this book, if you ignore the first main chapter and its use of critical theory, is simply as a collection of postmodernist essays on research method. Used in this way, there are chapters on interviewing, the main method used in qualitative research; on validity, the recurrent issue for all research perspectives; on 'archaeology' (three chapters — one of which is my attempt to describe a poststructuralist research method and the other two being applications of this latter methodology); and on my current archaeological thinking about research (the final chapter).

A third way is in contradiction to the first. This way of reading is in the temporal order they were written, and it shows that progress along some imagined logical or historical trajectory is simulacral. Chapter 1 was the first written and was written a few years before the others. Chapter 3 on interviewing was the second written. Chapters 4 and 6, in that order, were written very shortly after that. Next, I wrote chapter 2, followed by chapter 5 on policy archaeology. Finally, chapter 7 was the seventh written and chapter 8 the eighth.

Throughout the book, my central issue is that we as researchers operate from within certain philosophical or civilizational assumptions that structure how we think, what we think research is and what researchers are, how we do research, what we think the value or use of research is, and what we think the outcome of research is. In fact, in the last decade or so the rising tide of paradigm or epistemology discussions have, to some extent, been arguments about these issues. As a result of these discussions, we typically think, in the middle of the 1990s, that we now live within a multi-paradigm research world filled with all kinds of different philosophical orientations. I would like to suggest, however, that with all of the 'new' positions that have emerged and the old ones that have reemerged within social science research, we are still holding onto some primary assumptions, including a relatively autonomous individual subjectivity that thinks, decides, does, turns the wheel of life. In contrast, I suggest this latter assumption is an imperial one, congruent with the subjectivity of elite powerbrokers who expect to manage large populations and the nature of life itself. Alternatively, in these chapters I will explore a non-subject centered view, a view that I suggest may be more inciteful of a culture that sees itself as interwoven, interdependent, historicized, modest, and respectful of the full circle of all that is.

Notes

1 I have little interest in all of the debates about the possible differences among postmodernism, postmodernity, and poststructuralism (see, for example, Peters, 1996, for one such discussion of these debates).

2 At a Division D gathering that I attended at the 1996 American Educational Research Association annual meeting, I heard a presentation on a highly technical statistical issue. While I am sufficiently conversant in statistics to teach doctoral courses in it, and have done so, within five minutes I could not understand anything that the presenter was saying. However, I have never heard colleagues complain about the technical language of statistics being so inaccessible to the lay public that we ought to drop it, though I frequently have heard this kind of collegial criticism of postmodernist work. It is an interesting question, then, as to why some complex writing is complained about, while other equally complex writing is not.

3 I would agree with Lincoln and Guba (1985) that the 'postpositivist' label has been appropriated by those, like Campbell, who now advocate a kind of neorealism or neopositivism that they call 'postpositivist'. What we called postpositivist five or ten years ago, I would now call 'interpretivist' or 'constructivist', much as Schwandt (1994) does.

References

BHABHA, H.K. (1985) 'Signs taken for wonders: Questions of ambivalence and authority under a tree outside Delhi, May 1817', *Critical Inquiry*, **12**, pp. 144–65.

FOUCAULT, M. (1972) *The Archaeology of Knowledge and the Discourse on Language*, New York, Pantheon.

FOUCAULT, M. (1973) *The Order of Things: An Archaeology of the Human Sciences*, New York, Vintage.

FOUCAULT, M. (1979) *Discipline and Punish: The Birth of the Prison*, New York, Vintage.

FOUCAULT, M. (1988) *Madness and Civilization: A History of Insanity in the Age of Reason*, New York, Vintage.

GARCIA, E. (1986) 'Bilingual development and the education of bilingual children during early childhood', *American Journal of Education*, **95**, pp. 96–121.

LADSON-BILLINGS, G. (1994) *The Dreamkeepers: Successful Teachers of African American Children*, San Francisco, CA, Jossey-Bass.

LATHER, P. (1986) 'Issues of validity in openly ideological research: Between a rock and a soft place', *Interchange*, **17**, 4, pp. 63–84.

LINCOLN, Y.S., and GUBA, E. (1985) *Naturalistic Inquiry*, Beverly Hills, CA, Sage.

MISHLER, E.G. (1986) *Research Interviewing: Context and Narrative*, Cambridge, MA, Harvard University Press.

PETERS, M. (1996) *Poststructuralism, Politics, and Education*, Westport, CT, Bergin & Garvey.

SCHWANDT, T.A. (1994) 'Constructivist, interpretivist approaches to human inquiry' in DENZIN, N.K. and LINCOLN, Y.S. (Eds) *Handbook of Qualitative Research*, Thousand Oaks, CA, Sage, pp. 118–37.

1 Educational Reforms Can Reproduce Societal Inequities: A Case Study

With Michael Imber

Often forgotten amidst appeals for the reform or restructuring of the public schools is the fact that those the schools most commonly fail to serve are low-income and minority students. It is not surprising, then, that numerous educational theorists have claimed that schools are strongly influenced by the inequitable distribution of knowledge, power, and resources in society and that schools tend to reproduce these same inequities within their policies and practices (Apple, 1982; Carnoy and Levin, 1976 and 1986; Giroux, 1981; Oakes, 1986; Rodriquez, 1987; among many others[1]). Bates (1980a, 1980b and 1987) and Foster (1986) have expanded this important line of argument by contending that educational administration plays an important role in this reproduction. Their critique, though, exists mostly at the theoretical, normative, or even ideological level, leaving interested educators with limited understanding of the mechanisms by which administrative practice contributes to the reproduction of societal inequities.

This chapter shows how such inequities can be reproduced within school systems in one crucial area of administrative responsibility, school reform. It begins by examining the dominant paradigms of educational organizational reform — functionalism, culturalism, and critical theory — and by showing how school reform decisions can have an unequal effect on different student or constituency groups. The second section of the chapter assesses notable examples of functionalist and culturalist scholarly work on educational reform and addresses the inadequate development of critical theory in terms of research on actual administrative practices. The third part of the chapter presents a case study of one school district's reform effort that illustrates how societal inequities can permeate both the process and product of school reform even when that is not the conscious intention of the participants. The final section offers suggestions for countering the influence of such inequities on administrative practices.

Throughout the 1980s, school reform has been prominent on the agenda of educational practitioners and theorists. Although various models of organizational change have been discussed in the administrative science literature, historically the discourse on reform in education has been dominated by the functionalist or instrumentalist approach, typified by the work of Cunningham (1982). During the past fifteen years, though, a compelling critique of the functionalist approach has been developed by several leading theorists, including March and Olsen (1976), Meyer

(1983), Scott (1987), and Weick (1979). In response to this criticism, a rival philosophy, often called the culturalist or interpretivist approach, has attracted attention both in business and education. Examples of this are the works of Kilmann (1986) and Peters and Waterman (1982) in business and Sarason (1982) in education. A third perspective is that of critical theory (Anderson, 1990; Bates, 1982; Foster, 1986; Sirotnik and Oakes, 1986; Yeakey, 1987). This approach rejects both the functionalist and the culturalist positions because they ignore the inequitable distribution of knowledge, power, and resources in society and the influence of that distribution on schools (Bates, 1980b and 1987; Foster, 1986). But critical theory also has critics who have questioned its application to educational administration on the basis of several issues, chief among which has been its lack of specific, verifying examples (Lakomski, 1987; Willower, 1985; Yeakey, 1987).

Regardless of which organizational paradigm is utilized, school reforms are policy decisions based on choices about the allocation or reallocation of limited public resources (Sarason, 1982). Several commentators have argued that these choices can inequitably benefit different student groups (such as gifted, at-risk, special education, low or high SES, and majority or minority race students) or different public constituencies (such as low or high SES parents, real estate developers, the local Chamber of Commerce, or residents of older neighborhoods) (Berman, 1985; Bernstein, 1975; Carnoy and Levin, 1986; Katz, 1975; Kirst, 1988; Metz, 1988; Oakes, 1986; Popkewitz, 1988; Whiteside, 1978). For example, a district reform effort may involve building a new elementary school that benefits powerful development interests in the community instead of revitalizing older, underutilized inner city facilities with large percentages of at-risk children. Or a district may choose to fund a new gifted student program, the beneficiaries of which are not likely to be the children of low-income parents, rather than to expand a program for special education students. Thus the question of who has the power to make decisions about school reform becomes particularly important.

Formally, school boards are the democratically elected representatives of the community, empowered to make resource decisions within the mandate given the board by the state (Campbell, Cunningham, Nystrand and Usdan, 1985). Nonetheless, because school boards have overwhelmingly been composed of lay people who have very little expertise in education or politics, they have developed various compensating strategies to assist in making major reform decisions. One strategy, consistent with the functionalist approach, has been to utilize administrators, academicians, or other consultants as technical experts. Another strategy, typical of the culturalist approach, has been to employ pluralistic constituency committees as representatives of community opinion. In the first instance, the school board is getting technical expertise; in the second, the board is creating an additional opportunity for community participation beyond the board's own democratically elected status.

Whenever either of these methods is used to develop recommendations on school reform, the ultimate power of the school board is eroded. If the board has turned to experts, those experts will either control the reforms or control the possible range of reform choices. If the board has turned to a community committee, the board will pay a heavy political price if it ignores the recommendations of that committee. Critical theorists assert that both methods can inadvertently reinforce the inequitable distribution of knowledge, power, and resources in society. Unfortunately, critical theorists have offered little in the way of research showing how educational administrative practices reinforce societal inequities or practical suggestions addressing how administrative practices might enhance or support equity.

The Discourse on Planned Educational Change

The Functionalist Approach

Cunningham's (1982) *Systematic Planning for Educational Change* typifies the functionalist approach to planned change with its emphasis on technical knowledge and expert control:

> The book presents a number of tools — planning process, context, and theory; participation, group process, and communication in planning; management by objectives; function line-item budgeting, planned programmed budgeting, and zero-base budgeting; task planning, Gantt charting, and program evaluation review technique; committee, nominal group, and Delphi techniques; decision making and decision-tree analysis; organizational development and team building; computer and management information systems; and planning for the future — these all have the potential for greatly improving one's skills as an educational planner and agent for change. (p. xiv)

> There is a growing body of systematized knowledge about process, context, theory, structure, tools, and techniques of planning that will improve the administrator's chance of accomplishing his or her organizational and individual goals. (p. xiii)

> The link between knowledge and action develops best when the planning process is built directly into the management system. (p. 8)

> Planning works best when it begins at the top and flows to the bottom. (p. 22 and 107)

This management-oriented approach is further solidified when Cunningham states that the purpose of the planning is control: 'Planning is used to gain control of the future through current acts' (*ibid*, p. 4). In other words, planned educational change 'works best' when it is systematically in the hands of the administrator or manager 'at the top' and flows from that position down 'to the bottom' of the organization for the purpose of controlling 'the future through current acts' (*ibid*, p. 4).

Formally, the school board has power over the administration, and the voters have power over the school board via democratic elections. However, in Cunningham's book there is very little discussion of the school board or its relationship to the administrator and planned change. When he does briefly mention the board, he says that although it 'theoretically' has control over policy, it 'leaves room for interpretation (of that policy and) . . . does not give the direction needed . . . It is the planner's task, then, to integrate a profusion of goals, on the one hand, and to deal with often ambiguous or vaguely defined goals, on the other' (*ibid*, pp. 38–9). In other words, while the position of the board is formally recognized, the power to make the reform decisions belongs to the administrator as the planner of the reform.

Cunningham (*ibid*) also discusses the relationship between the administrator as the reform expert and the school community. He says that involving the community in reform decisions:

> takes time, is costly, may cause issues to be aroused in the community, and may not produce the consensus or the majority for the direction needed. . . . the school community may become divided regarding what schools should be and what they should do. This sort of planning should therefore be regarded as potentially politically charged. The superintendent's review of such plans is advised. (p. 39)

Although obviously very hesitant about community participation, especially if there may be problems of control, Cunningham later devotes an entire chapter to 'Participation in the planning process'. In this chapter, he reviews the literature on participation, concluding that 'although the research seems clearly to suggest that participation is important to the effectiveness of the planning and decision-making process, there is still much debate on exactly how much participation should occur' (*ibid*, p. 115). He then discusses various technical methods for defining 'how much participation', but he maintains his consistent conclusion that ultimate power should rest with the expert, ending the chapter with the statement, 'The planner must obtain input and assistance through broad participation but never lose sight of his or her own ultimate responsibility for making the final decisions' (*ibid*, p. 121).

Essentially, Cunningham (*ibid*) replicates the traditional hierarchical bureaucracy of Weber with the concentration of power and knowledge at the top of the pyramid. But the application of this model to school reform raises the question of whose needs and interests the school administrator serves. If the ultimate power to control school reforms is in the hands of the superintendent or some other similarly positioned administrator, will the reforms tend to benefit some student or constituency groups more than others?

An answer to this question can be suggested by examining the personal characteristics of superintendents and the political context of the superintendency. According to Tyack and Hansot (1982), 'Superintendents in the twentieth century have almost all been married white males, characteristically middle-aged, Protestant, upwardly mobile, from favored ethnic groups, native-born, and of rural origins' (p. 169). Crowson (1987) in his review of the literature reports that this continues to be a correct portrayal. With virtually all holding master's degrees or higher, with an average of more than thirty years experience as professionals, and with salaries that place them in the top 10 per cent of all working Americans (Campbell, Cunningham, Nystrand and Usdan, 1985; Pounder, 1988), superintendents are certainly part of the upper-middle, professional class. In addition, both Tyack and Hansot (1982) and Crowson (1987) emphasize the conservative values of most superintendents.

If this portrait is correct, it is easy to surmise that superintendents will find it difficult to understand the needs and interests of many low-income and minority constituencies. This was confirmed by Campbell, Cunningham, Nystrand and Usdan (1985):

> Superintendents (during the time of activism in the late 1960s and early 1970s) . . . found it difficult to communicate and understand the sentiments of the poor and underprivileged. Some admitted, in interviews, their anxiety during such encounters. They expressed support for citizen participation publicly but were privately terrified of it. (pp. 181–2)
>
> As an outgrowth of the civil rights revolution, most city superintendents in recent years have had difficulty interpreting the will of communities made up largely of blacks or other minority groups. (p. 218)

Thus it can be concluded that superintendents are limited in their understanding of the needs and interests of significant segments of the community, specifically their least powerful constituents. This would suggest that superintendents' reform efforts are unlikely to be either representative of, or equitably beneficial to, these groups.

Even if superintendents do attempt to serve the whole community, it is highly improbable that they will succeed because of the political position of public schools. Since a public school system is rarely an important power center within a community, it is highly dependent on powerful players in each community for continued support (Campbell, Cunningham, Nystrand and Usdan, 1985; Kimbrough, 1964). The superintendent then is caught between the practical necessity of acquiring the support of the community power structure and the theoretical option of serving the needs of the whole community. In all but the most exceptional cases, the practical necessity will defeat the theoretical option: The superintendent will choose the needs and interests of the powerful over the powerless. The former group can more easily hurt both the district and the superintendent, while the latter will find it difficult to have even a minimal negative effect. For instance, a conflict between the superintendent and the owner of the local newspaper can mean continual bad press, potentially damaging to any effort requiring public support and thus to the superintendent's career. On the other hand, a conflict with one low-income black person, in all but the rarest cases, is likely to cause a small problem at worst.

The Culturalist Approach

Sarason's *The Culture of the School and the Problem of Change* (1982) is often cited as the leading culturalist commentary on school reform (Firestone and Corbett, 1987; Sirotnik and Oakes, 1986). As Sarason's title suggests, a major culturalist theme is that in order to create change it is necessary to understand and utilize the culture of the school as experienced both by those within the school and by those in the surrounding community. Sarason (1982) contended that without this understanding, school reform is doomed to failure. In addition, he is explicitly critical of the technical approach, labeling the functionalists' 'step-by-step recipe' as unworkable 'social engineering' that 'bypasses the task of coming to grips with the characteristics and traditions of the setting and the ways in which they ordinarily facilitate and frustrate change' (p. 78). For Sarason, the crucial issue is not technical knowledge but cultural knowledge.

Instead of leaving the power to control school reform in the hands of the expert, as the functionalists do, Sarason emphasizes the 'participation of all affected constituencies in any change effort' (*ibid*, p. 294). Moreover, he insisted that this participatory involvement be based on real power sharing: 'Constituency building is not a token gesture or a consequence of noblesse oblige. It is a willing alteration of power relationships through which the self-interests of participants stand a chance of being satisfied . . .' (*ibid*, pp. 293–4). He reiterated this viewpoint when he approvingly cited John Dewey who he argued:

> understood in an amazingly clear way that all those who would be affected by the educational enterprise should in some way be part of it, not out of consideration of courtesy or as token gestures to the implications of the legal status of schools, but because the goals of education would not be met unless they had the support of diverse constituencies. (p. 294)

For Sarason, the answer to the question of who should hold power in a reform effort is 'all affected constituencies'.

Sarason's belief in pluralistic participation is especially evident in his discussion of what he considers to be the most outstanding example of comprehensive research on school reform. He cited with approval Berman and McLaughlin's finding that 'to the extent that the effort at change identifies and meaningfully involves all those who directly or indirectly will be affected by the change, to that extent the effort stands a chance to be successful' (p. 79). He shared their view that 'a very large fraction of educators intent on change' simply do not grasp 'the significance of constituencies for the change effort' (*ibid*).

The culturalists' preference for giving control of school reform to 'all affected constituencies' follows from their focus on the culture of the school and its surrounding environment. Within the culturalist frame of reference with its phenomenological or interpretivist epistemology, those who participate in an enterprise like a school district maintain norms, behavioral regularities (Sarason, 1982), or myths and ceremonies (Meyer and Rowan, 1983) about what attitudes and behaviors are acceptable within that setting. Over time, these norms become a culture and assume a life of their own (Firestone and Corbett, 1987), the maintenance of which has great importance to its members. Accordingly, any effort to change the culture of the school must involve those who sustain that culture on an everyday basis. For schools, as Sarason points out, that means not only district staff, but also those in the surrounding community.

Implicit in the culturalist's analysis is the assumption that participation alone gives adequate voice to diverse constituencies. However, as Apple (1979) has argued, this kind of pluralism ignores the inevitable consequences of the prior-existing diversity of interest and power. Although representatives from 'all affected constituencies' may sit together in the best participatory fashion on a reform committee, those representatives do not leave the knowledge, power, and resources that they command in the community at the schoolhouse gates. Some of these committee members, like the manager of a local television station or a major real estate developer, may control substantial resources within the community. The power implicit in the control of these resources will not magically vanish nor will the need to protect and enhance these resources be set aside during school reform committee meetings. Other committee members with much formal education and experience in participating in professional meetings will also be adept at expressing themselves appropriately, at having the necessary knowledge and skills to persuade others, and at managing the committee process to the benefit of their constituencies.

On the other hand, members of the committee who are uneducated, who are unskilled workers, or who are unemployed or on welfare will tend to be less adept and effective. In fact, it is likely that a conflict between the more and less powerful will not even occur. The more powerful will often dominate the agenda to such an extent that their choice appears to be the choice of the whole committee and community, while the less powerful may have difficulty in appropriately verbalizing their needs (Bachrach and Baratz, 1970; Lukes, 1974). Although the ability of educated professionals and community power elites to exercise considerable control over local governmental policies and actions, often at the expense of the less powerful, is well established (Schumaker, 1990; Stone, 1989), culturalists seem to assume that such power differentials will disappear when all constituencies participate together on school reforms. Consequently, while the culturalist has a more democratic approach to reform than the functionalist, the culturalists' lack of attention to the considerable differences among community constituencies effectively allows the most influential constituencies to remain in control.

The Critical Theory Approach

Foster (1986) defined critical theory both as a focus on 'structural variables (in human relationships), particularly those of class and power' and as an effort to examine 'sources of social domination and repression' (p. 72). Yeakey (1987) extended that definition to the study of organizations when she says that the function of critical theory is:

> to analyze organizations and their structural and ideological features within the larger social context they inhabit. Prior to the contributions of the critical theorists in the larger body of organizational literature, certain phenomena were rarely discussed. Virtually nonexistent were explanations of organizations which entailed an exposition of how some individuals and groups have access to resources and others

do not; why some groups are underrepresented and others are not; why certain influences prevail and others do not. (p. 27)

Sirtonik and Oakes (1986) applied this organizational perspective to education when they defined critical theory as attending 'to how educational structures, content, and processes are linked to the social and economic context in which the school is situated' (p. 36). The central theme that runs through these and other conceptualizations of critical theory is a focus on interrelationships between society and its institutions and issues of race, ethnicity, gender, and social class. Specifically, this chapter focuses on whether schools as organizations reproduce within their reform efforts the inequitable distribution of power and resources that already exists in society.

There are three fundamental problems, though, with the application of critical theory to educational administration. First, the language that critical theorists use is frequently overly-dependent on a specialized Marxist terminology (Lather, 1986; Willower, 1985; Yeakey, 1987). Second, the stance critical theorists typically take toward school administration and administrators is often so negative that it discourages the interest of all but a few administrators (Willower, 1985). Third, critical theory analyses of educational administration are based almost exclusively on critiques of administrative theory with little supporting evidence from practice-based research (Lakomski, 1987; Willower, 1985).

With the publication of *Paradigms and Promises* in 1986, Foster made a major contribution to the solution of two of these problems. The book's avoidance of jargon combined with its method, language, and tone make it the most easily accessible discussion of critical theory for school administrators. Foster's stance toward administrators was a very sympathetic one, communicated through such statements as 'none (of the ways a crisis manifests itself) is more poignant than the everyday erosion in the self-image of . . . administrators' (p. 11) or 'we believe that administrators and students of administration can generally make a difference' (*ibid*, p. 14). The combination, then, of an accessible approach and a sympathetic tone is very effective in improving the reception of the work and its ideas by school administrators.

However, these strengths may also be the source of the work's primary weakness. In his effort to make the book accessible and sympathetic, Foster's analysis of educational administrative practice does not make a strong case for the practical need for critical theory. For the most part, his critique of the status quo is based on the inadequacies or failures of the functionalist model of school administration. But his characterization of critical theory is severely diluted. It is true that scattered throughout the text are brief allusions to 'insensitivity to culture and politics' (*ibid*, p. 9), 'the concentration of control in the hands of management' (*ibid*, p. 42), 'domination and repression' (*ibid*, p. 72), 'the bureaucratically and hierarchically structured way of running our schools' (*ibid*, p. 199), but these themes were never examined in depth. Moreover, although there are brief summaries of three empirical studies, none of these illustrates how school management practices reproduce cultural insensitivity or domination and repression. Without such a research-based portrait grounded in specific administrative practices, the need for critical theory in educational administration and the ability to convince administrative practitioners of its worth are substantially undermined.

Yeakey's (1987) discussion of 'critical thought and administrative theory' (p. 23) evidences the same strengths and weaknesses as Foster's. She decried the proliferation of Marxist terminology and did not needlessly alienate interested administrators by blaming them for the inequitable status quo in education. However, she based her entire critique on an evaluation of organizational theory without any correlation with actual organizational practices. Once again, educational practitioners are left with little understanding of how the central issue of critical theory, the effect on schools of the unequal distribution of societal power and resources, has any practical connection to educational administrative practices.

In contrast, Bates (1980a, 1980b, 1982 and 1987) has provided the most extensive and most sophisticated effort to apply critical theory to educational administration while avoiding the three problems discussed above. First, although his language was somewhat linked to Marxist terminology, it was not overly done. Second, while Bates did not display the obvious warmth of Foster, his sympathetic attitude toward school administrators was appropriately communicated. Third, he sometimes made good use of the research done by others to illustrate his conclusions. Nonetheless, Bates' orientation was extensively theoretical and not specifically grounded in his own research on the practical application of critical theory to administrative practices.

The remainder of this chapter builds on the works of Bates and Foster in using a critical theory approach to analyze specific instances of educational administrative practice. Three illustrative examples have been taken from a case study of one school district's efforts at reform to show how the inequitable distribution of knowledge, power, and resources within the community affected its educational reform efforts and to demonstrate how both the functionalist and culturalist methods can result in the reproduction of community inequities within the school system. As with any effort to match theories with actual occurrences, a perfect fit cannot be expected. In addition, the three examples presented here cover only a small portion of the reform effort, which also included policy decisions about new construction, new boundaries, the reorganization of the district, general educational goals, racial imbalances in enrollments, class sizes, and curricular changes.

The Johnsonville School District's Reform Effort[2]

The information presented is based on three sources. First, fifty-four newspaper articles covering the first three years of the district's reform effort were examined. Second, members of committees formed at various stages of the reform effort, including district staff, school board members, parents, and community representatives were interviewed in sessions lasting one to two hours each. Included among the parents and community members were representatives of the various socioeconomic groups, races, and constituencies that comprise the population of Johnsonville.

In addition, each interviewee was asked to name the most outspoken representative of the major competing viewpoints that the committee had considered, and those individuals were subsequently interviewed. There were eleven interviews in all. During the interviews, all participants were asked both the same common set of questions and various additional questions that arose out of answers to the common set. Consequently, approximately two-thirds of each interview session was fairly structured and about one-third was open-ended. And, finally, the third source of data was a large notebook of handouts for committee members, including letters summarizing the discussions that occurred at each meeting.

On 25 April 1984, the Board of Education of the Johnsonville school district, located within a small (approximately 60,000 population), midwestern city, decided to reconsider the organization of the school district. The next day the local newspaper reported that 'the school board members approved a long-range study' of the district. The newspaper also indicated that 'The study of the issues . . . will be conducted by a panel of parents, patrons and district employees' (*The Johnsonville Daily*, 27 April 1984, p. 1). In other words, the Board decided to pursue a major reform of the district system and to accomplish this through a pluralist method, somewhat like the one advocated by Sarason.

At the time of the Board's decision, the organization of the district had not been studied for over twenty years. The city was experiencing considerable physical growth, particularly in the Eastern direction, with much of this growth occurring in middle-class and upper middle-class suburban areas. Most of the older elementary schools, where much less growth was occurring, were located near each other in the older, central part of the city. Concurrently, the district's superintendent of over twenty years was retiring, and by the time the reform process actually began, the new superintendent was in place. The Board itself was also in a state of transition as four new members had recently been elected. In deciding to undertake a systematic program of reform, they and their more experienced colleagues were no doubt influenced by a pervasive call for school improvement from both state and national leaders.

In accordance with the Board's decision, a group of fifty-five parents and community members were invited to a meeting to develop the basic educational goals which would guide the district for the next five years. According to a district-level staff member, the superintendency team composed of the superintendent and three assistant superintendents decided that the method of selection of the participants for the goal-setting meeting would be to ask the principals of all attendance centers to choose representatives from the parent population of their schools. It was also reported that there was no discussion by the superintendency team as to whether this approach would bias the selection. It simply appeared to be an easy way to collect a group of school parents including at least some from each school. In addition, an ad was run in the local newspaper inviting any interested citizens to participate, but no one responded.

According to the same informant, the principals handled their task for choosing participants in two ways. Some turned the decision over to the president of the school's parent organization, while others chose the participants themselves. Whether these approaches yielded participants who truly represented the population of their school varied with the demographics of each school. The Johnsonville school district at that time had one high school (grades 10–12), three junior high schools (grades 7–9), and sixteen elementary schools (grades K–6). All the schools except the single high school served contiguous geographical areas with some minor exceptions. Some schools were known as 'rich' schools socioeconomically, others as 'poor'. For instance, while 24.5 per cent of all students in the district received free or reduced lunches (the district's only data on SES) and 17.4 per cent were minority students, Elkland Elementary School, serving the highest socioeconomic neighborhood, had only 0.6 per cent who were receiving free or reduced lunches and 6.5 per cent who were minority students. On the opposite end of the socioeconomic scale was the California Elementary School which had 80.7 per cent receiving free or reduced lunches and a 46.2 per cent minority population. If the two selection methods produced representative participation, it would be expected that the parents chosen from each school would closely reflect the class and race distribution of the students of each school. This result did not occur.

Participants from the wealthier schools were reasonably typical of their parent populations. They tended to be educated professionals, business owners, managers, and spouses of such individuals. Participants from the middle-income and working-class schools were mixed. They included some of the same kind of people that represented the wealthier schools and some more typically representative of their respective populations. For example, there were two blue-collar, white males from one elementary school dominated by middle-class and blue-collar populations. However, participants from the poorest schools were occupationally more typical of the wealthier schools than their own. For example, the only participants selected from the two poorest schools were two white, male professionals, even though one was selected by a principal and the other by the president of a parent organization. While these two men were characterized as liberal advocates for lower class and minority concerns by other committee members, they were not demographically or culturally representative of their schools' populations.

In addition, there was a total of ten representatives at the goal-setting meeting from the two elementary schools with the lowest number of free and reduced lunches, but there were only two representatives from the two schools with the highest number of free and reduced lunches. That is, the two elementary schools with the fewest free and reduced lunches (10 per cent of the district's schools and 7.3 per cent of the district's students) accounted for 18.2 per cent of the participants at the meeting, while the two elementary schools with the most free and reduced lunches (10 per cent of the district's schools and 4.7 per cent of the district's students) accounted for only 3.6 per cent of the participants. The two elementary schools with the fewest free and reduced lunches had over five times the representation of the two schools with the most free and reduced lunches. Consequently, at the meeting in which the district developed its basic educational goals for the next five years, the participants from the two poorest elementary schools were not only unrepresentative in terms of race and SES, but also substantially fewer in number than those from the two wealthier elementary schools.

Thus, although, according to several newspaper articles and several informants, the Board of Education and the superintendent supported a reform effort that was broad-based and representative of the whole school community, the group of people who participated in the goal-setting meeting chiefly represented the white, business, and professional classes. Interviews with district school officials, board members, and reform participants revealed no conscious effort to create a non-representative group; instead it appeared to have been an unplanned, inadvertent result of the selection process and of a lack of attention to the problem. Principals who chose their representatives apparently chose those who already were regular participants in school-related parent activities and who were thought reliable and capable to defend their school's and their neighborhood's interests during the reform effort. For the most part, this meant that they chose those parents who had the interest, knowledge, and resources to be effective in community-wide activities, and these people tended not to be low-income or minority parents. Parent organization presidents who chose the participants from their schools also chose those who were already active or who could be relied upon to participate. But even in the low-income and minority dominated schools the parents chosen were not the poor or minority ones.

There could have been several reasons for this result: (i) principals or parent organization presidents were unconsciously eliminating low-income and minority parents; (ii) these latter parents were eliminating themselves because their lives were already too difficult, because they were socialized not to participate, or because they felt uncomfortable or not understood in school meetings dominated by higher-income whites; or (iii) a combination of both. But whatever the cause, the fact is that the committee assigned to set the goals for the district's reform effort, despite the stated intention of representing all segments of the population, was dominated by middle to upper-middle class whites.

The main task of the goal-setting committee was to rate eighteen possible district goals from a list compiled by Phi Delta Kappa based on an analysis of other districts' reform efforts. Although it cannot be known what a proportionally representative committee might have done, the goals chosen were entirely consistent with the interests and needs of the white, middle, and upper-middle class constituencies that dominated the committee and much less focused on lower class and minority needs. While a number of purely academic goals (presumably of interest to all school constituencies) were chosen, a number of affective ('develop feelings of self-worth') and cultural ('appreciate culture and beauty in the world') goals of a type often associated with the professional and upper-middle class were emphasized as well. Rated lower were a number of goals that might have appealed to minority parents, notably, 'Learn how to get along with people who think, dress and act differently'. Among the lowest rated goals were two that working class parents might have chosen to emphasize: 'develop skills to enter a specific field of work' and 'gain information needed to make job selections'. Whatever the accuracy of these speculations, the fact remains that lower class and minority parents never had an equal opportunity to influence the choice of the basic educational goals selected for the district.

Near the end of the goal-setting meeting, the participants were asked to join one of two committees that would study the district and make recommendations to the Board of Education as to what changes were needed or desired. One of the committees was called the Organizational Structure and Auxiliary Services Committee. While several participants at this initial goal-setting meeting decided to join this new committee, district administrators also recruited additional participants from the district staff and from the community. The result was a thirty-two-member committee that met sixteen times for two to four hours each time. While the chair was a district-level staff member, other administrative staff — one secondary principal, two elementary principals, and two district-level directors of auxiliary services — were also included. Also participating were three teachers, one elementary and two secondary, two board members, a member of the Chamber of Commerce, the head of the city planning department, and a university professor. The rest were parents representing twelve of the district's twenty schools. There was one representative for each of the two poorest elementary schools, the two white, male, professionals mentioned above, and several representatives for the poorest junior high, one of whom was the spouse of a white, low to middle income farmer and another of whom was a white, low-income, single parent. In other words, all of the committee members were white, even though 17.4 per cent of the district's students were minorities, and only one was definitely not middle class or above, even though 24.5 per cent of the district's students received free or reduced lunches. The rest were middle-class to upper middle-class. Again, the membership of a committee crucial to the reform effort was homogeneous and non-representative in terms of race and SES.

This membership configuration became particularly troublesome when about halfway through the process the committee focused on the potential effects on black children of proposed boundary changes, busing, and closing or consolidating schools. At this point, the lack of representation of the parents of these minority children became all too obvious, even embarrassing, according to some on the committee. The chair of the committee then made special arrangements to add three low-income, black parents to the committee. These minority parents attended the one committee meeting dedicated to minority issues. The main focus of the discussion at this meeting was whether the blacks preferred that the district close their children's neighborhood schools and bus their children to wealthier white-dominated ones. The response of the black parents was unequivocal. They did not want their neighborhood schools closed, but they did want these schools to be upgraded, to have the same level of funds spent on them as they felt was spent on the wealthier schools. They wanted to keep their neighborhood schools, but they wanted them to be as good as the wealthier white schools. But as the committee continued to meet on subsequent occasions and on other topics, several interviewees reported that these black parents soon quit attending. Nothing, according to these informants, was said in the committee about the fact that the black parents were again not participating.

Thus, an avowedly participatory process of school reform proceeded with almost no input from a significant segment of the community. The only time this lack of representation was even noticed occurred when the specific topic of the committee's discussion was the attitude of black parents to certain proposals. What was never addressed was that all of the decisions faced by the committee, not just those related directly to the schools with a high percentage of low-income and minority students, would have an effect on the district's resources that were available for low-income and minority children. Partially in response to the committee's work, the school board later decided to build one new elementary school and to remodel and expand three others, all of which were located outside the low-income and minority-dominated areas of the city, even though two of the schools located in the latter areas were substantially underutilized. In other words, reform decisions were made that budgeted large expenditures for expansion in white-dominated areas when smaller expenditures could have been made for remodeling and use of the underutilized structures in two of the low-income, minority-dominated areas of the city.

One aspect of the final report of this committee to the school board particularly illustrates the effect of the non-representativeness of the group. The one real input that the committee received from otherwise unrepresented black parents was that they did not want their neighborhood school closed and their children bused to the newer schools dominated by middle and upper-middle whites and that they did want the physical and educational quality of their schools to be similar to that of the wealthier schools. However, the black parents expressed no objection to middle and upper-middle, white children being bused into their underutilized schools. Nonetheless, three out of four of the possible plans offered by the committee supported closing the older schools that the black parents wanted remodeled and busing the low-income and minority children throughout the city. The district administration also supported closing these schools. The committee and the administration claimed that the latter approach was in the best interest of the low-income and minority children, even though this was the exact opposite of what the parents of these children had said they wanted.

Early in the reform process, another, much smaller committee, called the Steering Committee, was created by the superintendent. All recommendations to the school board on possible reforms were to be reviewed by this committee prior to presentation to the board. The apparent effect of this committee was to allow a small, select group to exercise ultimate control over the reforms. The committee had eleven members including seven from within the educational power structure. Four of these were the administrative leadership of the district — the superintendent, who was the chair, the three assistant superintendents, two school board members, and the past president of the teachers' union. The remaining four participants on the committee were members of the power elite that dominated the city economically. One was the general manager of the local newspaper; another was the plant manager for one of the largest employers in the city and an active participant in numerous community issues. The other two were university professors both of whom were active in community affairs, including one who would soon be president of the local Chamber of Commerce, the center of economic power within the community.

Thus, the Steering Committee, for which there was no attempt at representativeness, was essentially a combination of the local educational elite (about two-thirds of the committee) and the local power elite (about one-third of the committee). Obviously the committee was overwhelmingly weighted in favor of the educational elite, a fact that was a source of irritation to one of the members of the power elite on the committee. During the interview he complained that the committee was simply meant to be a 'rubber-stamp' for the plans of the superintendent.

Although it appears that the intent of this committee was to provide a mechanism for control of the reforms by the superintendent, it had, according to all interviewees, virtually no actual impact on the reform effort except in one important instance. This exception was the issue of whether and when to build a new elementary school. At one point during the committee's deliberations, the leading member of the local power elite on the committee in an unusually frank statement complained to a newspaper reporter that 'The district was shifting away from the traditional policy of building schools in developing areas before the areas are fully built up.' In other words, he was suggesting that the school district should build new schools in new development areas before the development is completed, as the district had done in the past, so that home buyers would be drawn to the new areas. He further argued that 'it's a "negative influence" on development to tell families who build homes in the (newly developed) east part of the city that they will have to bus their children two miles to school' (*The Johnsonville Daily*, 29 April 1985, p. 3). He was complaining that real estate agents would have to tell potential buyers that their children would need to be bused, presumably making sales more difficult. The superintendent in the same newspaper article countered that the district could not continue the old pattern of building new schools during the early phases of a large development project. Instead, he argued that the school board should expand schools to handle the influx of new students throughout the district.

As a result of the reform effort the district over a two-year period (1987/88) substantially expanded three established elementary schools. Two of the expanded schools were located in blue-collar to middle-class neighborhoods that were showing growth, and the other, Elkland Elementary School, was located in a wealthy suburban locale near the newly developed area in which the local power elite wanted a new school to be built. In accordance with the wishes of the non-educators on the Steering Committee and despite the opposition originally voiced by the superintendent, this new elementary school desired by the local power elite was built exactly where the elite wanted. At the same time, two predominantly low-income and minority elementary schools in the older part of the city, about two miles from the new school, that were underutilized by half were ignored as sources of available space.

Due to the expansion of the three schools and the construction of a new one, the district added space for 950 more students, though by 1989 it was only using 750 of those spaces. The two older schools, the ones with high low-income and minority populations, together held 250–300 fewer students than their capacity. Thus the district built more than it needed, and it built to fit the needs of the wealthy developers. Although the district could have utilized the older schools and saved substantial funds through less construction, no-one on the various committees nor in the administration publicly suggested that the already existing space in the older schools be used to fill some of the space needs.

After the report of the conflict between the superintendent and the leading member of the local power elite on the Steering Committee, there were no other newspaper articles or public discussions addressing the conflict about whether to build a new school. While those of the local elite who were interviewed reported that the new school was built to meet the needs of local population growth, other informants were not so sure. Several of the informants were suspicious about why it was built at all, why it was built earlier than it needed to be, and why it was built exactly where the real estate developers wanted it. Other informants clearly supported the time and place of the new construction. Whatever the disagreements about the new school, there are four unquestionable points. First, the superintendent and the representative of the economic elite on the Steering Committee did publicly disagree about the construction. Second, there was un-utilized space in two schools, and those schools were two of the ones with the highest number of low-income and minority children. Third, several informants, all of whom participated in the reform process and some of whom were members of the educational elite, were suspicious about the construction decision. Fourth, the school was built when and where the local power elite wanted it to be.

None of these issues, though, was brought out prior to the bond election that would decide on funding the expanded schools and the new school. The broad support for the bonds included both the educational elite and the economic elite. In a sense, a compromise had been struck because the administration gained the school expansions that it wanted and the economic elite got its new school in the right location. But the needs of the low-income and minority schools, children, and parents were neither represented nor served. Neither were the best interests of taxpayers served. An appropriate footnote to this decision was that the district later decided to bus in some low-income students to this new school to provide some diversity to the student body.

Because the Steering Committee was created by the superintendent and since its membership consisted only of the local educational and power elites, the committee exemplifies Cunningham's functionalist approach to reform. That the local power elite was able to fulfill its needs even when the chief educational expert, the superintendent, opposed them supports the vulnerability of expert-driven reforms to the influence of powerful constituencies. In the case of the culturalist-oriented constituency committees — the goal-setting committee and the Organizational Structure and Auxiliary Services Committee, similar results occurred. First, even though there was apparently no conscious effort to exclude low-income and minority parents, they were clearly underrepresented on either committee. Second, even when there was some representation, as when the black parents were brought in to talk about black concerns, the recommendations of these minority parents were largely ignored by the middle and upper-middle class, white-dominated committee. Third, the output of both committees was arguably biased by this lack of representation. Consequently, even though the culturalist approach is more pluralistic and democratic than the functionalist method, an assessment of a culturalist-like reform effort from a critical theory perspective reveals culturalism's inherent limitations. There are, however, measures that any district can take to alleviate these limitations, and these are discussed in the final section of the chapter.

Discussion and Conclusions

School reforms are allocations or reallocations of scarce educational resources. Whoever controls the educational change process has the power to benefit some students or community constituencies more than others. The traditional model of educational administration, functionalism, concentrates power in the educational expert, usually the superintendent in the case of district-wide reforms. The Johnsonville Steering Committee's decision to build a new school in accordance with the wishes of the community's real estate development interests illustrates the defects of this approach. Because of the political weakness of local school systems, expert-driven reforms are vulnerable to control by local power elites. Thus, functionalist reforms tend to be to the disadvantage of the least powerful groups within the community. To avoid these problems, culturalists argue that 'all affected constituencies' should control school reform. The flaw in this approach, as critical theorists have pointed out, is that all affected constituencies are not equal in their ability to exercise power. Some groups have considerable economic resources that may directly or indirectly affect reform decisions. Other groups, such as educated professionals, have skills and knowledge to excel in participatory decision-making. On the other side, there are those that have neither economic power nor the skills to be effective in committee work. Consequently, constituency-based reforms also tend to produce results that favor the more powerful and more skilled over the less powerful and less skilled, even when there is no conscious conspiracy to create this inequitable result. In other words, the power inequalities in the community can bias even pluralistic school reform efforts in which there is no intentional effort to produce unfair results.

The findings of the Johnsonville case study, though, are entirely consistent with numerous reports of political scientists on the influence of community elites over local public policy (Schumaker, 1990; Stone, 1989). In his analysis of this influence, Schumaker (1990, p. xi) has coined the term 'critical pluralism' to describe a shared decision making process in which power, not just the opportunity to participate, is equitably distributed. If school reform is to become a truly democratic enterprise which affords equal opportunities that benefit all student groups and all community constituencies, the pluralism advocated by the culturalists must become a critical pluralism, one that is highly attentive to the significant differences in knowledge, power, and resources of various community constituencies and to the ways in which these differences affect school policy and decision-making.

The critical pluralist approach requires attention to two principles for its application to school reform. First, in a democracy, constituency committee-based reforms are superior to expert-driven reforms, but the participation on constituency committees must equitably represent the community. If a district's student population is 15 per cent black, blacks should occupy about 15 per cent of the places on school reform committees. If 30 per cent of the students come from blue-collar families, so should about 30 per cent of those who make decisions about school reform. No matter how good an excuse there seems to be, constituency-based committees should simply not proceed unless all groups are equitably represented. Second, while equitable representation is a necessary condition of critical pluralism, it is not enough. Critical pluralism requires that committees operate in such a way that all members have equal voice. There must be an equitable opportunity for all participants to exercise control over committee decisions, not simply to be present when decisions are made.

From this perspective, there are several steps that could have been taken in Johnsonville to assure a more truly representative, democratic reform process. First, there should have been aggressive measures to recruit minority and lower class committee members in approximate proportion to the district's student population. In order to do this, it might have been necessary to provide child care or other enabling incentives. Second, when the more representative committees first met, there should have been a frank, in-depth discussion of the differences among individuals that make it difficult to share power. Participants should have been encouraged to share their own backgrounds and biases and to each make a commitment to respect and consider each other's points of view. Third, it should have been made clear to all members that the point of the committees was not to engage in a power struggle but rather to develop plans designed to equitably benefit the community's constituencies even if that meant providing more resources to the least powerful constituencies. Fourth, the committees' decisions should not have been subject to review of an expert or elite-controlled Steering Committee. When the recommendations of constituency committees can be ignored if they do not coincide with administrative or power-elite desires, the community is not participating, it is being manipulated. Finally, these principles should have been addressed throughout the reform effort, not just enunciated early on and allowed to disappear like the black committee members in Johnsonville. If the Johnsonville school reform effort had proceeded in accordance with the principles of critical pluralism, it is likely that its benefits would have been more equitably distributed among the community's constituencies.

Notes

1   The literature on this is extensive, both in the United States and Europe (see, for example, Berman, 1985; Bernstein, 1975; Bourdieu and Passeron, 1977; Bowles and Gintis, 1976; Coleman *et al.*, 1966; Jencks *et al.*, 1972; Nasaw, 1979; Popkewitz, 1988; Sharp and Green, 1973; Sirotnik and Oakes, 1986; Whitty, 1985 and Young, 1971).

2   Johnsonville is a fictitious name used to provide anonymity to the schools and the district. Efforts have also been made to disguise the informants.

References

ANDERSON, G.L. (1990) 'Toward a critical constructivist approach to school administration: Invisibility, legitimation, and the study of non-events', *Educational Administration Quarterly*, **26**, pp. 38–59.

APPLE, M. (1979) *Ideology and Curriculum*, London, Routledge and Kegan Paul.

APPLE, M. (1982) *Education and Power*, Boston, MA, Routledge and Kegan Paul.

BACHRACH, P. and BARATZ, M.S. (1970) *Power and Poverty: Theory and Practice*, New York, Oxford University Press.

BATES, R.J. (1980a) 'Bureaucracy, professionalism and knowledge: Structures of authority and structures of control', *Education Research and Perspectives*, **7**, pp. 66–76.

BATES, R.J. (1980b) 'Educational administration, the sociology of science, and the management of knowledge', *Educational Administration Quarterly*, **16**, pp. 1–20.

BATES, R.J. (1982) *'Towards a critical practice of educational administration'*, paper presented at the annual meeting of the American Educational Research Association, New York.

BATES, R.J. (1987) 'Corporate culture, schooling, and educational administration', *Educational Administration Quarterly*, **23**, pp. 79–115.

BERMAN, E. (1985) 'The improbability of meaningful educational reform', *Issues in Education*, **3**, pp. 99–112.

BERNSTEIN, B. (1975) *Class, Codes and Control: Vol. 3, Towards a Theory of Educational Transmissions*, London, Routledge and Kegan Paul.

BOURDIEU, P. and PASSERON, J. (1977) *Reproduction in Education, Society and Culture*, London, Sage Publications.

BOWLES, S. and GINTIS, H. (1976) *Schooling in Capitalist America*, New York, Basic Books.

CAMPBELL, R.F., CUNNINGHAM, L.L., NYSTRAND, R.O. and USDAN, M.D. (1985) *The Organization and Control of American Schools*, Columbus, OH, Merrill.

CARNOY, M. and LEVIN, H.M. (1976) 'Introduction' in CARNOY, M. and LEVIN, H.M. (Eds) *The Limits of Educational Reform*, New York, David McKay, pp. 1–22.

CARNOY, M. and LEVIN, H.M. (1986) 'Educational reform and class conflict', *Journal of Education*, **168**, pp. 35–46.

COLEMAN, J.S., CAMPBELL, E.Q., HOBSON, C.J., MCPARTLAND, J., MOOD, A., WEINFELD, F.D. and YORK, R.L. (1966) *Equality of Educational Opportunity*, Washington, DC, US Department of Health, Education, and Welfare.

CROWSON, R.L. (1987) 'The local school district superintendency: A puzzling administrative role', *Educational Administration Quarterly*, **23**, pp. 49–69.

CUNNINGHAM, L.L. and HENTGES, J.T. (1982) *The American School Superintendency 1982: A Summary Report*, Arlington, VA, American Association of School Administrators.

CUNNINGHAM, W.G. (1982) *Systematic Polanning for Educational Change*, Palo Alto, CA, Mayfield.

FIRESTONE, W.A. and CORBETT, H.D. (1987) 'Planned organizational change' in LORSCH, J.W. (Ed) *Handbook of Organizational Change*, Inglewood Cliffs, NJ, Prentice-Hall, pp. 321–40.

FOSTER, W. (1986) *Paradigms and Promises: New Approaches to Educational Administration*, Buffalo, NY, Prometheus Books.

GIROUX, H. (1981) *Ideology, Culture, and the Process of Schooling*, Philadelphia, PA, Temple University Press.

JENCKS, C., SMITH, M., ACLAND, H., BANE, M.J., COHEN, D., GENTIS, H., HEYNS, B. and MICHELSON, S. (1972) *Inequality: A Reassessment of the Effect of Family and Schooling in America*, New York, Basic Books.

KATZ, M.B. (1975) *Class, Bureaucracy and Schools: The Illusion of Educational Change in America*, New York, Praeger.

KILMANN, R.H. (1986) *Beyond the Quick Fix*, San Francisco, CA, Jossey-Bass.

KIMBROUGH, R.B. (1964) *Political Power and Educational Decision-making*, Chicago, IL, Rand McNally.

KIRST, M.W. (1988) 'Recent state educational reform in the United States: Looking backward and forward', *Educational Administration Quarterly*, **24**, pp. 319–28.

LAKOMSKI, G. (1987) 'Critical theory and educational administration', *The Journal of Educational Administration*, **25**, pp. 85–100.

LATHER, P. (1986) 'Issues of validity in openly ideological research: Between a rock and a soft place', *Interchange*, **17**, pp. 63–84.

LUKES, S. (1974) *Power: A Radical View*, New York, Macmillan.

MARCH, J.G. and OLSEN, J.P. (1976) *Ambiguity and Choice in Organizations*, Bergen, Norway, Universitetsforlaget.

MEYER, J.W. (1983) 'Institutionalization and the rationality of formal organizational structure' in MEYER, J.W. and SCOTT, W.R. (Eds) *Organizational Environments: Ritual and Rationality*, Beverly Hills, CA, Sage Publications, pp. 261–82.

MEYER, J.W. and ROWAN, B. (1983) 'The structure of educational organizations' in MEYER, J.W. and SCOTT, W.R. (Eds) *Organizational Environments: Ritual and Rationality*, Beverly Hills, CA, Sage Publications, pp. 71–97.

METZ, M.H. (1988) 'Some missing elements in the educational reform movement', *Educational Administration Quarterly*, **24**, pp. 446–60.

NASAW, D. (1979) *Schooled to Order: A Social History of Public Schooling in the United States*, New York, Oxford University Press.

OAKES, J. (1986) 'Tracking, inequality, and the rhetoric of reform: Why schools don't change', *Journal of Education*, **168**, pp. 60–80.

PETERS, T.J. and WATERMAN, R.H. (1982) *In Search of Excellence*, New York, Harper and Row.

POPKEWITZ, T.S. (1988) 'Educational reform: Rhetoric, ritual, and social interest', *Educational Theory*, **38**, pp. 77–93.

POUNDER, D.G. (1988) 'The male/female salary differential for school administrators: Implications for career patterns and placement of women', *Educational Administration Quarterly*, **24**, pp. 5–19.

RODRIQUEZ, F. (1987) *Equity Education: An Imperative for Effective Schools*, Dubuque, IA, Kendall Hunt.

SARASON, S.B. (1982) *The Culture of the School and the Problem of Change*, Boston, MA, Allyn and Bacon.

SCHUMAKER, P. (1990) *Critical Pluralism: Evaluating Democratic Performance in the Resolution of Community Issues*, Lawrence, KS, University Press of Kansas.

SCOTT, W.R. (1987) *Organizations: Rational, Natural, and Open Systems*, Englewood Cliffs, NJ, Prentice-Hall.

SHARP, R. and GREEN, A. (1973) *Education and Social Control*, London, Routledge and Kegan Paul.

SIROTNIK, K.A. and OAKES, J. (1986) 'Critical inquiry for school renewal: Liberating theory and practice' in SIROTNIK, K.A. and OAKES, J. (Eds) *Critical Perspectives on the Organization and Improvement of Schooling*, Boston, MA, Kluwer-Nijhoff Publishing, pp. 3–93.

STONE, C.N. (1989) *Regime Politics: Governing Atlanta, 1946–1988*, Lawrence, KS, University Press of Kansas.

TYACK, D. and HANSOT, E. (1982) *Managers of Virtue: Public School Leadership in America, 1820–1980*, New York, Basic Books.

WEICK, K.E. (1979) *The Social Psychology of Organizing*, Reading, MA, Addison-Wesley.

WHITTY, G. (1985) *Sociology and School Knowledge*, London, Methuen.

WHITESIDE, T. (1978) *The Sociology of Educational Innovation*, London, Methuen.

WILLOWER, D.J. (1985) '*Marxian critical theory and educational administration: A criticism*', paper presented at the annual meeting of the American Educational Research Association, Chicago, April.

YEAKEY, C.C. (1987) 'Critical thought and administrative theory: Conceptual approaches to the study of decision-making', *Planning and Changing*, **18**, pp. 23–32.

YOUNG, M.F.D. (1971) 'Knowledge and control' in YOUNG, M.F.D. (Ed) *Knowledge and Control*, London, Collier Macmillan, pp. 1–17.

2 Social Relativism: (Not Quite) A Postmodernist Epistemology

How far the perspective character of existence extends or indeed whether exist-ence has any other character than this; whether existence without interpretation, without 'sense', does not become 'nonsense', whether, on the other hand, all exist-ence is not essentially an interpreting existence — that cannot be decided even by the most industrious and most scrupulously conscientious analysis and self-examination of the intellect; for in the course of this analysis the human intellect can-not avoid seeing itself in its own perspective forms, and only in these. We cannot look around our own corner. (Nietzsche, quoted in Spivak, 1976, pp. xxvii–xxviii)

Epistemology: An Introduction

Epistemology is the study of how we know or of what the rules for knowing are.[1] From my perspective how I see (my epistemology) must precede what I see (my ontology) because how I see shapes, frames, determines, and even creates what I see.[2] This description, however, could not be said to be accurate for all epistemolo-gical positions. Positivism, for instance, has attempted to derive rigorous 'scientific' rules for creating a one-to-one correspondence between what 'reality' is and how it is represented in research so that the representation is untainted by researcher bias or the ambiguity of language, among other possible threats to claims of valid-ity. From the positivist perspective, then, how knowing is accomplished does not shape, frame, determine, or create what is known; the positivist epistemology claims to mirror reality.[3] This position, according to Foucault (1977) assumes 'an eye whose entire substance is nothing but the transparency of its vision' (p. 45).

For positivists the rules for knowing (the positivist epistemology) guarantee or warrant the fact that the research representations of reality truly represent reality. If the researcher follows the positivist rules, the results are certified to represent reality accurately. Very few epistemologists think that the positivists succeeded in developing such rules: 'all of the main forms of positivism are now regarded as false, their key tenets clearly refuted' (Evers and Lakomski, 1991, p. viii).[4] As Minh-ha (1989) asserts, 'There is no such thing as a "coming face to face once and for all with objects"; the real remains foreclosed from the analytic experience . . .' (p. 76). Popper, however, as a friend and critic of the Vienna Circle put it most succinctly: 'Everybody knows nowadays that logical positivism is dead' (quoted in Culbertson, 1988, p. 18).

Polkinghorne (1983), though his epistemological target is more encompassing, contends that 'the logical-empirical philosophy of science . . . has failed to hold up under continued self-examination' (p. x). In fact, it could reasonably be argued that, as implied by Polkinghorne with his use of the word 'self-examination', much of the contemporary ferment in epistemology derives directly from the questioning of the positivist rules by the positivists themselves and their successors. Rorty (1979), for example, has argued that the analytic philosophers of England and the United States, who in many ways could be said to be in the positivist tradition, have played a major role in undermining their own tradition. The later Wittgenstein would be the most well-known example of this tradition turning against itself.

Realism

Though positivism is now seen as a failed attempt to create rigorous scientific rules for mirroring reality,[5] most social science research, including that in education, continues to take place within the general parameters derived from positivism, though largely without the almost fanatical logical purity sought by positivists. Social science researchers who want to retain the scientific method could be said to have returned, at least in terms of epistemology, to the general scientific frame that in many ways preceded the positivist heresy (for example, John Stuart Mill). Currently, realism has generally been divided into two groups — naive realists and scientific realists.

The most commonly practiced of these two epistemologies is labeled naive realism (Mishler, 1991), a somewhat unfair though also fairly accurate label. The overwhelming preponderance of research in education administration and in education in general, as in many other social and psychological science disciplines, is of this type. This perspective assumes that conventional social science research methods unproblematically insure accurate or valid representations of reality. It thus proceeds unreflexively as if the perspective of the researcher has no effect on what is seen. Accordingly, most of the scholarly work in education pays little, if any, attention to its epistemological assumptions.[6]

As an unself-conscious stepchild of positivism, naive realism assumes that the 'seen' or 'researched' world is reasonably transparent to conventional consciousness or, at least, to a consciousness trained in conventional social science research methods. For this transparency to exist the mind of the conventional researcher must be in a virtual one-to-one correspondence of understanding to 'the world'. That is, what the researcher thinks she/he sees accurately reflects that which the researcher is looking at in the world. In addition, the researcher assumes that the language used to represent the world in the linguistic presentation of the research is not so ambiguous that meaning becomes problematic.[7]

The second group of realists, whom I have labeled scientific realists, is itself divided into smaller sub-groups under labels such as neo-realism, scientific realism, coherentist realism, or critical realism, each of which is somewhat different from but mainly similar to the others. The entire group is much more sophisticated or reflective in terms of the numerous epistemological problems that have been raised against positivism. Indeed, this second group has tried to adjust the epistemology of science in terms of the criticisms that have been made of positivism so that the orthodox scientific method, albeit through a realist reconstruction, remains defensible as the preferred method of research.

The differences between the two groups of realists are fairly obvious. If, for instance, in studying a classroom a researcher assumes that the facts she/he 'sees' are unproblematically 'there' in the world without reference to any particular theoretical perspective, this researcher is a naive realist. Scientific realists, however, recognize that, even in the natural sciences, facts are always theory-laden because 'something' can only become a fact due to the theory that makes it recognizable as a fact. House (1991) explains the difference between naive and scientific realism thusly: scientific realism must also be distinguished from naive realism, which is clearly wrong. For example, a naive realist would hold that a lemon is really yellow. A scientific realist would hold that a lemon appears yellow because of the refraction of light off its surface, the particular nature of light waves, and the structure of the human eye, thus invoking the causal entities and structures that produce the phenomenon, that is, the yellow lemon. The analysis does not stop with surface events but examines the underlying patterns and tendencies (p. 4).

When it comes to describing events in a research setting, more often than not, naive realists assume that what you see is what you get. When they look at a classroom they are unaware that what they see, what they pick out as facts, are theory or perspective dependent. Different theories yield different facts: whereas one researcher may see 'yellow' in a classroom, another researcher, looking at the same classroom as the first, may see 'red'. House's scientific realism recognizes the theory dependency of facts. 'The world is known only under particular descriptions (or theories)', and thus theory 'does not mirror reality' (*ibid*, p. 5), as a naive realist would typically claim.

Another criticism that scientific realists have of naive realism is the latter's view of causation. The naive realists, House tells us, assume a view of causation that is derived from the philosophers David Hume, John Stuart Mill, and Bertrand Russell. Within this view the classic example is that of one billiard ball striking another. House depicts this phenomenon as 'a flat ontology' in which there is a flow of events and experiences such that our observations produce regular patterns (*ibid*, p. 5). The goal of science is to locate these regularities in the flat configurations. The problem with the naive realist conception of causality, according to the scientific realists, is that their primitive understanding of causation sees social reality in an analogously simple way. In contrast, 'A realist conception of causation might see events as being produced by the interaction of a multitude of underlying causal entities operating at different levels' (*ibid*, p. 7).

As an example, House cites evaluation of planned change. In the naive realist view, an evaluation of the same reform applied in several sites would expect the same result at each site. In other words, the naive realists have a traditional experimentalist orientation toward evaluation. But scientific realists, assuming that 'like causal features do not necessarily produce like results', would take a different approach as they viewed different sites or contexts (*ibid*, p. 7). As House explains:

> The program (being evaluated) would not be exactly the same from place to place but would differ with the multitude of factors that produce the program — for example, different teachers and students. In other words, the program would not be seen as a fixed entity, an 'X' in a design, but as itself varying from site to site however it is produced. Furthermore, even the same program can produce different results because of the complexity and interaction of all the structures that affect the results. (*ibid*, p. 7)

Scientific realists would have very different expectations with regard to program evaluation:

> A (scientific) realist conception of causation would call for evaluation approaches that expect and track variability and irregularity of events, for somehow describing programs and their outcomes so that influences can be registered and so that causal entities and their interactions can be understood. One might draw inferences from experiments, with (the) help of substantive knowledge, but one would not expect the studies to yield critical tests of the program (as a naive realist would). (*ibid*, p. 8)

Thus, while naive realists see evaluation as similar to a traditional experiment that tests the effects of a specific reform at different sites, scientific realists see a multisite evaluation as tracking and explaining differences that are not comparable in an experimental sense.

Scientific realists have several other criticisms of naive realists which I will not address here. For those who want to pursue a more thorough understanding of scientific realism, the House article and its references are a good beginning. Another good example, though much different in approach taken and in the references cited, is Evers and Lakomski's *Knowing Educational Administration* (1991). Chapters 1, 2, and 10 of this work are more specifically focused on epistemological issues, while the other seven chapters apply scientific realism to the theory debates in educational administration.

Simply put, from the scientific realist perspective the world and our judgments about it are substantially more complex and problematic than the naive realist view usually assumes. Indeed, in my opinion, epistemological judgments of the nature of reality are more problematic than even the scientific realists assume. As Greenfield (1978) has said, 'The relationship between explanation and reality is *at best* (my emphasis) uncertain' (p. 19). The next section will address my point of view on this issue.

Social Relativism

While I agree that the scientific realists have made the best attempt to date to reconstruct the scientific method in the face of the broad array of criticisms that have been made of positivism by both the positivists themselves (Phillips, 1983) and various postpositivists, including Popper, Toulmin, Kuhn and Feyerabend, I find their perspective to be inadequate. Instead of any version of realism for the social sciences, I would support what I call social or postmodernist relativism, even though relativism is, as Barnes and Bloor (1991) have said, 'everywhere abominated' (p. 21) (see, also, Donmoyer, 1985; Bernstein, 1988; Harding, 1991; Lather, 1991b; Phillips, 1983; among numerous others who oppose relativism).

What I mean by this term 'social or postmodernist relativism'[8] is the unabashed recognition that all epistemology, ontology, and the ways of thinking that yield such categories as epistemology and ontology are socially conditioned and historically relative or contextual.[9] More simply, 'ways of knowing are inherently culture-bound and perspectival' (Lather, 1988, p. 570). This is the same point that Habermas makes in *Knowledge and Human Interests* (1971) when he says:

> the interpreter cannot abstractly free himself from his hermeneutic point of depar-
> ture. He cannot simply jump over the open horizon of his own life activity and just
> suspend the context of tradition in which his own subjectivity has been formed in
> order to submerge himself in a subhistorical stream of life that allows the pleasur-
> able identification of everyone with everyone else. (p. 181)

Foucault (1977) makes a similar point in his essay 'Nietzsche, genealogy, history'. In this work he criticizes historians who write history as if they write from outside of history; instead Foucault praises Nietzsche's embrace of his own perspectival positionality. Similarly, in this study I criticize social scientists who do science as if they work from outside of their own historical positionality; instead I praise the embrace of the relativity of the social scientists' positionality.[10]

By the word 'social', I intend to signal that this postmodernist version of relativism is not 'anything goes' because there are always social and historical constraints on what is allowed, though what is allowed is always open to challenge and change. I also intend to signal that this postmodernist relativism is social and not individual. Although there are individual perspectives based on the idiosyncratic differences among individuals, the 'stuff' with which individuals construct and interpret 'reality', and are constructed and interpreted by 'reality', is social and not individual.

This social relativism flies in the face of any positivist or realist efforts to develop foundational or ahistorical truths or truth claims: 'paradigms and language games — to borrow from Kuhn and Wittgenstein — have been relativized' (Apple, 1991, p. vii). This position also undermines seemingly postfoundational efforts to establish some kind of criteria, standards, procedures, decision rules, or rationality which rises above the relativity of history. Both truth and any kind of postfoundational meta-criteria for establishing truth are in my view socially relative to a particular time and place. Even though in that particular time and place there may be a variety of truths competing with one another and even though there will be many possible truths or truth methods which are not allowed in that particular time and place, both the competing truths and the excluded truths are socially and historically located.

For instance, currently positivism, realism, critical theory, feminism, interpretivism, constructivism, and poststructuralism, among others, are all competing within the Western social sciences to name truth (or, as with some deconstructionists, to leave truth nameless). There are other truth games, such as fundamentalist Christianity, Tibetan Buddhism, or even earlier versions of science, which are not currently allowed within the social sciences. This does not mean that these or other alternatives are not viable possibilities for the social sciences, but only that they are outside the current, socially defined boundaries of what is considered valid approaches to the generation of knowledge. It also does not mean that the alternatives that I have named or other currently unrecognized possibilities will not in the future become allowable.

Social or postmodernist relativism, thus, accepts that there are social and historical constraints on what can be claimed as truth, or whatever other word we use to designate knowledge, in any particular social and historical location. It does not accept, however, that such social and historical constraints cannot be questioned or altered. While the acceptance of such social and historical constraints may at first appear conservative, it is in fact the opposite. It specifically locates where the struggle for truth or knowledge occurs. Truth is a social, historical, and, therefore, a political struggle. Truth is not power-free; it is power-laden. 'Discourse and politics, knowledge and power are . . . part of an indissoluble couplet' (*ibid*, p. vii). 'Power and knowledge directly imply one another . . .' (Foucault, 1979, p. 27). In the sense that this social relativist epistemology uncovers the truth-power relationship, it is radical rather than conservative: 'to politicize (knowledge production) means not to bring politics in where there were none, but to make overt how power permeates the construction and legitimation of knowledges' (Lather, 1991b, p. xvii).

The struggle for truth is a struggle for power because different truth games establish different relations between people or, as Foucault (1977) would say, between different 'constellation(s) of bodies' (p. 39).[11] For example, Habermas in *Knowledge and Human Interests* (1972) claims that the application of the positivist truth game to social issues inappropriately removes social decisions from the democratic community to the small, select community of truth game experts. It could also be argued, as Foster (1986) has done, that one of the reasons positivism and its sociological ally, functionalism, have been so dominant in the social sciences is that the advocates of positivism and functionalism have claimed to be value-free and apolitical. Positivists and functionalists could then avoid addressing the inequitable arrangements of power within which they worked.

Truth games, however, always imply in my view how people are arranged in relation to each other — different truth games, different relations. Another way of saying the same thing is that all truth games are political.[12] All truth games imply political arrangements, though what those political arrangements are for a particular truth game is itself open to argument. Habermas (1971), for example, argued for a more democratic truth game than the scientistic one he saw dominating the West. Others (Antonio, 1989, or Bernstein, 1988, for example) have contended that Habermas' truth game has an inherently elitist basis because of Habermas' transcendental claim that the fundamental nature of communication, a central facet of his theory of truth, is ahistorical and, thus, foundational. This would be elitist because Habermas could then argue that his truth was the real truth in relation to other possible truths that were not founded on the same communicative basis as his.

Poststructuralism, another example of a truth game, with its claim that the establishment of a truth game necessarily means the repression of other truth games yields an ongoing critique of the dominance of any truth game, whether the game is scientific, Marxist, or any other one (Merquior, 1985).[13] Foucault (1977) contended that 'humanity installs each of its violences in a system of rules and thus proceeds from domination to domination' (p. 151). This poststructuralist truth-game implies a social arrangement in which there is a constant undermining of unitary dominance in any form. Habermas, however, in his criticisms of Foucault claimed that poststructuralism was inherently conservative because it undermined key democratic values developed through the Enlightenment (Bernstein, 1992). According to Habermas' critique, Foucauldian poststructuralism would, in effect, support social relations in which the most powerful were unchecked in their actions by any commitment to such Enlightenment values as democracy and individual liberty.

Three Criticisms of Social Relativism

The latter contention — that relativism undermines protections against 'might makes right' — is in fact one of the criticisms of the type of relativism I support.[14] The argument goes as follows: If there is no foundational truth, no right way to determine what is the good, the true, and the beautiful, whichever group is strongest will simply establish its choices for these categories, and, most certainly, establish self-serving choices at that. More simply, might makes right. Harding (1991), the widely respected feminist epistemologist, makes a similar point when she says, 'There have to be standards for distinguishing between how I want the world to be and how, in empirical fact, it is. Otherwise, might makes right in knowledge-seeking . . .' (p. 160). This argument, however, depends on the positivist assumption that a non-power related truth game is possible.[15] It is doubtful, at least in the social sciences, that such a power-free truth-game has ever existed.

This argument against relativism also depends on a totalizing view of power. Choices about truth games are always made within specific social and historical contexts. Such contexts are never simple, and they are rarely totally dominated by a single 'might'. For example, there is little question that the most powerful group in a particular community has more ability to establish its truth game than less powerful other groups; for example, people of color or working people do not dominate such truth games. So on average the most powerful group is going to 'win' more often than any other group whenever and wherever the more powerful group chooses to fight for its interests. (The more powerful groups in a community often ignore many decisions, such as many decisions about schools, because they see no vital interest of theirs at stake.) But this is only part of the picture: 'Power in a society (or in any community, school, etc.) is never a fixed and closed regime' (Gordon, 1991, p. 5). There are, as Fraser (1989), a poststructuralist-oriented feminist, says, 'multiple axes of power' (p. 10). The more powerful groups are often divided among themselves. In such cases they sometimes make alliances with other less powerful groups.[16] Less powerful groups are sometimes sufficiently united to defeat the more powerful. The less powerful also tend to resist domination in multiple and creative ways both as individuals and as groups (Apple, 1982; Giroux, 1983; Weiler, 1988).

In addition, there are often social constraints on the powerful that are historically rooted in values that both the powerful and the less powerful accept to a greater or lesser degree. For instance, in the West the emerging capitalists, along with other social groups, used the promise of democratic values and practices like universal suffrage to 'defeat' the royalist truth game, but now, at least to some extent, the capitalists have to abide by those democratic values and practices. This is not to say that the powerful do not often abrogate, ignore, or corrupt such historical arrangements; this is also not to say, though, that they always abrogate, ignore, or corrupt such arrangements. In other words, the powerful are also constrained, to some extent, by their truth games.

The same picture could be drawn of schools. On average, the formal power hierarchy usually dominates. In specific contexts, however, there are often multiple centers of power in constant struggle, conflict, compromise, and negotiation. Sometimes within a particular school district a principal is more powerful than the superintendent. Sometimes a teacher is more powerful than a principal. Sometimes teachers are more powerful in some areas, while principals are more powerful in other areas. Sometimes a student or group of students is more powerful within a particular classroom than the teacher. Often these relations of power shift over the course of a school year.

While there may be a dominant truth game in a particular school, there are virtually always alternative truth games with different degrees of power in different situations. There are, in addition, consensual values and interpretations that constrain what is allowable within a school or a classroom. For instance, in many states corporal punishment is not allowed even if the formally most powerful person in the classroom (i.e., the teacher) wants to utilize such punishment.

Similar things could be said about the dominance of the social sciences by the conventional science approach to epistemology.[17] While it is true that conventional science has dominated methods departments in education and while the advocates of this approach have often acted arrogantly like the powerful often do, many in education (like Lincoln and Guba, 1985) have fought against this dominance. Sometimes the new alternatives are supported by conventional scientists who think like Feyerabend that science should remain very open to new ideas and methods. The advocates of alternative orientations have thus been able to gain ground in educational research partially because there are constraints within which the conventional social scientists had to exist. For many reasons, then, those who have resisted the dominance by conventional social scientists have attained some power and, in some situations, could now be said to have established a new dominance.[18]

Consequently, while 'might' or the more powerful groups certainly make right or truth more often than anyone else does (and this inequity must repeatedly be emphasized), the most powerful in any situation only rarely, and perhaps never, possess totalized control for a very long period of time. To argue, then, that relativism in the social sciences leads to a totalized control by the most powerful is to ignore the past historical connections between power and truth (which positivists only assumed they had overcome) and to ignore that power is rarely or only fleetingly totalized. Instead of permitting a dominance of power over knowledge, social or postmodernist relativism leads to an unmasking of the historical relations between these two and of the illusion that any dominance is comprehensive or total.

A second, and related, criticism of relativism is that it undermines emancipatory struggles and epistemologies: the 'undercutting of foundational Enlightenment tenets causes many intellectuals with emancipatory concerns to question the politics of postmodernism' (Lather, 1991b, p. 37).[19] Those who make this critique, such as some feminists (see Nielsen, 1990; or Lather, 1991b, pp. 26–31, for example), argue that relativism undermines factual or empirical determinations that certain social groups, such as women or people of color, are oppressed or have less power or are exploited.[20] These critics are reluctant to set aside some kind of foundationalism or empirical criterion from which they can argue that it is really *true* that certain groups are socially oppressed.

Another argument which some feminist critics have made is that the current fascination with relativism is a male response to the growing power of feminism. Since feminists have effectively questioned masculinist versions of foundationalism, so this argument goes, males have strategically switched to a relativist philosophy that makes all positions equal and thus undermines foundationalism as successfully revised by feminists. According to Harding (1991), 'Historically, relativism appears as a problematic intellectual possibility only for dominating groups at the point where the hegemony of their views is being challenged' (p. 153).

While I too would sometimes wish that there were ahistorical foundations for justice and equality, I do not agree that the social relativism I support is a threat to feminism or other emancipatory positions. Indeed, I would argue the opposite. The Enlightenment values of justice and equality were never ahistorical or foundational. These Enlightenment values have evolved out of multiple historical struggles reaching back hundreds of years. The idea or the belief that women are equal to men is not an ahistorical truth but a social creation constructed within historical human activity.

Women, and the men who supported their struggles, have fought to create the 'truth' of gender equality in the face of immense opposition, an opposition that, not incidentally, often couched its resistance to equality in foundational truth claims, such as the 'natural' role of women. The equality of women as a truth was not created by Enlightenment values; instead both the equality of women and other Enlightenment values are historical social constructions. This does not mean that feminists did not in their struggles draw on already recognized Enlightenment values. They certainly did. Feminists obviously used Enlightenment values with which to develop rationales that would convince other women and men of the justice of their cause. Many or even most of the early feminists may have believed that these values were foundational or ahistorical. Nonetheless, such values or truths and the partisan use of such values always arise out of and evolve within historical conditions and struggles.

A third criticism of relativism is that it has meaning only as one side of a binary opposition between a correspondence theory of truth and an 'everything is relative' truth (Bernstein, 1988; Harding, 1991; Lather, 1991b). One way of pursuing this critique is to contend that once a correspondence theory of truth is disposed of, the other side of the binary, relativism, is no longer meaningful. This is similar to the argument Barone (1990) used to say that since objectivism was dead, subjectivism had lost any useful meaning.

Another way of pursuing this critique is to make both sides of the binary problematic as some poststructuralists and feminists have done (Haraway, 1988; Harding, 1991; Lather, 1991b). While I agree with the effort by feminists and poststructuralists to think outside of the traditional sexist or logocentric binaries, I do not agree with how this has been done by Haraway, Harding, and Lather. The effort to move beyond the foundationalism/relativism binary violates a basic tenet of postmodern thought, according to Derrida (1981). This tenet is that it is not possible to completely free oneself from the discourse out of which the issues arose in the first place. Decisive breaks are not possible: 'I do not believe in decisive ruptures. . . . Breaks are always, and fatally, reinscribed in an old cloth that must continually, interminably be undone' (*ibid*, p. 24). In fact, Derrida would claim that our concepts are 'marked through and through by referential . . . assumptions, and there is no way of simply breaking their hold by a kind of deconstructionist fiat' (Norris, 1987, p. 54). That is, the social-cultural academic matrix, which includes the foundationalist/relativist binary and within which Bernstein, Lather, and Harding think and write, cannot be escaped by simply declaring one's escape. One Derridian alternative is

> to criticize . . . from *within* (his emphasis) an inherited language, a discourse that will always have been worked over in advance by traditional concepts and categories. What is required is a kind of internal distancing, an effort of defamiliarization which prevents concepts from settling down into routine habits of thought. (*ibid*, p. 16)

Another postmodernist response is to think and write at the margins of the old binary and thereby signal an awareness of one's own limits (Hutcheon, 1989). An additional postmodernist alternative, and the one I have tried to pursue, is to transform the binary from within by recognizing and using its classical meaning, moving with and against that meaning, and altering it by pushing it in new directions.

Several of those who want to move beyond the foundationalism/relativism binary, and I count Bernstein (1988), Harding (1991), Lather (1991b) in this group, want to retain some degree of foundationalism, especially in terms of the idea that there is a 'real' that can really be known in some sense.[21] But all three are difficult to pin down because they all have commitments that straddle both sides of the binary. While I have no quarrel with their relativist commitments, I do disagree with their foundationalist ones. For Bernstein (1988) this retained foundationalism is contained in such statements as: 'We must avoid the fallacy of thinking there are no fixed, determinate rules for distinguishing better from worse interpretations . . .' (p. 91).

For Harding (1991), who for me is more complex and persuasive than Bernstein (1988), this retained foundationalism is 'a strong objectivity'. While this strong objectivity recognizes that all views are historical — 'a strong notion of objectivity requires a commitment to acknowledge the historical character of every belief or set of beliefs' (Harding, 1991, p. 156), it still includes a commitment to a scientific idea of objectivity that is inescapably ahistorical. For example, she claims that it is possible to have 'a critical evaluation . . . (that would determine) which social situations tend to generate the most objective knowledge claims' (*ibid*, p. 142). Her expansion of objectivity from the traditional sphere of the context of justification to the sphere of discovery leaves the idea of objectivity intact. Even her argument that the 'bias' of feminism leads to a stronger objectivity leaves the idea of objectivity intact. In fact, she takes a position that is similar to Bernstein's when she indicates that strong objectivity can discriminate between 'Which ones (truth claims) generate less and which more partial and distorted accounts of nature and social life' (*ibid*, p. 161).

Lather (1991b) has a range of criticisms of relativism. It has no meaning outside of the binary. It undermines the objective reality of the oppression of women. It is a masculinist maneuver to undermine feminism. It ignores context and positionality. Of the three scholars discussed in this section — Bernstein, Harding, and Lather — she is the most thoroughly committed to a postmodernist social relativism and, thus, is more willing to undermine foundationalist ideas of all sorts. She is, however, somewhat divided in this commitment as is appropriate to her deconstructionist inclinations. For example, she says her goal, and the goal of desconstruction as a method, is to transcend 'a binary logic by simultaneously being both and neither of the binary terms' (*ibid*, p. 13). It is not surprising then that in 'being both' she is committed, like Harding (1991), to retaining an objectivism that confirms inequitable power arrangements in terms of class, race, and gender. Contrary to Bernstein (1988), Harding (1991), and Lather (1991b), I resist the idea of placing anything outside of the relativity of specific social and historical conditions. I would suggest that what Bernstein, Harding, Lather, and others are against is a modernist definition of relativism, one that is 'anything goes' and individualistic and one that is idealistic and separated from its moorings in particular historical contexts. Their idea of relativism is itself ahistorical. 'Anything goes' is a phantom; historically 'anything goes' is never possible. What is possible, truth games or otherwise, is always embedded in historical conditions. The argument against individualistic relativism proceeds similarly. Humans are social, historical beings. While an individual may become an idiosyncratic (individual) combination of the bits and pieces of her/his social and historical positionality, she/he cannot reach outside time and place for these bits and pieces. In fact, what most of us become individually is well within the accepted patterns of our time and place. Social relativism, rather than resisting our positionality, recognizes and valorizes the social and historical contingency of human existence and our truth games.

I would argue that a poststructuralist view of relativism, as I am trying to develop here, dissolves many of the prior problems with relativism. This I think is the point of view that Alcoff (1987) arrives at in her meditation on the problems of positivism and relativism for a feminist social science:

> What happens to the problem of relativism if we drop out from the above picture
> of the transcendent, independent reality lying beyond our discourse or web? It
> seems to me this is what Foucault and Gadamer at least want to do. Our beliefs
> (truth claims) are still relative to a discourse, but they cannot be characterized as
> therefore 'less true' because they are not being compared to a transcendent real-
> ity . . . it is not just the criterion of truth that is relative, but truth itself is relative . . . it
> would appear to make relativism less formidable by undercutting the usual ground
> its critics take. (p. 98)

It would, thus, seem to me that it is possible to maintain the ongoing critique of
foundationalist truth games and to posit nothing — no criterion, no rationality, no
objectivity of any kind, no anything — as outside particular historical contingencies
and positionality without falling into the problems that Bernstein (1988), Harding
(1991), and Lather (1991b), among others fear. I have, for instance, no problem
with 'strong objectivity' as a criterion according to Harding's (1991) definition, but
I strongly resist the idea that this criterion is not historically mediated. I can see that
this criterion is useful and meaningful for the social struggle to establish equitable
social arrangements, but I cannot see that arguing that this criterion is itself unmediated by socially located truth games is helpful to that struggle.

And, finally, I am not as sanguine as Harding is about a standpoint approach.
In fact, I am not sanguine about any one position, mine included. I am as suspicious
as Fraser (1989) of the claim that a standpoint approach, like that of Harding and
others, solves our epistemological dilemmas. I would agree with the poststructuralists
that all perspectives imply political arrangements and invariably exclude some
groups, some voices. Some sort of social relativist or postmodernist epistemology
is necessary but certainly not a romanticized 'everyone is equal' one or an 'all
positions are equal' one. A contentious, self-critical pluralism, an Ellsworth (1989)
style pluralism of shifting coalitions and conflicts, might be best.

Two Postfoundational or Pragmatic Alternatives to Social Relativism

As was briefly mentioned in the prior section, there have been numerous efforts to
develop postfoundational or pragmatic alternatives to relativism. A wide range of
scholars have attempted to derive postfoundational alternatives that would provide
us with a middle range choice between the Scylla of foundationalism and the
Charybdis of relativism.[22] Bernstein's *Beyond Objectivism and Relativism* (1988) is
obviously a classical example of this approach, but here I want to consider two
other scholars whose work is more specifically located within the field of education. In both cases, however, I will contend that their postfoundationalism or pragmatism fails.

Donmoyer (1985), in an article that was partially entitled 'The rescue from
relativism', used Toulmin's claim

that there are ways to rationally assess the relative worth of conflicting claims
... (and) that differing purposes (of the particular research) will inevitably result
in different criteria for appraising the relative adequacy of conflicting conceptual
schemes or languages. (p. 18)

Donmoyer does recognize that 'different theoretical languages (different perspectives) will lead researchers to employ quite different dependent variables, and these
variables will profoundly influence research findings' (*ibid*, p. 19). He, nonetheless,
wants to privilege some sort of rationality procedures that rises above politics, tradition, and error (i.e., meta-paradigmatic standards which rule over all truth games):

Whenever they (educational researchers) make decisions about funding research
or allocating journal space, questions of purpose must be answered. Answers,
however, normally emerge more from the exercise of political power or from an
appeal to tradition or from an inappropriate application of methodological canons
than from *rational deliberation* (my emphasis). There is a need, therefore, for
methodologists to develop (such rational) procedures. . . . The development of such
procedures will not be easy. The work remaining, however, is *largely procedural
rather than epistemological* (emphasis added) . . . (*ibid*, p. 19)

The oppositional deployment is clear: 'political power', 'tradition', and 'inappropriate application of methodological canon' on the negative side and 'rational
deliberation' on the positive. He follows this rhetorical strategy with a further
valorization of 'rational deliberation' by citing the need for 'methodologists to
develop procedures' that would facilitate the implementation of such rationality.
Finally, he makes sure we understand his commitment by stating that the epistemological issues are settled and only procedural work remains. In short, rationality,
rational deliberation, and rational procedures provide the warrant for decisions
about knowledge claims.[23]

Mishler's (1990) application of disciplinary exemplars, which are adapted
from Kuhn (1970), is a second example of an effort to develop postfoundational
standards. In this case, however, it is not standards or procedures of rationality
which are privileged but the research exemplars which come to dominate 'a community of scientists as they (the scientists) come to share nonproblematic and
useful ways of thinking about and solving problems' (Mishler, 1990, p. 421). That
is, Mishler sees respected exemplars of past research within specific disciplinary contexts as postfoundational guides to social science research. Obviously he is
more oriented to a relativistic point of view than Donmoyer (1985) by the fact that
such exemplars are socially and historically embedded. For example, Mishler (1990)
agrees with my contention that epistemological issues are located in 'the social
world — a world constructed in and through our discourse and actions, through
praxis' (p. 420). He also agrees that 'Since social worlds are endlessly being remade
as norms and practices change, it is clear that judgments . . . may change with time,
even when addressed to the "same" findings' (*ibid*, p. 420).

From my social relativist perspective each of these examples commit different
errors, but the source of the errors, in my view, is due to their desire or need to

avoid relativism. While Donmoyer (1985) agrees that there are 'different theoretical languages' (p. 19), he appears to think that there are rationality procedures which rise above such languages.[24] Is there, however, only one kind of rationality that is applicable to all situations and all theoretical languages? Are there rationality procedures to which all theoretical language advocates would agree? Could we not have different rationalities and different sets of rationality procedures, a condition Bachelard (who both mentored and strongly influenced Foucault (Eribon, 1991)) suggests already exists even in the natural sciences (Gutting, 1989), or could we not have different 'logic fragments' as Barth (1991, p. 125) suggests?

Merquior (1985) says that Cassirer in *The Philosophy of the Enlightenment* concludes that

> the Enlightenment significantly changed the concept of reason. While, for Descartes, Spinoza or Leibniz, reason was 'the territory of eternal truths', the next century no longer saw reason as a treasure of principles and fixed truths, but simply as a faculty, the original power of the mind, to be grasped only in exercise of its analytical functions. (p. 69)

Foucault (1977) suggests that what we label as reason historically 'arose from the passion of scholars, their reciprocal hatred, their fanatical and unending discussions, and their spirit of competition — the personal conflicts that slowly forged the weapons of reason' (p. 142) Deleuze (1992) asserts that 'reason is forever bifurcating; there are as many bifurcations as there are foundations, as many collapses as there are constructions . . .' (p. 163) Derrida says the rule of reason is logocentric (Flax, 1990). Habermas (1971) argues that 'Representations and descriptions are never independent of standards. And the choice of these standards . . . cannot be either logically deduced or empirically demonstrated' (p. 312). In addition, feminists and race-oriented theorists (see, for example, Stanfield, 1985 or Minh-ha, 1989), among others, have contended that privileging the rationality of conventional social science is unfairly or unduly providing legitimacy to only one kind of possible rationality. These critics would advance other kinds of rationality.

If there are multiple rationalities and multiple sets of rationality procedures, as I would contend there are, Donmoyer (1985) has simply moved relativity from one domain of concern to another without settling anything, without establishing the apparently desired Archimedean point. My critique, though, does not mean that rationality and rationality procedures do not exist. They do. My point is that there are many rationalities and many sets of rationality procedures (some of which overlap, some of which conflict, some of which are incommensurable), all of which operate within particular social, historical, and disciplinary contexts.

Mishler (1991), though he is closer to my position than Donmoyer (1985), makes a different set of mistakes. First, he unproblematically appropriates Kuhn's natural science-oriented 'shared exemplars' approach to the social sciences. While I agree that the old, assumed epistemological differences between the social and natural sciences are less meaningful or defensible than they once were, an exemplar that is guiding research in the social sciences is different from an exemplar that is guiding research in the natural sciences. According to Kuhn (1970), a particular discipline within the natural sciences is guided by the same paradigm except in the rare revolutionary periods. Thus, those utilizing an exemplar in a natural science discipline generally agree epistemologically; the exemplar simply guides their research within that agreement.

The social sciences, as Kuhn himself has pointed out, are much different. Rarely does any particular discipline in the social sciences have the kind of epistemological consensus that Kuhn saw in the natural sciences. In addition, the history of the social sciences looks more like succeeding ideologies (Bernstein, 1988; Polkinghorne, 1983) rather than Kuhn's 'normal (progressively accumulating) science' followed by occasional eruptions of 'revolutionary science'. Consequently, in the social sciences presiding exemplars serve more to establish the dominance of one epistemological voice over others. The research which such exemplars guide serves to exclude alternative research voices as much as it supposedly serves to simply guide research.

Shakeshaft's (1987) feminist research in educational administration well illustrates this point. She contends that the dominant exemplars in educational administration privilege male administrators and the viewpoint of those men over women administrators and the viewpoint of those women. The result, according to Shakeshaft, has been that male perspectives and experiences are privileged while female perspectives and experiences are marginalized or silenced. Mishler's privileging of a discipline's 'shared exemplars', thus, tends to privilege the discipline's status quo over other possible contending voices.

This same point was also made by Scheurich and Lather (1991). They found that in a specific journal conversation about epistemological perspectives in supervision, only two of several possible epistemological perspectives were being included in the exchange within the journal. Even if the two included perspectives, and the exemplars representative of those two, are considered the 'normal science' of supervision, they were not the only perspectives possible. Other perspectives exist in supervision; they were simply not represented within this journal conversation. Consequently, an acceptance of the dominant two perspectives in supervision, as was done by those conducting the conversation, reinforced the dominance of the status quo and the exclusion of other voices.

A second problem for Mishler (1990) is that he argues, following Kuhn, that 'shared exemplars' are an accurate description of the way that scientists do science. I would suggest, following Bachelard, Canguilhem, and Foucault, that scientists are much more non-standardized than this in how they do science (Gutting, 1989). I would contend that some follow exemplars, some follow orders, some pursue various other approaches, and most do all three of these. (For descriptions of scientific work that that are different than 'exemplar-oriented' approaches, see Latour and Woolgar's *Laboratory Life: The Construction of Scientific Facts*, 1986.) In addition, Mishler ignores how idiosyncratic the individual scientist is in her/his perception and use of a particular exemplar. In other words, Mishler in a certain sense totalizes the use of exemplars both by assuming that exemplars are the best description of how scientists proceed and that the use of exemplars proceeds in the same fashion for all scientists. This privileging of a totalized version of shared exemplars serves, once again, to marginalize or silence other, equally defensible research approaches. In response to Donmoyer's and Mishler's postfoundational approaches I counsel extreme suspicion toward any effort to privilege or totalize any postfoundational approach, whether that approach be some kind of meta-criteria or meta-guide to how research ought to be done. Instead I would call for the literal multiplication of *bricolage*[25] methods which are reflectively aware of their social and historical contextuality and of their politics.[26]

A Social Relativist Critique of Scientific Realism

Earlier, after reviewing scientific realism, I indicated that although I thought that it was superior to either positivism or naive realism, I still considered it to be inadequate.[27] I make this judgment primarily on the basis of two conclusions. First, although scientific realists think that 'knowledge is a social and historical product' (House, 1991, p. 3), they still believe that a body of knowledge can be developed which accurately describes the 'complex and stratified' 'real world' (*ibid*, p. 3). This combination of assumptions hides two connected problems. One is that 'social and historical' implies a single, unified social and historical context; otherwise many knowledges would be elicited from many social and historical contexts, which is what I as a social relativist or *bricoleur* would say. The other problem is that the scientific realists, subsequently, assume that the one knowledge/one context produces essentially one best description. While there may be conflict between various contending descriptions of the 'real world', one will be eventually judged the best, according to the scientific realists. If the scientific realists do not support this 'one best description' conclusion, then they must accept the existence of a range of equally possible but different descriptions, which is what I would accept.

A second way that scientific realism is inadequate is similar to Donmoyer's (1985) postfoundationalism. They assume that they can develop rational criteria which rise above historically positioned and mediated social and cultural constructions. This is clearly apparent in the recent work of Evers and Lakomski (1991), who consider themselves scientific or coherentist realists. They privilege a set of coherency standards, but they would not agree that their standards are meta-paradigmatic because they think that only realism is acceptable and that a multiple-paradigms position is unacceptable. They call their coherentist standards 'extra-empirical'. In their view

> theory choice needs to be guided by a consideration of the extra-empirical virtues possessed by theories. These virtues of system include simplicity, consistency, coherence, comprehensiveness, conservativeness, and fecundity, though they are often referred to collectively as coherence considerations or as elements in a coherentist account of epistemic justification. (p. 4)

These 'extra-empirical virtues' are meant to guide choices between theories. From my perspective Evers and Lakomski (1991) have several problems with these 'virtues'. First, they have the linguistic problem of how to define each of their criteria, a problem logical positivists and analytical philosophers have found to be difficult indeed. What I think they will find as they attend to these definitional issues is that relativism will simply reappear in decisions about appropriate definitions. Second, the decision of which criterion is more important in any particular situation is equally difficult. What if, in comparing two theories, one is high (whatever that means) on simplicity, consistency, and coherence and the other is high on comprehensiveness, conservativeness, and fecundity? Which is better? What is the appropriate balance amidst all of these terms?

Third, and most devastating, these extra-empirical virtues themselves have no empirical foundation even though they are supposed to rule over empirical judgments. Even Quine, upon whom Evers and Lakomski (1991) assert much of their theory is dependent, indicates that 'these extra-empirical criteria are based neither on empirical nor rational foundations' (Hesse, 1980). If no empirical or rational reasons exist for these coherency criteria, they are historically relative to derivation in particular social or disciplinary contexts (i.e., socially relative). As Hesse argues, the 'adoption of such criteria, which can be seen to be different for different groups and at different periods, should be explicable by social rather than logical factors' (*ibid*, p. 33). Moreover, she contends that, even in the natural sciences,

> Conflicting (natural) scientific paradigms or fundamental theories differ not just in what they assert as postulates, but also in the conceptual meaning of the postulates and in their criteria of what counts as a good theory; criteria of simplicity and good approximation: of what is to be an 'explanation' or a 'cause' or a 'good inference', and even what is the practical goal of scientific theorizing. All such differences are inexplicable by the logic of science, since they are precisely disputes about the content of that logic. The historian must make them intelligible by extra-scientific causation. (*ibid*, p. 33)

All three of these issues — definition of the coherence terms, the weight given to each term in relation to the others, and the lack of foundations for the coherency criteria — will simply lead back to relativity. As Hesse, following Barnes (1974), says,

> all attempts to find demarcating criteria, that is, necessary and sufficient conditions for a belief system to be a science, have failed. These failures include all verifiability and falsifiability criteria, and all specific appeals to experimentation and/or particular kinds of inductive or theoretical inference. At best, he (Barnes, 1974) argues, the concept 'science' must be regarded as a loose association of family resemblance characteristics involving, among other things, aversion to all forms of anthropomorphism and teleology, and consequent tendencies to secularism, impersonality, abstraction and quantification. Moreover, we must not impose our own scientific criteria on the past; the subject matter of the historian of science can only be demarcated by recognizing (ex post facto) what it is in the past that exhibits causal continuity with present science. (*ibid*, p. 47)

As with Donmoyer (1985), Evers and Lakomski (1991) have attempted to solve the 'problem' of relativism but have only succeeded in moving it elsewhere. More importantly, however, I do not accept that reality, whatever that is, can be encapsulated under the sign of any single, dominant epistemology, scientific or coherentist realism in this case. As Foucault (1991) says, 'I am a pluralist' (p. 53). Further, as fits my emphasis on the politics of all epistemology, I find such single-epistemology dominance highly dangerous. Again, I would support the proliferation of many ways of seeing and the dominance of none. Foucault (1977, p. 168) puts this much more poetically when he says, 'we should welcome the cunning assembly that simulates and clamors at the door' of knowledge.[28]

A Postmodernist Politics of Epistemology

If, as in my view, epistemology or truth games are 'grounded' not in foundational truth claims nor even in such apparently postfoundational claims as rationality procedures (Donmoyer, 1985) or disciplinary exemplars (Mishler, 1990) but are located in shifting and diverse historical human practices, politics and power become central epistemological or doxological issues. As Eisner (1988) says, 'There is no such thing as a value-neutral approach to the world . . .' (p. 19). Epistemology as doxology is then no longer limited either to the explication of particular truth games or to the competition between truth games. Epistemology is thus expanded to include the history, sociology, and politics of truth games.[29]

For example, scientific realism, as discussed previously, is a currently advocated truth game. In the earlier discussion I covered in a traditional way some of what this position was about and how it compared to other positions, such as positivism and naive realism. From the social relativist position I have been exploring, a consideration of scientific realism would be expanded to include an additional set of questions. If scientific realism were the ruling paradigm, who would benefit? Does it require expert knowledge and thus privilege experts over others? Is its view of the technological products of science unproblematically positive? Does it view science and technology in an idealistic way or does it view science in terms of its 'real' practices? What is its social history? Under what social and historical conditions did it arise? As a way of thinking, does it privilege some social groups over others? From what social groups in terms of class, race, and gender would it tend to draw its advocates? What does it mean if its advocates are chiefly members of a single social group? Does it then, historically and socially, serve particular class, race, and gender interests?

Fraser (1989), a feminist who rejects both a correspondence-oriented positivist approach and a standpoint approach (pp. 181–2) like that of Harding (1991), raises similar kinds of questions in reference to choices about better or worse 'interpretations of people's needs' (Fraser, 1989, p. 181). She says that

> First, there are procedural considerations concerning the social processes by which various competing need interpretations are generated. For example, how exclusive

or inclusive are various rival discourses? How hierarchical or egalitarian are the relations among the interlocutors? In general, procedural considerations dictate that, all other things being equal, the best need interpretations are those reached by means of communicative processes that most closely approximate ideals of demo-cracy, equality, and fairness.

In addition, considerations of consequences are relevant in justifying need interpretations. This means comparing alternative distributive outcomes of rival interpretations. For example, would widespread acceptance of some given inter-pretation of a social need disadvantage some groups of people vis-a-vis others? Does the interpretation conform to, rather than challenge, societal patterns of dominance and subordination? . . . In general, consequentialist considerations dic-tate that, all other things being equal, the best need interpretations are those that do not disadvantage some groups vis-a-vis others. (*ibid*, p. 182)

In this more specific application, Fraser illustrates the kinds of political analysis that need to be applied to epistemological questions in general and to specific applications of particular epistemologies. When she asserts that there are no privil-eged foundational, postfoundational, or, even, standpoint reasons for judging one interpretation better than another (*ibid*, pp. 181–2), and she turns instead to political judgments, she is evidencing the kind of approach I have tried to develop and explain in this work.

Similar kinds of questions would also be applied to the definition of such key research terms as 'empirical', 'data', or 'reality'. Such terms draw their meaning from the epistemology in which they exist. For example, Farran's (1990) feminist constructivist definition of data or Lather's (1991b) postmodernist feminist defini-tion of 'data' are different than Kerlinger's (1986) meaning of the same word within his positivist orientation. Farran (1990) says that ' "data collection" is "data construction" ' (p. 91). Lather (1991a) says that 'Data might be better conceived as the material for telling a story where the challenge becomes to generate a poly-valent data base that is used to *vivify* (her emphasis) interpretation as opposed to "support" or "prove" ' (p. 10). It is not difficult to imagine that Kerlinger would have formidable problems with Farran's and Lather's definitions.

Similarly, what is 'really' happening in a classroom and what 'facts' are used to support a particular perspective may be different for a naive realist, for a critical theorist, and for a poststructuralist. As Kuhn (1970) says of two groups of scientists working out of two different paradigms, 'Practicing in different worlds, the two groups of scientists see different things when they look from the same point in the same direction' (p. 148). A naive realist might say that what is really happening is the teacher is attempting to teach a particular lesson to the students. A critical theorist might say that what is really happening is that the teacher is attempting to get the students to believe in the dominant ideology even though doing so is not in their own interests and even though some students are resisting. A poststructuralist might say that what is really happening is all of the above and more: The teacher is teaching subject content and dominance among many other things, and the students are learning, accepting and resisting dominance, socializing, fighting, sleeping, etc. Which of these is 'true', however, depends upon whose truth story is being told.[30]

The issue, in this instance, is not that different perspectives 'see' different 'facts'. Most contemporary epistemologists agree that they do (though they would certainly not agree that all of the currently competing epistemologies are equally valid). The issue is the political dimension of the definition of specific terms like 'empirical', 'facts', or 'reality'. From a social relativist viewpoint the issue is not whether the term 'empirical' refers to some observable reality. 'Observable' and 'reality' are also relative terms. As Minh-ha (1989) notes, 'The *real* . . . (is) nothing else than a (social) *code of representation* (her emphases)' (p. 94). The contestable meanings of these terms — 'empirical', 'data', 'reality', 'facts' — float historically within particular epistemologies or within certain disciplinary communities dominated by particular epistemologies.

While the advocates of these epistemologies or the members of these communities may claim that 'empirical' is a referent to 'observable reality', I would say that their claim is simply relative to their epistemology or their community, both of which exist within specific historical and sociological contexts: 'the categories or concepts by and through which we structure experience (or reality or research) are themselves historically and culturally variable' (Flax, 1990, p. 35). None of these terms — 'empirical', 'data', 'reality', 'facts' — rise above their location in space and time and thus point somehow to a real reality; they are all contextually relative. This contextual relativity leads then to the issue of what are the politics of a particular use of such terms as 'empirical' or 'facts'.

An example will serve to illustrate this point. Suppose we take the question of whether a generalized bias against people of color and women exists in the United States public school system. This would conventionally be considered an empirical question. Bias would be defined. Data or facts would be gathered. An empirical determination would be made. This process, though, is problematic or relativistic in at least two ways. First, there would be disagreements over the definitions of bias, and there would be no external standards by which to solve the disagreements. In addition, each definition would have a certain politics. For instance, a radical feminist might suggest that the educational system is not only biased in terms of test composition or teacher wait time but also in terms of the basic idea of what knowledge is. A conventional social scientist of liberal inclinations might want to define bias only in measurable or behavioral terms. Each of these researchers embed their politics in their definitions.

Second, what are considered data or facts is open to epistemological debate. Naive realists would see facts in one way; scientific realists would see facts in another way. A critical theorist might see facts in still a different way, and so on. Therefore, in social science research the nature of reality, according to certain definitions and facts, is debatable. Furthermore, since the nature of reality is debatable and since different portraits of reality include different political arrangements of people, debates over the nature of reality are, in effect, political debates. Determinations of whether the United States public school system is generally biased against people of color and women only become 'empirical' questions once several prior issues are decided, issues which are fundamentally political or ethical.

Perhaps my position can be illustrated better by comparing truth game enactments to policy enactments. Donmoyer (1985) says that Toulmin specifically exempts policy studies from being a social scientific discipline, but I would argue that the social sciences are in much the same situation as policy studies. We seem to have no problem recognizing that different policy enactments yield different arrangements of people (i.e., have a politics). We also seem to have no problem accepting that policy enactments are political or, even, ethical enactments. Finally, we also seem to have no problem recognizing that it is acceptable for people to differ on policy enactments. But we want truth games to be special sorts of games that rise above such relativistic political struggles. I would, in contrast, claim that epistemological enactments are very similar to policy enactments. Truth games in the social sciences are not about some sort of privileged truth; they are socially constrained perspectives that have significant political implications. In short, truth game enactments are political or ethical enactments (Hesse, 1978).[31]

The result is that researchers in terms of their epistemological enactments are in the same position as a school administrator or teacher who has to make policy choices. An administrator or teacher can choose to base her or his decisions on effectiveness, cost, equity, career needs, or on some combination of several possibilities. Each decision will have a certain politics (i.e., it will benefit some people or groups over others). For example, cutting funds for a gifted program will tend to hurt upper-middle-class white families, while cutting funds for an at-risk program will tend to hurt lower-class families of color. Each policy decision of the administrator or teacher will express, explicitly or implicitly, the politics of that person and her/his social, historical positionality.

It is, thus, not the purposes of research that drives these choices about which epistemology to utilize, as suggested by Donmoyer (1985). Critical theorists like Foster (1986) or Bates (1980 and 1982) who contend that positivism is politically questionable cannot ethically or politically choose a positivist perspective from which to conduct their research no matter what the purpose of the research is. The same is true for feminists or Afrocentrists who have similarly criticized conventional social science research approaches. Those who assume that they can choose any epistemology to fit the needs of the research situation restrict the array of epistemologies to only those which are considered to be value-free, believe that only value-free epistemologies are acceptable in the social sciences, or ignore the politics of the research they conduct. Obviously, in my view and others, such as critical theorists, feminists, or race/culture theorists, the third possibility — ignore their politics — is the most likely.

From a social relativist position, each epistemological enactment, like the policy enactments of the administrator or teacher, is a political enactment. No specific epistemology or particular research situation can remove the researcher from this predicament. The result is that the enactment of an epistemology can no longer be founded on picking the best epistemology in terms of which one brings the researcher closer to some sort of foundational truth or in terms of which one coheres most closely to some postfoundational standard or criterion. It is now based on which epistemology best expresses the politics of the researcher.[32] Truth game enactments or epistemological enactments are ultimately political or ethical enactments.

Notes

1   In this case I am using a very broad and loose definition of the word 'epistemology', a use which is common throughout education and the social sciences in general. For those whose who might label themselves as epistemologists or as philosophers, there are often more technical or exacting definitions of epistemology. For example, Bernstein (1978) indicates that epistemology as an endeavor is more connected to scientific methodology than to the methods of other paradigms. Polkinghorne (1983, pp. 9–10) makes a similar point. He says that Plato in *Theatetus* distinguished between *doxa* ('what we believe to be true') and *episteme* ('what we know to be true'). Thus, 'epistemology (the *logos* or study of *episteme*) has become the search for methods and foundations which enable us to be assured of the truth of our beliefs.' I would claim, however, that currently the use of the word 'epistemology' is not restricted in this way. But if we were to restrict ourselves to the classical definition, I would label what I do and what everyone else in the social sciences does as doxological rather than epistemological.

Also, in this discussion of epistemology I will focus exclusively on the social sciences for which there is little evidence of a succeeding accumulation of better and better approximations of the truth of the kind that Popper and Lakatos, for instance, argue can be found in the natural sciences. There are, however, numerous scholars who argue against the idea of steadily improving knowledge even in the natural sciences. This latter group would include Feyerabend, Rorty, and Bernstein, among others. There are also, more recently, scholars of the natural sciences who argue that the natural sciences are more like the social sciences than has previously been recognized (see Rouse, 1987, for an excellent example of one such an approach).

2   In my opinion, the separation of epistemology and ontology is artificial. In practice and in theory my epistemology cannot be separated from my ontology. What I see and how I see are intimately interwoven.

3   If we look across many of the texts addressing these issues, we find that the definitions of such terms as epistemology, positivism, realism, and the like are different in different texts. For instance, Polkinghorne (1983) uses the phrase 'pragmatic science' to mean something similar to House's (1991) 'scientific realism'. Though there are differences in their descriptions, there is also considerable overlap. There is, thus, really no way to stipulate definitions that would apply across all or most texts, nor is there even really a need to do so. Instead my approach is sometimes to define explicitly a term I am using, but more often I let the context implicitly indicate the meaning, which always remains somewhat slippery and ambiguous.

4   See, also, Phillips (1983) who contends there are at least four versions of positivism, some of which are considered to be dead and some of which are considered to be 'still alive in one form or another' (p. 6). Donmoyer (1985) argues that Phillips in this same article is defending a 'reconstructed version of positivism' (p. 14), a kind of pragmatic or common sense version of positivism. Lincoln and Guba (1985) however, vilify positivism, as do many others. In fact, positivism is the most common straw-philosophy of those interested in defending alternative viewpoints. Lather (1991b), on the other

hand, is a good example of a scholar who positions herself as thoroughly and deeply critical of positivism but does not give much space to attacking it. She is much more interested in developing a postmodernist emancipatory perspective than maligning positivism. Lather (in press) does assert that 'Positivism is not dead, as anyone knows who tries to get published in most journals, obtain grants from most funding agencies or have research projects accepted by theses and dissertation committees. What is dead, however, is its theoretic dominance and its "one best way" claims over empirical work in the human sciences' (pp. 6–7).

5   I would contend that positivists were not a complete failure; through their self-critique they showed that the positivist dream was not possible. In addition, it is often forgotten in the current vilification of positivism that the positivists saw their rigorous rules as an enhancement of democracy. As Fuller (1988) says, 'Returning to the positivists, it is well known that their chief ideologue, Otto Neurath (1962), saw the Unified Science movement as, in part, a way of driving out the politically conservative and elitist tendencies of hermeneutical thinking in the "human sciences" . . . and driving in the more radical and egalitarian, specifically Marxist, politics associated with a naturalistic approach to the "social sciences". Less well known is how Neurath's preoccupation with the status of "protocol statements", those fundamental building blocks of evidential warrant in the natural sciences, contributed to the overall project. . . . Neurath's concern with protocol statements, along with other positivist attempts at formulating a principal of verification, may perhaps be seen as raising to self-consciousness the values of *equality* (his emphasis) (of the individual knowers) and *progress* (of the collective body of knowers) which were first asserted in the Scientific Revolution' (pp. 6–7).

6   One example of work that does not attend to its epistemological biases is the new work on micropolitics (for example, Blase, 1991). While I think this work is a very important in expanding our understanding of the complexity of classrooms and schools, I find Blase to be unreflexive in an epistemological sense. The proponents of the micropolitics of school settings seem to understand the complexities of such settings but not the complexities of their own epistemology. How they see what they see and thus what they see itself is much more problematic than they seem to understand.

7   Naive realism would accurately describe the epistemological basis of most work in educational administration, just as it does in almost all areas of education. Positivism itself became influential in educational administration in the 1950s with 'the theory movement' under the leadership of Getzels, Griffiths, and Halpin, but only a few of its practitioners were serious theorists in a positivist sense. By the 1960s, however, Halpin himself had begun to question the legitimacy and limitations of positivism (and functionalism, the sociological version of positivism) for educational administration (Culbertson, 1988; Griffiths, 1988). In retrospect, naive realism would be a better descriptor for the research practices of most adherents of this movement. Whatever label is applied, however, this perspective continues to be influential among the great majority of professors of educational administration as shown by a study of the syllabi and textbooks used in the United States by participants in the University Council for Educational Administration (UCEA) (Nicolaides and Gaynor, 1989), which incidentally was founded to further the theory movement (Culbertson, 1988).

8   As with the other perspectives that I address in this study, I will not try to present an exhaustive description or explanation of socially constrained relativism. I think that a comprehensive coverage is not only impossible in practice but theoretically impossible. Instead I will discuss certain aspects of this perspective or certain issues raised by it that I think are particularly important. This will obviously and necessarily leave a range of

issues unaddressed and questions unanswered, some of which may or may not be encountered in future conversations or written work.

9 Nielsen (1990) maintains that 'the critical tradition', of which I would, in general, consider myself an advocate, supports a similar position as mine: 'the critical tradition rejects the idea that there can be "objective" knowledge. Proponents of the tradition argue that there is no such thing as an objectively neutral or disinterested perspective, that everyone or every group (including themselves) is located socially and historically, and this context inevitably influences the knowledge they produce. Knowledge, in short, is socially constructed' (p. 9).

10 One important theme that will not be developed in this work is an explication of postionality. This is obviously a complicated concept, especially in terms of social relativism. In lieu of a more extended discussion, I would say that positionality encompasses history, class, race, and gender, among other possible factors. One's historical position, one's class (which may or may not include changes in one's class over the course of a lifetime), one's race, one's gender, one's region, one's religion, and so on, all of these interact and influence, limit and constrain productions of knowledge. Without a doubt these interactions are extremely complex. Nonetheless, they cannot be overlooked, especially where one social group, like white middle class males, tends to dominate knowledge production. The social positionality of such dominant groups and the maintenance of that positionality has an immense impact on knowledge production. Many, however, would dispute that positionality and relativity, even as I have defined them, are related. Indeed, positionality is a position that is often used to escape the bane of relativism. As can be surmised by the end of this chapter, I disagree that the non-relativist version of positionality attains this escape.

11 Foucault (1979) takes the relation between power and knowledge several steps farther when he asserts that 'Perhaps, too, we should abandon a whole tradition that allows us to imagine that knowledge can exist only where the power relations are suspended and that knowledge can develop outside its injunctions, its demands and its interests. Perhaps we should abandon the belief that power makes mad and that, by the same token, the renunciation of power is one of the conditions of knowledge. We should admit rather that power produces knowledge (and not simply by encouraging it because it serves power or by applying it because it is useful); that power and knowledge directly imply one another; that there is not power relation without the correlative constitution of a field of knowledge, nor any knowledge that does not presuppose and constitute at the same time power relations' (p. 27).

12 I define the word 'political' somewhat differently from what is most common. Most frequently the word 'political' is used in such statements as 'The principal's choice as to which teacher is to chair the committee was very political.' My definition encompasses this latter use for the most part, but it is also much broader than this. I use the word to indicate alignments, arrangements, or relationships of power, resources, and people.

13 One line of thought in poststructuralism, following Nietzsche (Taylor, 1986), suggests that the pursuit of knowledge is a facade for a will to power on the part of Western civilization. Lubiano (1991) calls it the 'Euro-American territorial and cultural will to power' (p. 181). Foucault (1977) says that Nietzsche thought that 'The historical analysis of this rancorous will to knowledge reveals that all knowledge rests upon injustice . . . and that the instinct for knowledge is malicious' (p. 163). Young in an excellent work entitled *White Mythologies* (1990) contends that the Western knowledge project is an academic version of Western imperialism.

14   As I have said previously, I will not attempt to be comprehensive. In this instance I will not try to answer all of the criticisms of relativism. Even if this task were possible, there would be little room in this work for little else. Instead, I will attempt to address three criticisms that are particularly important to me and are relevant to developing my perspective. I will not address, in particular, the argument that is widely thought to destroy relativism (i.e., that it is self-refuting). According to one way this argument goes, if everything is relative, then relativity itself is relative and thus refuted. Hesse (1980) has successfully, in my opinion and in the opinion of Barnes and Bloor's (1991), answered this criticism of relativism. Nonehtheless, I do not think that someone who is strongly against relativism will accept her argument. In a certain sense, the unwillingness to listen to Hesse's arguments reasserts relativism.

   Poststructuralism addresses the apparently self-refuting character of relativism in a different way. Poststructuralists such as Minh-ha (1989) and Spivak (1988) have developed a way of writing that both asserts and undermines the assertion. Lather (1991b) in education has also focused on this manner of rhetorical presentation of a text. In this way, these authors always foreground the contingency of all statements. Although this poststructuralist style was not specifically developed to answer the critics of the supposed self-refuting character of relativism, it flows out of a similar understanding that all positions are problematic.

15   See feminist (Alcoff, 1987; Harding, 1986 and 1991; Lather, 1991b; Minh-ha, 1989; Nielsen, 1990; Shakeshaft, 1987), race-oriented (Gordon, Miller and Rollock, 1990; Stanfield, 1985), and critical theorist (Bates, 1980 and 1982; Foster, 1986; Habermas, 1971) critiques of positivism as a power-free truth game.

16   Stone (1989) has written a book about Atlanta, Georgia, that details the long-term alliance between the African-American community (middle class and lower class) of Atlanta and its largely white business community. Because African-American leaders were able to develop a large, consistent block of voters and because the white business community saw its success dependent on the support of that block of African-American voters, a reasonably successful coalition was developed between what is traditionally seen as a less powerful group, the African-Americans, and a more powerful group, the business community.

17   See, for example, Merquior's (1985) comment about epistemological dominance as seen by Foucault in *The Archaeology of Knowledge* (1972): 'the dominance of an episteme does not mean that every single mind thought along the same line in a given age and culture' (p. 61).

18   Another good example is the Greenfield-Griffiths-Willower debates. Greenfield raised what he called a phenomenological challenge to the positivism of the theory movement in educational administration. Proponents of the theory movement, like Griffiths and Willower, responded with aggressive repudiations of Greenfield. Although this debate continues to simmer (Culbertson, 1988; Greenfield, 1991), in many ways the challenger, Greenfield, has 'won' the debate, at least theoretically. This was verified by Griffiths (1988) himself when he admitted that 'the demise of the theory movement came at the 1974 meeting' where Greenfield first presented his phenomenological critique (p. 30). This powerful effect of Greenfield's critique was also verified by Culbertson (1988) when he concluded that Greenfield 'fired a shot at the theory movement that was heard around the world. Striking hard at the key suppositions of the theory movement, he precipitated controversy which is not yet ended' (p. 20). That most professors of educational administration continue to operate from within the positivistic frame of the theory movement (Nicolaides and Gaynor, 1989) means, though, that while the theory

movement may be dead theoretically, it is still thriving in departments of educational administration and, presumably, among school administrators.

19 This criticism is particularly important to me because I am a strong advocate for the numerous emancipatory perspectives, such as feminism, critical theory, Afrocentrism, and so on. In fact, my perspective is located amidst the work of scholars who position themselves within one of the critical perspectives. Part of my purpose in this work, however, is to disagree with such scholars that relativism is not the threat it is seen to be and that relativism is a 'better representation' of their work than foundational or the various postfoundational perspectives. (For examples of two critical theorists who, as Lather, 1991b, says, are both 'attracted' and 'ambivalent' toward a relativist position, see Giroux, 1988, and McLaren, 1988.)

20 For example, Lather (1991a), who considers herself to be working at the 'intersection of postmodernism and the politics of emancipation' (p. 1), says that 'While "the real" is mediated through language, it has not disappeared' (p. 31), especially the 'realities of poverty, racism, sexism, imperialism' (p. 30). I would argue otherwise: these 'realities' are not real in the sense that Lather hopes they are; they are historically located social constructions that have arisen out of past and present political struggles. Bakhtin (1986) says that the meanings of all words 'always exists among other meanings as a link in the chain of meaning, which in its totality is the only thing that can be real' (p. ix). I will have more to say, however, about this as this particular section progresses.

21 One of the arguments that I would pursue in opposition to Bernstein's (1988), Harding's (1991), and Lather's (1991b) ideas of the 'real' is that the very idea that there is a something called reality that is 'out there' to be known by humans is itself a cultural construction. To go around thinking that there is something out there is a Western cultural construct. Other cultures, some Native American cultures and some African cultures, for instance, do not appear to think this say. To think in the Western way is to assume that there is some kind of separation between the thinker and the 'out there' reality. In addition, the insertion of something called 'knowing' that is located in between the thinker and this thing called reality is equally dependent on the same dualism of humans and reality. Some non-Western cultures, and some marginalized cultures within the West, think, instead, that humans and reality are one interdependent whole. They would thus not posit some process like 'knowing' that existed between human existence and the larger world, nor would they posit the humans/world dualism.

22 Rorty (1989) argues, and I agree, that these postfoundational efforts arise out of the same impulse or needs that lead to foundational standards. He advises that we simply give up this way of thinking.

23 Donmoyer (1991) has an article in *Educational Administration Quarterly* that, in my opinion, suggests a very different position from the one he maintained in 'Rescue from relativism'. In this 'postpositivist' article he suggests that the evaluation of a school program be conducted as a parent-teacher committee process. He even suggests, contrary to his prior position on rationality (Donmoyer, 1985), that there are 'limits . . . (to) rational discourse' and that these limits 'challenge some of the fundamental assumptions that undergird a deliberative approach' (p. 285). Such an approach seems very social relativist to me. It apparently posits that there is no correct evaluation of the program that rises above the socially located committee process. Thus, in this case, 'knowledge' is a social production with no ahistorical foundation or postfoundational meta-criteria. Moreover, he even discusses the fact that the parent-teacher committee

process is basically political. In this case, the ideology of the teachers was able to dominate complaints about the program by the parents with the result that the evaluation was judged to be inequitable by Donmoyer. The main limitation of the article from my point of view, however, is that Donmoyer is not self-reflective of his own positionality and politics within the study.

The issue could be raised that this case raises the very problems that are cited in reference to relativism (i.e., relativism leads to might makes right). I would simply say, as I have said previously, that power and knowledge are always operative in all knowledge production situations, no matter what epistemology was used. Knowledge production is always a political process: 'The postpositivist critique suggests that ideological issues can never be avoided, they can only be unconscious' (Donmoyer, 1991, p. 293). That the more powerful or the more articulate usually win is nothing new, as the less powerful and less articulate well know. But social relativism foregrounds that there is always a politics. In addition, as I have also contended, the powerful rarely, and perhaps never, have total dominance for any meaningful period of time. It is my opinion that if Donmoyer had been looking for indications that the dominance of the teachers on the committee was not total, he would have been able to find such evidence.

24 Poststructuralists would suggest that the only way one sort of rationality can be privileged over other possible alternative rationalities would be through a (hidden) violent suppression of these other alternatives. They would argue that any kind of epistemological privilege involves a kind of violence (Flax, 1990; Foucault, 1977; Minh-ha, 1989; Norris, 1987; Scheurich and Lather, 1991; Young, 1990).

25 *Bricolage* is a French word which means 'the ad hoc assemblage of miscellaneous materials and signifying structures' (Levi-Strauss, quoted in Norris, 1987, p. 134). Spivak (1976) says 'the *bricoleur* makes do with things that were meant perhaps for other ends' (p. xix). Levi-Strauss used this word to describe how pre-Western cultures 'made sense of the world in a way quite remote from our own, more logical and regimented habits of thought' (Norris, 1987, p. 134). 'The *bricoleur* is a kind of Heath Robinson figure, happy to exploit the most diverse assortment of mythemes — or random combinatory elements — in order to create a working hypotheses about this or that feature of social life. The opposite approach is that of the typecast "engineer", one who starts out with a well-defined concept of a machine (or explanatory theory) he want to construct, and who follows this blueprint through to its logical conclusion' (Norris, 1987, p. 134).

26 I think my socially constrained relativism also overcomes postpositivist positions, as typified by Donmoyer (1987), that argue that relativism eliminates any possibility of making decisions or judgments about theories or paradigms. My reply is simply that decisions or judgments are made, but they are made within the political struggles of a particular social, historical, and, often, disciplinary context. From a relativist position the decisions or judgments made are not 'better' according to any postfoundational reasoning that is itself ahistorical or apolitical. Such judgments are only 'better' in terms of a particular perspective within a specific context.

27 In light of this statement and the prior discussions of social relativism, it might be argued that I have no basis for judging any position as inadequate. If this argument, however, is thought to be inconsistent with my explanations of social relativism, then I have failed to communicate clearly. A social relativist does not contend that judgments cannot be made between various perspectives or various theories within a single perspective. Instead a social relativist claims that such judgments, including those made

in this work, are themselves within social, historical contexts and are, thus, relative. In addition, I have tried repeatedly to make the point that all perspectives, theories, and judgments have a politics, though what those politics are for a particular perspective, theory, or judgment is always debatable.

28 For a critique of realism in philosophy, see Rorty (1982, pp. xxi-xxxvii). Rorty's pragmatism has been criticized as being relativistic. Thus, the realist based 'anti-pragmatist backlash' (p. xxi) that he is responding to would be similar to criticisms that might be made of relativism.

29 There are numerous scholars who claim that epistemological discussions should include historical, sociological, and, especially, political issues. See, for example, Bernstein (1982 and 1988), Burrell and Morgan (1979), Clegg (1989), Foster (1986), Greenfield (1991), Habermas (1971), Harding (1986 and 1991), Lather (1986a, 1986b; 1991a and 1991b), Richardson (1988), and Stanfield (1985). These examples, of course, reflect my political and epistemological interests; there are many other examples reflecting other political and epistemological interests.

30 Donmoyer (1991) makes this same point but from a more practical angle: 'Few people would disagree with the proposition that schools should promote learning, but the term *learning* (his emphasis) will mean different things to a kindergarten teacher influenced by Piaget, a process-product researcher, an art teacher who wants to promote productive idiosyncracy, and a parent who wants the schools to go back to basics. Each of these meanings reflects a different conception of what learning is, and what teaching ought to be. Each can be said to reflect a different paradigm of reality' (p. 179).

31 Fraser (1989), whose work I greatly admire, insists that 'you can't get a politics straight out of epistemology, even when the epistemology is a radical antiepistemology like historicism, pragmatism, or deconstruction. On the contrary, I argue repeatedly that politics requires a genre of critical theorizing that blends normative arguments and empirical sociocultural analysis in a "diagnosis of the times" ' (p. 6). To some extent I simply disagree with her if she defines politics as a general political orientation. In fact, I would say that you do not 'get a politics . . . out of epistemology'; instead I would say that an epistemology is a politics, again if by politics is meant a general orientation that arranges bodies and things. Moreover, I would also suggest that this issue is best examined in terms of specific applications or practices of particular epistemologies. In such cases, it seems to me, the equation of epistemology and politics is even more evident. I would emphasize, however, as I have before, that what the politics of a particular epistemology is in general or in a specific application is always debatable.

32 See Lather (1986b) and Gitlin, Siegel and Boru (1988) for discussions that move beyond this one to the necessary political relationship between the researcher's epistemology and her/his research methods.

References

ALCOFF, L. (1987) 'Justifying feminist social science', *Hypatia*, **2**, 3, pp. 85–103.
ANTONIO, R.J. (1989) 'The normative foundations of emancipatory theory: Evolutionary versus pragmatic perspectives', *American Journal of Sociology*, **94**, 4, pp. 721–48.
APPLE, M.W. (1982) *Education and Power*, Boston, MA, Routledge and Kegan Paul.

APPLE, M.W. (1991) 'Series editor's introduction' in LATHER, P. (Ed) *Getting Smart: Feminist Research and Pedagogy With/in the Postmodern*, New York, Routledge.

BAKHTIN, M.M. (1986) *Speech Genres and Other Late Essays* (V.W. McGee, trans.) Austin, Texas, University of Texas Press.

BARNES, B. (1974) *Scientific Knowledge and Sociological Theory*, London, Routledge and Kegan Paul.

BARNES, B. and BLOOR, D. (1991) 'Relativism, rationalism and the sociology of knowledge' in HOLLIS, M. and LUKES, S. (Eds) *Rationality and Relativism*, Cambridge, MA, MIT Press, pp. 21–47.

BARONE, T.E. (1990) *'Subjectivity'*, paper presented at the annual meeting of the American Educational Research Association, Boston, MA, April.

BARTH, R.S. (1991) 'Restructuring schools: Some questions for teachers and principals', *Phi Delta Kappan*, **73** 2, pp. 123–28.

BATES, R.J. (1980) 'Educational administration, the sociology of science, and the management of knowledge', *Educational Administration Quarterly*, **16** 2, pp. 1–20.

BATES, R.J. (1982) *'Towards a critical practice of educational administration'*, paper presented at the annual meeting of the American Educational Research Association, New York, March.

BERNSTEIN, R.J. (1978) *The Restructuring of Social and Political Theory*, Philadelphia, PA, University of Pennsylvania Press.

BERNSTEIN, R.J. (1988) *Beyond Objectivism and Relativism*, Philadelphia, PA, University of Pennsylvania Press.

BERNSTEIN, R.J. (1992) *The New Constellation: The Ethical-political Horizons of Modernity/ Postmodernity*, Cambridge, MA, MIT Press.

BLASE, J. (1991) *The Politics of Life in Schools: Power, Conflict, and Cooperation*, Newbury Park, CA, Sage.

BURRELL, G. and MORGAN, G. (1979) *Sociological Paradigms and Organisational Analysis*, Portsmouth, NH, Heinemann.

CLEGG, S.R. (1989) *Frameworks of Power*, London, Sage.

CULBERTSON, J. (1988) 'A century's quest for a knowledge base' in BOYAN, N.J. (Ed) *Handbook of Research on Educational Administration*, New York, Longman, pp. 3–26.

DELEUZE, G. (1992) 'What is a *dispositif*?', (T.J. Armstrong, trans.) in *Michel Foucault: Philosopher*, New York, Routledge, pp. 159–66.

DERRIDA, J. (1981) 'Semiology and grammatology: An interview with Julia Kristeva' (A. Bass, trans.) in *Positions*, Chicago, IL, University of Chicago Press.

DONMOYER, R. (1985) 'The rescue from relativism: Two failed attempts and an alternative strategy', *Educational Researcher*, **14**, 10, pp. 13–20.

DONMOYER, R. (1987) 'Beyond Thorndike/Beyond melodrama', *Curriculum Inquiry*, **17**, 4, pp. 353–63.

DONMOYER, R. (1991) 'Postpositivist evaluation: Give me a for instance', *Educational Administration Quarterly*, **27**, 3, pp. 265–96.

EISNER, E. (1988) 'The primacy of experience and the politics of method', *Educational Researcher*, **17**, 5, pp. 15–20.

ELLSWORTH, E. (1989) 'Why doesn't this feel empowering? Working through the repressive myths of critical pedagogy', *Harvard Educational Review*, **59**, 3, pp. 297–325.

ERIBON, D. (1991) *Michel Foucault* (Betsy Wing, trans.) Cambridge, MA, Harvard University Press.

EVERS, C.W. and LAKOMSKI, G. (1991) *Knowing Educational Administration: Contemporary Methodological Controversies in Educational Administration*, Oxford, Pergamon Press.

FARRAN, D. (1990) 'Producing statistical information on young people's leisure' in STANLEY, L. (Ed) *Feminist Praxis: Research, Theory and Epistemology*, London, Routledge, pp. 91–102.

FLAX, J. (1990) *Thinking Fragments: Psychoanalysis, Feminism, and Postmodernism in the Contemporary West*, Berkeley, CA, University of California Press.

FOSTER, W. (1986) *Paradigms and Promises*, Buffalo, NY, Prometheus Books.

FOUCAULT, M. (1972) *The Archaeology of Knowledge and the Discourse on Language* (A.M. Sheridan Smith, trans.) New York, Pantheon Books (original work published 1969).

FOUCAULT, M. (1977) *Language, Counter-memory, Practice* (D.F. Bouchard, trans.) Ithaca, NY, Cornell University Press.

FOUCAULT, M. (1979) *Discipline and Punish: The Birth of the Prison* (A.M. Sheridan Smith, trans.) New York, Vintage Books (original work published 1977).

FOUCAULT, M. (1991) 'Politics and the study of discourse' (C. Colin, trans.) in BURCHELL, G., GORDON, C. and MILLER, P. (Eds) *The Foucault Effect: Studies in Governmentality*, Chicago, IL, University of Chicago Press, pp. 87–104.

FRASER, N. (1989) *Unruly Practices: Power, Discourse, and Gender in Contemporary Social Theory*, Minneapolis, MN, University of Minnesota Press.

FULLER, S. (1988) *Social Epistemology*, Bloomington, IN, Indiana University Press.

GIROUX, H. (1983) *Theory, Resistance, and Education*, South Hadley, MA, Bergin and Garvey.

GIROUX, H. (1988) 'Border pedagogy in the age of postmodernism', *Journal of Education*, **170**, 3, pp. 162–81.

GITLIN, A., SIEGEL, M. and BORU, K. (1988) 'The politics of method: From leftist ethnography to evaluative research', *International Journal of Qualitative Studies in Education*, **2**, 3, April, pp. 235–53.

GORDON, E.W., MILLER, F. and ROLLOCK, D. (1990) 'Coping with communicentric bias in knowledge production in the social sciences', *Educational Researcher*, **19**, 3, pp. 14–19.

GORDON, C. (1991) 'Governmental rationality: An introduction' in BURCHELL, G., GORDON, C. and MILLER, P. (trans.) *The Foucault Effect: Studies in Governmentality*, Chicago, IL, University of Chicago Press, pp. 1–51.

GREENFIELD, T.B. (1978) 'Reflections on organization theory and the truths of irreconcilable realities', *Educational Administration Quarterly*, **14**, 2, pp. 1–23.

GREENFIELD, T.B. (1991) 'Re-forming and re-valuing educational administration: Whence and when cometh the phoenix?', *Organizational Theory Dialogue*, April, pp. 1–17.

GRIFFITHS, D.E. (1988) 'Administrative theory' in BOYAN, N.J. (Ed) *Handbook of Research on Educational Administration*, New York, Longman, pp. 27–51.

GUTTING, G. (1989) *Michel Foucault's Archaeology of Scientific Reason*, Cambridge, Cambridge University Press.

HABERMAS, J. (1971) *Knowledge and Human Interests* (J.J. Shapiro, trans.) Boston, MA, Beacon Press.

HARAWAY, D. (1988) 'Situated knowledges: The science question in feminism and the privilege of partial perspective', *Feminist Studies*, **14**, 3, pp. 575–99.

HARDING, S. (1986) *The Science Question in Feminism*, Ithaca, NY, Cornell University Press.

HARDING, S. (1991) *Whose Science? Whose Knowledge?*, Ithaca, NY, Cornell University Press.

HESSE, M. (1978) 'Theory and value in the social sciences' in HOOKWAY, C. and PETTIT, P. (Eds) *Action and Interpretation: Studies in the Philosophy of the Social Sciences*, Cambridge, Cambridge University Press, pp. 1–16.

HESSE, M. (1980) *Revolutions and Reconstructions in the Philosophy of Science*, Brighton, Harvester Press.

HOUSE, E.R. (1991) 'Realism in research', *Educational Researcher*, **20**, 6, pp. 2–9 and 25.

HUTCHEON, L. (1989) *The Politics of Postmodernism*, London, Routledge.

KERLINGER, F.N. (1986) *Foundations of Behavioral Research* (3rd ed) New York, Holt, Rinehart and Winston.

KUHN, T.S. (1970) *The Structure of Scientific Revolutions* (2nd ed), Chicago, IL, University of Chicago Press.

LATHER, P. (1986a) 'Issues of validity in openly ideological research: Between a rock and a soft place', *Interchange*, **17**, 4, Winter, pp. 63–84.

LATHER, P. (1986b) 'Research as praxis', *Harvard Educational Review*, **56**, 2, pp. 257–77.

LATHER, P. (1988) 'Feminist perspectives on empowering research methodologies', *Women's Studies International Forum*, **11**, 6, pp. 569–81.

LATHER, P. (1991a) 'Deconstructing/Deconstructive inquiry: The politics of knowing and being known', *Educational Theory*, **41**, 2, pp. 24–35.

LATHER, P. (1991b) *Getting Smart: Feminist Research and Pedagogy With/in the Postmodern*, New York, Routledge.

LATHER, P. (in press) 'Critical frames in educational research: Feminist and poststructural perspectives', *Theory Into Practice*.

LATOUR, B. and WOOLGAR, S. (1986) *Laboratory Life: The Construction of Scientific Facts*, Princeton, NJ, Princeton University Press.

LINCOLN, Y.S. and GUBA, E.G. (1985) *Naturalistic Inquiry*, Beverly Hills, CA, Sage.

LUBIANO, W. (1991) 'Shuckin' off the African-American native other: What's "po-mo" got to do with it?', *Cultural Critique*, **20**, Winter, pp. 149–86.

McLAREN, P. (1988) 'Schooling the postmodern body: Critical pedagogy and the politics of enfleshment', *Journal of Education*, **170**, 3, pp. 53–83.

MERQUIOR, J.G. (1985) *Foucault*, Berkeley, CA, University of California Press.

MINH-HA, T.T. (1989) *Woman Native Other*, Bloomington, IN, Indiana University Press.

MISHLER, E.G. (1990) 'Validation in inquiry-guided research: The role of exemplars in narrative studies', *Harvard Educational Review*, **60**, 4, pp. 415–41.

MISHLER, E.G. (1991) 'Representing discourse: The rhetoric of transcription', *Journal of Narrative and Life History*, **1**, 4, pp. 255–80.

NEURATH, O. (1962) *Foundations of the Social Sciences*, Chicago, IL, University of Chicago Press.

NICOLAIDES, N. and GAYNOR, A. (1989) *The Knowledge Base Informing the Teaching of Administrative and Organizational Theory in UCEA Universities: Empirical and Interpretive Perspectives*, Charlottesville, VA, The National Policy Board for Educational Administration, December.

NIELSEN, J.M. (1990) 'Introduction' in *Feminist Research Methods: Exemplary Readings in the Social Sciences*, Boulder, CO, Westview Press.

NORRIS, C. (1987) *Derrida*, Cambridge, MA, Harvard University Press.

PHILLIPS, D.C. (1983) 'After the wake: Postpositivistic educational thought', *Educational Researcher*, **12**, 5, pp. 4–12.

POLKINGHORNE, D. (1983) *Methodology for the Human Sciences: Systems of Inquiry*, Albany, NY, State University of New York Press.

RICHARDSON, L. (1988) 'The collective story: Postmodernism and the writing of sociology', *Sociological Focus*, **21**, 3, pp. 199–208.

RORTY, R. (1979) *Philosophy and the Mirror of Nature*, Princeton, NJ, Princeton University Press.

RORTY, R. (1982) *Consequences of Pragmatism*, Minneapolis, MN, University of Minnesota Press.

RORTY, R. (1989) *Contingency, Irony, and Solidarity*, Cambridge, Cambridge University Press.

ROUSE, J. (1987) *Knowledge and Power: Toward a Political Philosophy of Science*, Ithaca, NY, Cornell University Press.

SCHEURICH, J.J. and LATHER, P. (1991) 'Paradigmatic compulsions: A response to Hills's issues in research on instructional supervision', *Journal of Curriculum and Supervision*, **7**, 1, pp. 26–30.

SHAKESHAFT, C. (1987) *Women in Educational Administration*, Newbury Park, CA, Sage.

SPIVAK, G.C. (1976) 'Translator's preface' in DERRIDA, J., *Of Grammatology*, Baltimore, MD, The Johns Hopkins University Press, pp. ix–xc.

SPIVAK, G.C. (1988) *In Other Worlds: Essays in Cultural Politics*, New York, Routledge.

STANFIELD, J. (1985) 'The ethnocentric basis of social science knowledge production', *Review of Research in Education*, **12**, pp. 387–415.

STONE, C.N. (1989) *Regime Politics: Governing Atlanta, 1946–1988*, Lawrence, KS, University Press of Kansas.

TAYLOR, M.C. (1986) 'Introduction: System . . . structure . . . difference . . . other' in TAYLOR, M.C. (Ed) *Deconstruction in Context: Literature and Philosophy*, Chicago, IL, University of Chicago Press, pp. 1–34.

WEILER, K. (1988) *Women Teaching for Change: Gender, Class and Power*, New York, Bergin & Garvey.

YOUNG, R. (1990) *White Mythologies: Writing History and the West*, London, Routledge.

3   A Postmodernist Critique of
Research Interviewing

Both positivist[1] and postpositivist views of research interviewing are inadequate from a postmodernist perspective. This chapter addresses that inadequacy by critiquing both characterizations of interviewing and by offering some initial considerations of what a postmodernist characterization might look like. First, I critique the positivist conception of interviewing and contrast it with my postmodernist view. Second, I critique what I consider to be the best comprehensive postpositivist work on research interviewing. Third, I offer a postmodernist reconceptualization of power within the interview, as an example of how one aspect of interviewing might be reconstructed from a postmodernist perspective. Fourth, I conclude with a discussion of the implications for research interviewing of the radical openness or indeterminacy within the intersection of language, meaning, and communication and with an advocacy for 'playful' experimentation that exceeds the constraints of a determinate, knowable ordering of 'reality'.

Conventional Interviewing Critiqued

Interviewing as a research method can be artificially separated into two parts. The first part is actually doing the interview; the second is interpreting the interview. In the conventional one-to-one interview the researcher or interviewer asks the subject or interviewee some questions, which may be predetermined (close-ended interviews) or developed within the interviewing process (open-ended interviews) and records the answers, usually on audio tape (Bogdan and Biklen, 1982). The audio tape is transcribed and then treated as a text. This text is analyzed and coded in order to support or develop some generalization or theory.

Within this view, research interviewing is seen as an unproblematic method for gathering qualitative data. Bogdan and Biklen (*ibid*) write that 'An interview is a purposeful conversation, usually between two people . . . that is directed by one in order to get information' (p. 133). Patton (1990) maintains that 'The purpose of interviewing is to find out what is in and on someone else's mind . . . to access the perspective of the person being interviewed' (p. 278). Lincoln and Guba (1985) describe interviewing as simply 'a conversation with a purpose' (p. 268).

From this conventional or positivist perspective, the researcher is purposeful and knows what she/he is doing. The researcher can devise questions whose meaning is bounded and stable. The questions can be stated in such a way that different interviewees understand the question in the same way. The researcher can deliver those questions so that the interviewee is not influenced by the delivery or by the particular researcher asking the questions. In the conventional view, the specific context of the particular researcher interviewing a particular person at a particular time in a particular setting is largely inconsequential (Mishler, 1986).

The transcribed text of the interview becomes data in a sense very similar to quantitative data (Bogdan and Biklen, 1982; Strauss and Corbin, 1990). The physical, non-verbal aspects of communication disappear. The variations in tone, intensity, and rhythm disappear. Even the pauses often disappear[2]. The words, as Mishler (1986) points out, are totally decontextualized. The lines of the text are numbered. The words and lines are divided into monads of supposedly unambiguous meaning. In Strauss and Corbin's (1990) words, 'During open coding the data are broken down into discrete parts' (p. 62). In fact, Bogdan and Biklen (1982) reductively compare the analysis of communicated meaning to sorting different kinds of toys by size, color, country of origin, and so forth. The reductive monads of meaning are then assembled into 'discovered' aggregates, that is: 'The process of grouping concepts that seem to pertain to the same phenomena is called *categorizing*' (Strauss and Corbin, 1990, p. 65). These aggregates or categories are compared across interviewers, interviewees, times, and places.

In contrast, my postmodernist perspective suggests that the researcher has multiple intentions and desires, some of which are consciously known and some of which are not. The same is true of the interviewee. The language out of which the questions are constructed is not bounded or stable; it is persistently slippery, unstable, and ambiguous from person to person, from situation to situation, from time to time. As Berman (1988) explains, 'Words do not . . . serve as markers that convey notions of a world whose structure and order are received into the mind through perceptions and afterward objectively described through, represented by, language' (p. 115). Sign and signification are only loosely linked (Saussure, 1983); 'signifiers . . . float in relation to referents' (Poster, quoted in Lather, 1991, p. 21). '(L)anguage wherever used is composed of structured signifiers, systematized among themselves by differences or oppositions and linked to signifieds in a way more tenuous than even Saussure realized' (Berman, 1988, p. 136).

The relationship between language and meaning, thus, is 'contextually grounded, unstable, ambiguous, and subject to endless reinterpretation' (Mishler, 1991, p. 260). What a question or answer means to the researcher can easily mean something different to the interviewee. What a question or answer means to the researcher may change over time or situations. What a question or answer means to the interviewee similarly may change. Meaning and understanding shift, in large and small ways, across people, across time, and across situations. What occurs in a specific interview is contingent on the specifics of individuals, place, and time (Mishler, 1986). The same set of questions asked by the same interviewer of the same interviewee can often elicit significantly different answers at different times or different places. Changing the interviewer changes the interview results, even if the new interviewer asks the same set of questions (Warren, 1988; Wax, 1979; Zinn, 1979). Even holding people, place, and time constant, however, will not guarantee that stable, unambiguous communication occurred in all or even most of the interview.

Data analysis is the second stage of interviewing as a research method. This stage, however, is not the development of an accurate representation of the data, as the positivist approach assumes, but a creative interaction between the conscious/ unconscious researcher and the decontextualized data which is assumed to represent reality or, at least, reality as interpreted by the interviewee.[3] Unfortunately, this creativity is severely bounded by the restrictions of modernist assumptions about selves, language, and communication. As Mishler (1991) notes, 'Transcriptions of speech . . . reflexively document and affirm theoretical positions about relations between language and meaning' (p. 271). One indication of this restriction is an elaborate and arcane focus on the mechanics of coding, such as that in Strauss and Corbin (1990), with no corresponding focus on the complex ambiguities of language, communication, and interpretation:

> As transcription has become both more routine and precise . . . emphasis on it as a technical procedure has tended to detach the process from its deeper moorings in this critical reflection on the intractable uncertainties of meaning-language relationships. (Mishler, 1991, p. 260)

Use of the technical procedures, adopted to reproduce the systematic rigor of the scientific method, masks the 'intractable uncertainties' and the unstable ambiguities of linguistically communicated meaning.

The decontextualized interview text which is transformed through the coding process becomes that from which the conventional researcher constructs her/his story. The bricks of the construction are the reductive monads of meaning, coded in categories in the transcript. These bricks are formed, however, from a mold that is then shaped from the researcher's conscious and unconscious assumptions and orientations. The claim of accurate or valid representation, especially in terms of such techniques as line numbering, identification and quantification of comparable meaning monads, statistical techniques, or even discourse analysis, simply serves to hide the overwhelming absent presence of the researcher and her/his modernist assumptions.

I am not saying that a modernist analysis of an interview text is a pure creation. The data are the words of the interviewee. For instance, the researcher cannot say the interviewee said yellow when she said green. The results and conclusions are interactively connected to the words the interviewee used: 'All theoretical explanations, categories, hypotheses, and questions about the data, . . . need to be checked out, played against the actual data' (Strauss and Corbin, 1990, p. 45). The modernist representation is not sheer fabrication, but all of the juice of the lived experience has been squeezed out, all the 'intractable uncertainties' and the unstable ambiguities have been erased. This research representation, in relation to the actual conversation between the researcher and the research 'subject', is a 'rhetorical reduction of complexity to simplicity, of differential relations to firm identities, . . . of diffusely textured situations to tightly boundaried containers, of webs of feeling to numbing objectifications' (Ryan, 1989, pp. 1–2).

The researcher uses the dead, decontextualized monads of meaning, the tightly boundaried containers, the numbing objectifications, to construct generalizations which are, in the modernist dream, used to predict, control, and reform, as in educational practice.[4] While these generalizations are said to represent reality, in my view they mostly represent the mindset of the researcher. That is, modernist researchers believe their research methods mirror reality; postmodernists believe modernist research methods (predominantly) mirror the representational ideology of the modernist researchers. Modernist research does not describe; it inscribes (Tyler, 1985).

My point is straightforward. The conventional, positivist view of interviewing vastly underestimates the complexity, uniqueness, and indeterminateness of each one-to-one human interaction. The reason it does this is not, as Mishler (1986) explains, to replicate a stimulus-response model. While I agree that the conventional view of interviewing frequently fits the S-R model, I think it does so for a more fundamental reason. Both the S-R model and the conventional view of interviewing are developed out of the same basic modernist assumptions about the nature of reality and research.

This modernist perspective situates the researcher as a kind of god who consciously knows what she/he is doing, who (if properly trained) can clearly communicate meanings to another person, and who can derive the hidden but recoverable meanings within the interview to support an abstract generalization. If this appears to be a caricature, we need only to look at the various articles and books written by researchers like Bogdan and Biklen (1982) or Strauss and Corbin (1990). What we find is a startling lack of discussion about the unresolvable ambiguities of consciousness, language, interpretation, and communication. From a postmodernist perspective, this severe modernist reduction of the exquisiteness of each lived moment borders on a kind of violence. As Campioni and Grosz (quoted in Lather, 1991) ask, 'Why is it necessary to unify/solidify what may be fluid, diverse and changing, if not in order to block and control it?' (p. 24).

But postmodernists have not been the only ones who have critiqued conventional, positivist interviewing; postpositivists have also questioned various facets of conventional interviewing. The best comprehensive example both to criticize the positivist approach and to develop a postpositivist alternative is, in my opinion, Mishler's *Research Interviewing* (1986). Unfortunately, from a postmodernist point of view, Mishler's alternative is also insufficient. The following section, then, is a brief postmodernist critique of the key modernist assumptions in this book.

Mishler's Postpositivist Alternative Critiqued

In *Research Interviewing* (*ibid*) Mishler first questions the conventional approach to interviewing and then suggests ways that an alternative interviewing approach needs to be formulated. While I generally applaud his critique of the conventional approach, I think his reformulation of interviewing retains some thoroughly modernist assumptions. This is particularly true of his conceptions of communication, narrative, and empowerment. In addition, he retains a modernist-derived belief that once the interview is better represented (more comprehensively, more contextually), its meaning can be elicited through 'systematic' analysis.[5]

Mishler's Chapters 1 and 2

Mishler's (*ibid*) modernist inclinations are apparent in his critique of the conventional approach to interviewing (his chapter 1), but they become much clearer when he turns to his postpositivist reformulation of interviewing. He begins his second chapter by quoting Hymes (a linguistic structuralist) who, Mishler says, defines speech events as '"activities, or aspects of activities, that are directly governed by rules for the use of speech"' (Hymes, quoted in Mishler, 1986, p. 35). Mishler (*ibid*) then points out that 'Hymes is concerned with developing a taxonomy of social units that provides a comprehensive sociolinguistic description of the varieties of talk that take place in communities' (p. 35). By defining interviews in this way, Mishler 'marks the fundamental contrast between the standard anti-linguistic, stimulus-response model (the conventional or positivist view) and an alternative (postpositivist) approach to interviewing as discourse between speakers' (pp. 35–6).

While it is true that Mishler is marking his contrast with the conventional view of interviewing, he is also marking his modernist inclinations. This is particularly apparent in his use of a structuralist taxonomy of language. In contrast to Mishler's modernist taxonomy, I am reminded of the postmodernist (or poststructuralist[6]) taxonomy of Borges that Foucault quotes in the 'Preface' to *The Order of Things: An Archaeology of the Human Sciences* (1973):

> animals are divided into: (a) belonging to the Emperor, (b) embalmed, (c) tame, (d) sucking pigs, (e) sirens, (f) fabulous, (g) stray dogs, (h) included in the present classification, (i) frenzied, (j) innumerable, (k) drawn with a very fine camel hair brush, (l) et cetera, (m) having just broken the water pitcher, (n) that from a long way off look like flies. (p. xv)

What this latter/poststructuralist taxonomy does, in contrast to Hymes' structuralist taxonomy, is to break 'up all the ordered surfaces and all the planes with which we are accustomed to tame the wild profusion of existing things' (Foucault, 1973, p. xv). Borges' 'taxonomy' critiques structuralist taxonomies by foregrounding, through caricature, the modernist need to order and encapsulate 'reality'.[7]

Mishler (1986), in fact, repeatedly indicates a need or desire 'to tame the wild profusion'.[8] While he asserts that 'even questions that are apparently simple in both structure and topic leave much room for alternative interpretations by both interviewer and interviewee' (p. 45), he adds that 'ambiguities are resolved through the discourse itself' (p. 47). My reading of this is that although he is critical of mainstream interviewing, which disregards alternative interpretations and ignores the ambiguities of communication, he still believes that ambiguities in understanding can be resolved, that through systematic research procedures 'reality' can be properly or accurately interpreted. It only takes, in Mishler's view, a more comprehensive, more contextualized approach than that practiced by conventional researchers.

For instance, he ends his second chapter by saying that he wishes 'to reemphasize the point that *systematic transcription procedures* (emphasis added) are necessary for valid analysis and interpretation of interview data' (*ibid*, p. 50). He follows this with the statement that 'it seems clear . . . that the value of succeeding stages of a study — coding, analysis, and interpretation — depends on the adequacy of the description of the phenomenon of interest, and in interview research this means *a carefully prepared transcript* (emphasis added)' (*ibid*). His assumption that 'systematic transcription procedures' and 'a carefully prepared transcript' will yield 'valid analysis and interpretation of interview data' reveals his philosophical commitment to modernist assumptions about method and data, particularly the assumption that there is a 'reality' out there that the researcher can accurately capture or represent, given the use of improved research methods.

Mishler's Chapter 3

Mishler's modernist commitments are repeated in his chapter on 'The Joint Construction of Meaning'. He begins this chapter with the following statement:

> In this chapter I explore implications of the proposition stated earlier that the discourse of the interview is jointly constructed by interviewer and respondent. I will show how both questions and responses are formulated in, developed through, and shaped by the discourse between interviewers and respondents. Further, I will argue that an adequate understanding of interviews depends on recognizing how interviewers reformulate questions and how respondents frame answers in terms of their reciprocal understanding of meanings emerge during the course of the interview. (*ibid*, p. 2)

Erroneous assumptions about the interviewer-interviewee interaction are, in my opinion, embedded in this statement. Interview interactions do not have some essential, teleological tendency toward an ideal of 'joint construction of meaning', no matter how Rogerian the researcher-interviewer might be.[9] Human interactions and meaning are neither unitary nor teleological. Instead, interactions and meaning are a shifting carnival of ambiguous complexity, a moving feast of differences interrupting differences.

Mishler seems to recognize some of this complexity when he says, in reference to a specific part of an interview, 'Is this one story with related subplots or a series of different stories? Interpretations will differ depending on how we view the separate episodes' (p. 73). But he undermines this recognition when he also says prior to the above quote that '*Systematic methods* (emphasis added) of narrative analysis must resolve a variety of problems' (p. 73). Again, Mishler occasionally seems to recognize the fundamental indeterminateness of language, meaning, and communication, but then repeatedly reverts to a modernist assumption that reality can be accurately known through careful, comprehensive, systematic study.

I suggest that the 'reality' of interviews is much more ambiguous, relative, and unknowable than Mishler assumes. Some of what occurs in an interview is verbal. Some is non-verbal. Some occurs only within the mind of each participant (interviewer or interviewee), but it may affect the entire interview. Sometimes the participants are jointly constructing meaning, but at other times one of them may be resisting joint constructions. Sometimes the interviewee cannot find the right words to express herself/himself and, therefore, will compromise her/his meaning for the sake of expediency. There may be incidences of dominance and resistance over large or small issues. There may be monologues. There may be times when one participant is talking about one thing but thinking about something else. A participant may be saying what she thinks she ought to say; in fact, much of the interaction may be infused with a shift between performed or censured statements and unperformed and uncensured statements. Indeed, the 'wild profusion' that occurs moment to moment in an interview is, I would argue, ultimately indeterminable and indescribable. As Spivak (1988) writes, by 'explaining, we exclude the possibility of the *radically* heterogeneous' (p. 105).

A simple experiment that anyone can perform will illustrate my point. Have someone interview you for one hour about some salient aspect of your work. Wait one week and have them continue the interview for another hour. During each interview monitor what is going on in your consciousness. Watch your conscious self drift away from the conversation at times. Watch your conscious self become defensive at times. Watch your self brag or posture or perform or say what you think the interviewer wants you to say. Watch your self censure or censor at one point and blurt out the truth at another. Do this experiment with different interviewers and notice how you 'feel' different and, thus, 'say' different things to different interviewers even if the questions are the same. Watch how changing the race, class, gender, age of the interviewer changes what you say.

As you experience this process, watch how quickly you shift internally from one thing to another. Watch how difficult it is to pinpoint from moment to moment what it is you are doing internally and externally. Watch how your internal consciousness is this indeterminable, ultimately undefinable swirl of activity, only part of which gets 'reported' as spoken words. Add to this the experience the understanding that much of what we do, verbally and non-verbally, is not available to our consciousness. Then add that the interviewer is engaged in the same internal process. Unless I am substantially different 'inside' than everyone else, the result is that the idea that there is some definable or determinable thing or pattern that can be discovered through an interview interaction is more than erroneous. It is the projection onto the interpretation of the interview of an unconscious, but not innocent, modernist conclusion about the nature of reality and our ability to 'know' that reality through research. The postpositivist interviewer's construction, much like that of the positivist, is being overlaid onto the interview. The constructed overlay is then 'discovered' through 'systematic' analysis and (mis)labeled as the 'valid' meaning of the interview.

Mishler's Chapter 4

Mishler's assumptions about what a narrative is, which dominates his fourth chapter, is also modernist. First, he essentializes story-telling by quoting several scholars who claim that story-telling is universal, that it is ' "built into the human mind" ' (Rayfield, quoted by Mishler, 1986, p. 67), that story-telling is ' "*the* primary way . . . human beings make sense of their experience" ' (Gee, quoted by Mishler, 1986, p. 68). Later, he reaffirms this essentialization when he remarks 'That stories appear so often supports the view of some theorists that narratives are one of the *natural* (emphasis added) cognitive and linguistic forms through which individuals attempt to order, organize, and express meaning' (p. 106).

It would be ridiculous to argue that narratives are not common across most cultures, but scholars of color, feminists, and postmodernists have made us very wary of promoting any kind of essentialization. What is often found is that such essentializing turns out to be the projections of a particular social group, as in the case with male characterizations of women or of mainstream Western characterizations of marginalized cultures. I would argue, in fact, that Mishler's idea of a narrative that can be validly represented through his narrative analysis posits a particularly modernist idea of a story or narrative as a knowable or specifiable unity.

The problem with Mishler's (1986) idea of a story or narrative becomes apparent in his later work (Mishler, 1991) in which, I would argue, his viewpoint has shifted closer to mine. While he continues to evidence modernist inclinations in this later article,[10] he clearly recognizes that what the definition of a narrative is, has a cultural or racial basis. In this later article, Mishler tells a story about 'a 7-year-old Black girl' telling her story. He says that 'This child's story does not have the preferred well-formed structure and was not understood by her teacher, who found it hard to follow, inconsistent, unclear, and perhaps not true' (*ibid*, p. 265). However, the child's story was later reanalyzed by a person of the same race and gender as the girl. This reanalysis indicated that the story was 'coherent, well-organized, and meaningful, but that it achieves these criteria through linguistic strategies of the oral rather than the literate narrative tradition' (*ibid*, p. 265). The teacher applied the 'literate (mainstream white Western) narrative tradition' and found that it failed the standards of that tradition. The reanalysis used 'the linguistic strategies of the oral (African-American) . . . tradition' and found that the story succeeded by those standards.

The question that I am raising with this example is: Whose definition of a story gets to be essentialized. Who is permitted to define what a story is or what story-telling is? Lubiano (1991) pointedly raises this same issue when she, as an African-American addressing the value of postmodernism to the African-American community, begins her article with the following quote from *The Sun* newspaper of 12 June 1988, published in England:

> Remember the time when stories had a beginning, a middle, and an end?
> In that order. . . .

> Three things made Britain great. A strong navy. The white race. And narrative closure. Don't let's throw them away. (*ibid*, p. 49)

The author of this newspaper article draws a telling connection between certain kinds of story-telling and the dominance of colonialism. Lubiano (*ibid*) draws a telling connection between certain story forms (definitions of story-telling) and a politics of dominance.

However, the centerpiece of Lubiano's (*ibid*) article is an explication of McPherson's 1977 novel, *Elbow Room* (1977). The novel is about an African-American novelist trying to get his novel accepted by a white editor and about the problems created by the white editor's failure to recognize that the story does not follow conventional (white) presumptions about the nature of a story. In addition, the novel itself does not follow those conventions. Lubiano (1991) asserts that

> The narrator (of the novel) . . . shatters the illusion of accurate and controlled representation by interrupting the story to argue *against* the imposition of a single narrative form, reminding the reader that he is not telling his story along the lines or within the boundaries that would reassure the editor or reinstate a 'white' aesthetic in 'black' face. (p. 167)

Later, Lubiano (*ibid*) says, 'The narrative decenters the authority of Western tradition and declines to replace it with another authority, *not even a narrative authority* (emphasis added)' (p. 177). Lubiano's point is that the choice of whose story is essentialized has serious social consequences. Moreover, she questions even the idea of characterizing or defining what a story is.

Mishler's Chapter 5

The final criticism I want to make of Mishler's *Research Interviewing* (1986) is to question his concept of empowerment. He begins this chapter by saying that 'In the mainstream tradition the interviewee-interviewer relationship is marked by a striking asymmetry of power; this is the central structuring feature of interviews as research contexts' (p. 117). Later, Mishler makes a stronger, more comprehensive statement about the asymmetries of power in interviewing:

> In a standard interview respondents are presented with a predetermined scheme of relevances: topics, definitions of events, categories for response and evaluation are all introduced, framed, and specified by interviewers, who determine the adequacy and appropriateness of responses. Finally, researchers through their analyses and reports define the 'meaning' of responses and findings, whereas respondents have no opportunity to comment upon interpretations of their words and intentions. This way of doing research takes away from respondents their right to 'name' their world (Freire, 1970). Stated somewhat extremely and from the perspective of respondents, interview research by excluding the biographical rooting and contextual

> grounding of respondents' personal and social webs of meaning bears a resemblance to a 'degradation ceremony' (Garfinkel, 1956, quoted in Mishler) or an identity-stripping process (Goffman, 1961, cited in Mishler). (p. 122)

While I agree that he raises important issues about the play of power within traditional interviewing,[11] I would suggest that Mishler's modernist presumptions constrain his ability to 'see' and address that play of power.

Mishler says that 'The alternatives to standard practice that will be discussed here (in chapter 5) are directed toward the empowerment of respondents' (*ibid*, p. 117). On the next page, he makes a similar statement: 'A central task in what follows is to find ways to empower respondents so that they have more control of the processes through which their words are given meaning' (*ibid*, p. 118). In my opinion, there is a kind of paternalism in these statements. The word 'empowerment', as he uses it, implies that the researcher can give power to the interviewee. The researcher is the superordinate who has the power to give, and the interviewee is the subordinate who needs the power that can be given by the researcher. In contrast, in the next section, I will develop a different view of the power relationship between researcher and the research 'subject' that illustrates how a postmodernist might reconstruct this aspect of research interviewing.

Dominance, Resistance, and Chaos/Freedom

I agree with Mishler (*ibid*) that in many ways the positivist conceptualization of interviewing is characterized by asymmetries of power. The interview is drawn from the researcher's project, especially in terms of the researcher's social and institutional position. The researcher develops the questions, and the interviewee answers them. The interviewee is under the spotlight, while the researcher remains hidden: 'The transcript (of the interview) should, paralleling the interview, be dominated by the subject's remarks' (Bogdan and Biklen, 1982, p. 95). The research label for the interviewee, 'the subject', signals her/his proper position. The interviewer's transcribed words are what is under the control of the researcher. From a postmodernist view, the 'wild profusion' of the Other (the interviewee) is reduced and refashioned to fit the modernist prison of the Same (the researcher's project).

If this is all that is happening in a mainstream interview, then Mishler's call to 'empower' the interviewee is appropriate. If this power asymmetry is a complete characterization of what occurs in an interview, what we have is a totalization, a seamless encapsulation of researcher and interviewee in what Hegel characterized as the Master-Slave relationship. If Mishler is correct, the only equity avenue for the interviewee is the benevolence of the researcher. But I disagree that the mainstream conceptualization of interviewing is an appropriate description of what is occurring in such interviews. Instead, I would argue that it is his modernist frame that predisposes Mishler to this view. I am not arguing, however, that power asymmetries do not exist. They certainly do. I agree with Mishler that the relationship between interviewer and interviewee is frequently inequitable and that this inequity is an underlying, but hidden facet of positivist notions of interviewing. But this is only one facet of the interview interaction; the asymmetry of power is not a total description of the interaction.

Classical Marxists and some critical theorists, such as Bernstein (1979), Bourdieu and Passeron (1977), and Bowles and Gintis (1976), have also totalized the asymmetries of power in the same way. While I respect these theorists for their commitment to an unflinching focus on power inequities and for making all of us pay attention to such inequities, they have tended to totalize this focus until all of social life is encapsulated by this totalization of inequity. More recently, however, various critical theorists, such as Apple (1982), Bates (1980), Foster (1986), Giroux (1983), and Weiler (1988) (most of whom draw on Freire [for examples, Freire, 1973] and Gramsci [for examples, Gramsci, 1973]), have emphasized the equal importance of resistance. In this view, those with less power are not simply trapped within the totalization of an asymmetrical power relation; the less powerful find innumerable, creative, even powerful ways to resist inequity. Weiler (1988) writes: 'The concept of resistance emphasizes that individuals are not simply acted upon by abstract "structures" but negotiate, struggle, and create meaning of their own' (p. 21); and Clegg (1989) concludes: 'Control (or dominance) can never be totally secured, in part because of agency. It will be open to erosion and undercutting by the action, embodied agency of those people who are its object . . .' (p. 193).

In the best instances of this view, this resistance is not romanticized. Often the resistance has a two-sided character that, on one side, interrupts domination, but which, on the other side, can also have negative consequences for the less powerful. For example, the less powerful may engage in resistance (such as acting-out in class) to the race, class, gender, or sexual-orientation dominance of schooling, but that same resistance may inhibit the learning of employment skills.[12]

This critical theory focus on dominance and resistance also applies to interviewing. Critical theorists would contend that if the researcher is open to 'seeing' resistance, she or he will find that interviewees are not just the subjects of researcher dominance, they are also active resistors of such dominance. I have found this to be true in my own interviewing as a researcher. Interviewees do not simply go along with the researcher's program, even if it is a structured rather than open one. I find that interviewees carve out space of their own, that they can often control some or part of the interview, that they push against or resist my goals, my intentions, my questions, my meanings. Many times I have asked a question which the respondent has turned into a different question that she or he wants to answer. While sometimes this may be an effect of misunderstanding, other times it is the interviewee asserting her/his own control over the interview. In other words, interviewees are not passive subjects; they are active participants in the interaction. They, in fact, often use the interviewer as much as the interviewer is using them.

This dominance-and-resistance view of the play of power is much different than Mishler's idea of empowerment in which power is given to the subject by the researcher. There is, thus, in Mishler's view a kind of paternalism based on modernist assumptions about who has power and how power operates. Classical Marxists have also held a view similar to Mishler's, but critical theorists have corrected the Marxist totalization by focusing on the resistance of the less powerful to dominance. Unfortunately, the dominance-resistance binary can itself become a new totalization that is in need of critique. That is, the critical theorists, while destroying the prior totalization of the classical Marxists, have created a new totalization by attempting to enclose or capture or interpret social life largely within the dominance-resistance binary. As Lather (1991) says, 'overtly oppositional work, while at war with the dominant systems of knowledge production . . . (often rein-scribes dominance) in what it hopes to transform' (p. 26).[13]

To displace the dominance-resistance binary, I would add an open-ended space which I sometimes, with irony, call chaos.[14] I will explain what I mean by this, but first I do not intend that the recognition of this third space (or term) erases the important focus on dominance or resistance. Our social life, including research, is riddled with dominance and inequity to the detriment of everyone. In addition, the understanding that the less powerful are not passive participants in the drama of dominance is a profound insight that is a necessary part of any move toward equity. But to enclose social life within the dominance-resistance binary is but another prison house of language, meaning, and communication.

What I first labeled as chaos might, however, be better labeled as 'chaos/ freedom'. What I mean by 'chaos/freedom' is everything that occurs that is neither dominance nor resistance; everything that escapes or exceeds this binary is chaos (because it is not encapsulated by the binary) and an openness or freedom for the interviewer and interviewee. Resistance to dominance is a positive necessity, but it is also necessarily tied to dominance. Dominance creates the need for resistance. Dominance is the master; resistance is the slave's reaction to this master. The condition of resistance persists as long as dominance persists. Resistance is, thus, not freedom. Resistance is not an open possibility; it is a closed determination. Much of living, however, occurs outside the confines of the dominance-resistance binary. People work with horses, grow plants, invent or make or fix machines. They write poetry. They raise children. They have intense, intimate one-to-one relation-ships. They fish, ski, climb, go spelunking. They not only pursue the wild profu-sion; they are the wild profusion. It is not that dominance and resistance do not exist within these activities, but there is more to living, working, and interviewing than can be circumscribed by the dominance-resistance binary.

We can, therefore, look at an interview and conclude that there is dominance of the interviewee by the researcher, resistance of the interviewee to researcher dominance, and chaos/freedom enacted by both the interviewer and the interviewee. Within this chaos/freedom, there are speech enactments which cannot be encapsu-lated or captured by the dominance of the researcher or the resistance of the inter-viewee. For instance, the researcher may perform for the interviewee for reasons that have nothing to do with dominance or the goals of the research. The researcher may use the interview experience to satisfy her/his relational or emotional needs. The same is true of the interviewee. The interviewee may play out a persona just for the satisfaction of the play. The interviewee may use the researcher to satisfy her or his need to communicate about some issues related to the research. The interviewee may practice stories about herself or himself to the researcher. Many aspects of the interview interaction simply exceed either the dominance of the researcher (including the foci or purposes of the research) and the resistance of the interviewee to that dominance.

Implications for Research Interviewing

If my critique of positivist and postpositivist views of interviewing is accepted, it could be concluded that I completely reject interviewing as a research method. This, however, is not my position. I have tried to undermine positivist and post-positivist conceptions of interviewing, both of which are based on modernist assumptions, but I do not reject interviewing itself. I am suggesting, instead, is that we need to critically rethink what occurs in research interviewing and how we report (represent) our results. But whether we continue to call the interview inter-action 'interviewing' is not crucial to me; the meanings of words continually migrate and change. For example, the meaning of the word 'validity' has changed consider-ably since it first emerged as a criterion in testing (Wolcott, 1990). Consequently, whether we call the interview interaction 'interviewing', 'conversation', 'story-telling', or simply 'an interaction' is of much less importance than what we think occurs in this interaction.

I have tried to argue that the interview interaction is fundamentally indeter-minate — the complex play of conscious and unconscious thoughts, feelings, fears, power, desires, and needs on the part of both the interviewer and interviewee cannot be captured and categorized. In an interview there is no stable 'reality' or 'meaning' that can be represented. The indeterminate totality (though, of course, there is no totality since we cannot circumscribe the interaction) of the interview always exceeds and transgresses our attempts to capture and categorize. When we think we 'interpret', through various data reduction techniques, what the mean-ing or meanings of an interview are, we are overlaying indeterminacy with the determinacies of our meaning-making, replacing ambiguities with findings or con-structions. When we proceed, then, as if we have 'found' or 'constructed' the best or the key or the most important interpretation, we are misportraying what has occurred. And techniques like prolonged interaction or joint construction (or even triangulation or collaboration) will not lead to a more correct interpretation because, again, an indeterminate ambiguity, 'a wild profusion', lies at the heart of the inter-view interaction.

The crux of the issue is the interpretive moment as it occurs throughout the research process. And, into this moment, the researcher brings consider-able conscious and unconscious baggage — other related research, training within a particular discipline (such as anthropology), epistemological inclinations, institu-tional and funding imperatives, conceptual schemes about story-telling or power, social positionality (the intersection of race, class, gender, sexual-orientation, among other key social locations), macro-cultural or civilizational frames (including the research frame itself); and individual idiosyncracies, the interactions of which are themselves complex and ambiguous. This plethora of baggage, in the guise of the interviewer, interacts with an interviewee, who, of course, brings her/his own baggage to the interaction. That the written result, the final interpretation, of the interview interaction is overloaded with the researcher's interpretive baggage is, therefore, inevitable. In a very important sense this written representation is largely, though not completely, but a mirror image of the researcher and her/his baggage.

But contrast what the researcher brings to the written representation with what I argue is the radical, indeterminate ambiguity or openness that lies at the heart of the interview interaction itself, at the lived intersection of language, meaning, and communication. The researcher then fills this indeterminate openness[15] with her/his interpretive baggage, imposes names, categories, constructions, conceptual schemes, theories upon the unknowable, and believes that the indeterminate is now located, constructed, known. Order has been created. The restless, appropriative spirit of the researcher is (temporarily) at peace.

Should we desire, however, to refuse this false order and, instead, foreground the indeterminate ambiguity, how might we redefine or reconceptualize research interviewing? First, we could highlight the baggage we bring to the research enterprise. Many feminists now name their social positionality, and numerous scholars now name their epistemological orientation. Although it is simply not possible to exhaustively name all of the conscious and unconscious baggage that the researcher brings to the interpretive moment, a reasonably comprehensive statement of disciplinary training, epistemological orientation, social positionality, institutional imperatives, and funding sources and requirements could be provided so that the reader has some sense of what the researcher brings to the research enterprise.

Second, we can foreground the open, indeterminacy of the interview interaction itself. But merely announcing this indeterminacy in an introduction and then proceeding to name 'reality' is not sufficient. As we conduct the interview and interpret the interview 'data', we can illustrate, though never completely, the shifting openness within the interview itself. For instance, I conducted an open-structured interview with a principal of an elementary school on how she was trying to restructure her school. During the second interview, we discussed the text of the first interview which I had provided to her prior to the second interview. Although the preliminary reason for our discussion of the first interview was a member check, what emerged instead in our discussion was the considerable ambiguity in our prior interaction. This ambiguity could, subsequently, have been represented in a written report.

What is needed is research on interviewing itself; some 'playing around' or experimentation with interviewing and with ways to represent interviews that highlight the indeterminacy of interview interactions, ways that allow for the uncontrollable play of power within the interaction. Although it may seem difficult, based on our traditional understanding of interviewing, to envision these kind of changes, we could look to art for examples of such changes. In painting, for example, abstract expressionism was a change to a different way of representing reality. Free form poetry was a change to different way of representing reality. For those artists who were committed to prior forms of painting or poetry, the new methods may have been difficult to understand; for the abstract expressionists and the free-form poets, these new methods fit their new understanding of reality.

There is no reason that a similar change in how interviewing is understood, conducted, and represented cannot occur in research interviewing. Though such efforts may already exist, I currently know of no published example. Patai's (1988) creative conversion of interview text into poetry is certainly provocative in this regard since poetry tends not to fear ambiguity or indeterminacy. But we cannot be limited either to poetic representations of interviews or to the two suggestions I have made above. What we need are some new imaginaries of interviewing that open up multiple spaces in which interview interactions can be conducted and represented, ways that engage the indeterminate ambiguity of interviewing, practices that transgress and exceed a knowable order.

Notes

1 I use four key terms throughout this article — positivism, postpositivism, modernism, and postmodernism, the meaning of which will become reasonably apparent throughout the article, but here I will provide a preliminary comparison of the terms. While I agree with Phillips (1983) that positivism means very different things to different scholars, many of which have little to do with its 'original' meaning, it has come to be widely accepted as a label for the application of the scientific method to the social sciences. In regard to interviewing, I take positivism (which I also call the 'traditional' or 'conventional' approach) to assume that the individual interview context (including, for instance, the personality or gender of the interviewer) is not a critical consideration and that a category-based reduction of the verbal text of the interview can be taken as a valid representation of the interview itself and of the perceptions of the interviewee. In contrast to positivism, I take postpositivism, following Mishler (1986), to assume that interviews are highly contextualized events and, thus, the representations of such events must be contextualized. But both positivism and postpositivism make the modernist assumption that the appropriate research method will yield the real or best meaning of an interview. Postmodernism, in contrast, suggests that there is a radical indeterminacy at the heart of the interview interaction which cannot be overcome by any methodology.

2 See, for example, an excerpt of an interview transcript in Bogdan and Biklen (1982, pp. 94–5) or a sample of a coded transcript (p. 168).

3 Even though the correspondence theory is little accepted any longer by research epistemologists, Strauss and Corbin (1990) assume that data correspond to reality: 'We are constantly comparing hypotheses against *reality (the data)* (emphasis added)' (p. 187). Throughout this work they repeat this equation; but they also contradict themselves. For example, they say, 'Building theory, by its very nature, implies interpreting data, for the data must be conceptualized and the concepts related to form a theoretical rendition of reality (*a reality that cannot actually be known, but is always interpreted* [emphasis added])' (p. 22). In my opinion, the idea that research interviewing can represent reality is their predominant view. If the interpretive view were their primary perspective, the entire orientation of the book would be changed. They, in fact, typify a mainstream or conventional view of interviewing.

4   See, for example, Strauss and Corbin (1990) who say that one of the goals of qualitative research is 'to allow some measure of control over' the world (p. 9) and that grounded 'theory should provide control with regard to action toward phenomenon' (p. 23).

5   I should point our that in a later article Mishler (1991) has, in my opinion, moved significantly toward a more postmodernist perspective. I focus mainly on his earlier book because it represents well some of the recent postpositivist, but still modernist, revisions of research.

6   'Poststructuralism' is a more accurate label for my point of view in this article, but in the US there is substantially more familiarity with and use of the term 'postmodernism' for the kind of work I do. In a more accurate sense 'postmodernism' is a label for a historical period; 'poststructuralism' is a kind of thinking that grew up largely in France that, among other things, rejected many of the structuralist assumptions, hence 'poststructuralist'.

7   Foucault's (1977) critique of categorization is similar to his critique of taxonomies. Foucault writes that 'the most tenacious subjection of difference (the other) is undoubtedly that maintained by categories . . . Categories organize the play of affirmations and negations, establish the legitimacy of resemblances within representation, and guarantee the objectivity and operation of concepts. They suppress the anarchy of difference, divide differences into zones, delimit their rights, and prescribe their task of specification . . . (Categories) appear as an archaic morality, the ancient decalogue that the identical (the Same) imposed upon difference (the Other)' (p. 186). A postmodernist concern, then, that Foucault and I share is about the modernist assumption that 'reality' can be named or defined through research. I argue that what occurs in conventional research is not a naming of 'reality' but rather is an interactive construction overweighed or overdetermined by the modernist assumptions (often labeled the Same in postmodernist work) of the researcher which are projected onto the Other (the speech acts of the interviewee). Foucault and others argue that this naming is violent and imperial.

8   Lubiano (1991) indicates that the need to represent or capture the 'wild profusion' (Foucault, 1973, p. xv) is an imperial need of white Western civilization. Poststructuralists would say that this need is the typically Western attempt to turn the other into the Same (Flax, 1990). For other examples of this point of view see Minh-ha (1989), Spivak (1988), Taylor (1986) or Young (1990).

9   Lengthening the duration of the interaction between the interviewer and the interviewee does not necessarily (teleologically) lead to better communication or better understanding, even if the researcher intends it so. Increased interaction may have many different meanings or effects for the interviewee: it may be boring; it may mean new performed elaborations of previous interview themes; it may mean new and different though not deeper and better themes; it may simply be circular and repetitive; it may satisfy emotional needs for interaction, connection, positive attention from another person; it may just be entertaining. There is literally no end to what increased interactions may mean to the interviewee, but there is nothing in the increase in time spent interviewing that teleologically inclines the course of the interview toward deeper or better communication and understanding. To assume increased interaction leads to better communication is the imposition of a modernist (humanist psychology) viewpoint on the event that we call interviewing.

10 Near the end of Mishler's (1991) more recent article, he says that 'Transcripts are our constructions and making them is one of our central research practices' (p. 277). I agree with this, but, in the very next paragraph in my opinion he contradicts the above postmodernist position with a modernist one. He says 'How we arrange and rearrange the text in light of our discoveries is a process of testing, clarifying, and deepening our

understanding of what is happening in the discourse' (p. 277). While I do not oppose his support for an intense and prolonged interaction with the interview transcript, I do not think that his interaction with the transcript 'tests, clarifies, or deepens' his understanding of what is happening in the interview. His extended interaction with the interview transcript is not a process that leads to a 'better' understanding of the interview; it is an interactive process of interpretive construction. The interpreter of the interview transcript is actually a larger and more formative part of the process than is the interview transcript. The process of prolongation is a creative process of construction, but it is not necessarily a road to clearer and deeper understanding.

11   Although I have not addressed the issue in this paper, there is a peculiar contradiction in Mishler's (1986) characterization of an interview as 'joint construction' in his chapter 3 and as an 'asymmetry of power' in his chapter 5. Joint construction seems to imply some kind of equal participation that is contradictory to Mishler's conclusions about the relationship of power between researcher and interviewee. Postmodernists often make the point that texts (and everything can be seen as a text) are not coherently unified, just like subjectivities are not coherently unified. From a postmodernist perspective the test of a single author has many 'voices', some of which conflict with others. I think this is the case with the above contradiction. Mishler has two contradictory commitments in *Research Interviewing* (1986). It is my opinion that his commitment to a kind of liberal humanist idea of discourse as a jointly constructed conversation is the stronger commitment. His second commitment to an exposure of the asymmetry of power in the interview is the weaker commitment. Indeed it almost seems tacked on to the larger project rather than integral to it. Otherwise, his ideas about discourse as a jointly constructed conversation would be more interrupted by his attention to power asymmetries. This is but one example of how his text deconstructs itself.

12   This two-sided aspect of resistance is particularly apparent in Willis' *Learning to Labour* (1977), even though this is not the central purpose of this influential work. Willis' project was to show the complex workings of class reproduction on 'the lads'; the two-sided aspect of resistance is but one part of this complexity.

13   Gitlin, Siegel and Boru (1988) and Lather (1986 and 1991), as advocates of emancipatory research, have also criticized emancipatory approaches that reinscribed dominance within research assumptions and methods. For instance, Lather (1991) writes that 'Poststructuralism positions Marxism as a movement of controlling, labelling, and classifying which denies its complicity and investment in dichotomy at the expense of the Other. Transforming difference into dichotomous oppositions, it reduces multiplicities and plurality into a single oppositional norm' (p. 24).

14   By using the word 'chaos', I am *not* referring to chaos theory. What I mean by this word is an open space in which occur events or actions that exceed the dominance-resistance binary.

15   I would suggest that, rather than being negative, the radical indeterminacy or openness in language, meaning, and communication is generative; it is a constant source of new forms, new spaces, new possibilities.

References

APPLE, M. (1982) *Education and Power*, Boston, MA, Routledge and Kegan Paul.

BATES, R.J. (1980) 'New developments in the new sociology of education', *British Journal of Sociology of Education*, **1**, 1, pp. 67–79.

BERMAN, A. (1988) *From the New Criticism to Deconstruction: The Reception of Structuralism and Post-structuralism*, Chicago, IL, University of Illinois Press.

BERNSTEIN, B. (1979) *Class, Codes, and Control*, London, Routledge and Kegan Paul.

BOGDAN, R.C. and BIKLEN, S.K. (1982) *Qualitative Research for Education: An Introduction to Theory and Methods*, Boston, MA, Allyn and Bacon.

BOURDIEU, P. and PASSERON, J-C. (1977) *Reproduction in Education, Society, and Culture*, Beverley Hills, CA, Sage.

BOWLES, S. and GINTIS, H. (1976) *Schooling in Capitalist America*, New York, Basic Books.

CLEGG, S.R. (1989) *Frameworks of Power*, London, Sage.

CONNELLY, F.M. and CLANDININ, D.J. (1990) 'Stories of experience and narrative inquiry', *Educational Researcher*, **19**, 5, pp. 2–14.

EISNER, E.W. (1991) *The Enlightened Eye: Qualitative Inquiry and the Enhancement of Educational Practice*, New York, Macmillian Co.

FLAX, J. (1990) *Thinking Fragments: Psychoanalysis, Feminism, and Postmodernism in the Contemporary West*, Berkeley, CA, University of California Press.

FOSTER, W. (1986) *Paradigms and Promises*, Buffalo, NY, Prometheus Books.

FOUCAULT, M. (1973) *The Order of Things: An Archaeology of the Human Sciences*, New York, Vintage Books.

FOUCAULT, M. (1977) *Language, Counter-memory, Practice* (D.F. Bouchard, trans.), Ithaca, NY, Cornell University Press.

FREIRE, P. (1973) *Education for Critical Consciousness*, New York, Seabury Press.

GIROUX, H. (1983) *Theory, Resistance, and Education*, South Hadley, MA, Bergin and Garvey.

GITLIN, A., SIEGEL, M. and BORU, K. (1988) 'The politics of method: From leftist ethnography to evaluative research', *International Journal of Qualitative Studies in Education*, **2**, 3, pp. 235–53.

GRAMSCI, A. (1973) *Letters from Prison* (L. Lawner, trans.), New York, Harper & Row.

HARDING, S. (1991) *Whose Science? Whose Knowledge? Thinking from Women's Lives*, Ithaca, NY, Cornell University Press.

HEGEL, G.W.F. (1977) *The Phenomenology of Spirit* (A.V. Miller, trans.), Oxford, Clarendon Press.

LATHER, P. (1986) 'Research as praxis', *Harvard Educational Review*, **56**, 2, pp. 257–77.

LATHER, P. (1991) *Getting Smart: Feminist Research and Pedagogy With/in the Postmodern*, New York, Routledge.

LINCOLN, Y.S. and GUBA, E. (1985) *Naturalistic Inquiry*, Beverly Hills, CA, Sage.

LUBIANO, W. (1991) 'Shuckin' off the African-American native other: What's "po-mo" got to do with it?', *Cultural Critique*, **20**, winter, pp. 149–86.

MINH-HA, T.T. (1989) *Woman Native Other*, Bloomington, IN, Indiana University Press.

MISHLER, E.G. (1986) *Research Interviewing: Context and Narrative*, Cambridge, MA, Harvard University Press.

MISHLER, E.G. (1991) 'Representing discourse: The rhetoric of transcription', *Journal of Narrative and Life History*, **1**, 4, pp. 255–80.

PATAI, D. (1988) 'Constructing a self: A Brazilian life story', *Feminist Studies*, **14**, 1, pp. 155–77.

PATTON, M.Q. (1990) *Qualitative Evaluation and Research Methods*, Newbury Park, CA, Sage.

PHILLIPS, D.C. (1983) 'After the wake: Postpositivistic educational thought', *Educational Researcher*, **12**, 5, pp. 4–12.

RYAN, M. (1989) *Politics and Culture: Working Hypotheses for a Post-revolutionary Society*, London, Macmillan.

SAUSSURE, F. (1983) *Course in General Linguistics* (R. Harris, trans.), London, Duckworth.

SPIVAK, G.C. (1988) *In Other Worlds: Essays in Cultural Politics*, New York, Routledge.

STRAUSS, A. and CORBIN, J. (1990) *Basics of Qualitative Research: Grounded Theory Procedures and Techniques*, Newbury Park, CA, Sage.

TAYLOR, M.C. (1986) 'Introduction: System . . . structure . . . difference . . . other' in DERRIDA, J. (ED) *Deconstruction in Context: Literature and Philosophy* (M.C. Taylor, trans.), Chicago, IL, University of Chicago Press, pp. 1–34.

THE GROUP FOR COLLABORATIVE INQUIRY (1993) 'The democratization of knowledge', *Adult Education Quarterly*, **43**, 4, pp. 1–8.

TYLER, S. (1985) 'Ethnography, intertextuality, and the end of description', *American Journal of Semiotics*, **3**, 4, pp. 83–98.

WARREN, C.A.B. (1988) *Gender Issues in Field Research*, Newbury Park, CA, Sage.

WAX, R.H. (1979) 'Gender and age in fieldwork education: No good thing is done by any man alone', *Social Problems*, **29**, 5, pp. 505–22.

WEILER, K. (1988) *Women Teaching for Change: Gender, Class & Power*, New York, Bergin & Garvey.

WILLIS, P. (1977) *Learning to Labour*, Westmead, Saxon House.

WOLCOTT, H.F. (1990) 'On seeking — and rejecting — validity in qualitative research' in EISNER, E.W. and PESHKIN, A. (Eds) *Qualitative Inquiry in Education: The Continuing Debate*, New York, Teacher's College Press, pp. 121–52.

YOUNG, R. (1990) *White Mythologies: Writing History and the West*, London, Routledge.

ZINN, M.B. (1979) 'Field research in minority communities: Ethical, methodological, and poltical observations by an insider', *Social Problems*, **27**, 2, pp. 209–19.

4   The Masks of Validity:
A Deconstructive Investigation

While many, widely different kinds of validity have been delineated across the growing array of research paradigms, the central point of this investigation is that, despite the ostensible differences, the myriad kinds of validity are simply masks that conceal a profound and disturbing sameness. This conclusion, however, is at odds with both conventional (positivist) and postpositivist[1] understandings of validity. If the different types of validity across and within all research paradigms were gathered together and compared, many of these types would appear to be unlike one another. For example, Cook and Campbell's (1979) 'statistical conclusion' validity is substantially different from Lather's (1986) 'catalytic validity', due since the epistemological orientations of Cook and Campbell and of Lather are extremely dissimilar. Even within the same paradigmatic perspective, however, there are efforts to distinguish between different kinds of validity. For instance, Maxwell (1992), working within a realist frame of reference, derived five different forms of validity from the practices of qualitative researchers.

These numerous and apparently dissimilar constructions of validity are simply different masks that conceal an underlying sameness, a singularity of purpose or function, that transgresses the supposedly incommensurable differences or boundaries dividing various research epistemologies. The central question of this chapter, then, is to define this sameness, this singularity. The path I will travel in addressing this is, first, to follow the curious paradigmatic transgressions of validity as it is carried out of its originary 'home' in conventional social science research by the postpositivist diaspora. Next, I will interrogate these transgressions. Third, I will name and discuss the singularity that wears the masks of validity. Finally, I will consider three types of validity that do not reinscribe this singularity.

Originary Validity[2]

Although the concept of validity was originally 'associated almost exclusively with testing' (Wolcott, 1990, p. 122), where it meant 'a test has validity if it measures what it purports to measure' (Allen and Yen, 1979, p. 95), validity became one of the necessary truth criteria of conventional social science research: no validity, no truth. Campbell and Stanley in their 1966 classic on research design contend that 'internal validity is the *sine qua non* of research design' (p. 5). This importance of validity has also been verified by Kerlinger in his equally classic *Foundations of Behavioral Research* (1986). 'Validity . . . is much more than technique. It bores into the essence of science itself' (p. 432). My point is that respected research methodologists of the traditional perspective agree about the primary importance of validity as a research criterion. This consensus underscores that the validity concept is a central issue within the conventional social science orientation (Mishler, 1990; Salner, 1989).

Conventional social scientists asserted that they could establish value-free, objective truth, or at least a probabilistic estimate of that truth, if the proper scientific methods were followed (Polkinghorne, 1983). To warrant this claim, it was necessary to develop appropriate methodological strategies. Validity, in all of its many reconstructions from face to construct validity, became one of the, if not the most, important criteria for establishing veridicality (Mishler, 1990). For instance, in measurement, reliability is a necessary but not sufficient condition; validity provides that sufficiency. In theory building, construct validity 'precedes, chronologically and epistemologically, other validity issues, inferences, and interpretation of research findings' (Cherryholmes, 1988, p. 428). The essential meaning of validity came to be, as Lincoln and Guba (1985) correctly surmised, the warrant of trustworthiness. If a research study had the appropriate validity, the results could be trusted (Campbell and Stanley, 1966). Validity became the line of bifurcation for a two-sided map. On one side of the map was that research which had passed the test of validity (i.e., was valid); on the other side of the map was that research which had not passed the test (i.e., was invalid), along with aspects of 'reality' that had not yet been researched. Validity as a set of research practices within the conventional social sciences is, thus, the name for the boundary line separating research that is acceptable from research that is not and from the, as yet, unresearched.

Since conventional social science has repeatedly been declared dead, at least theoretically, by postpositivist critics (for example, Barrone, 1990; Eisner, 1990; Guba, 1990; Howe and Eisenhart, 1990; Phillips, 1983), it is curious that many postpositivists continue to retain validity even though they are quite willing to dump conventional science, the nomological net from which validity derived its meaning. What is it about validity that it exceeds its paradigmatic birthplace? What compels the epistemological travelers of the postpositivist diaspora to 'not leave home without it'?

The most ready answer, and one that has been most frequently discussed, is that postpositivists, like Miles and Huberman (1984) or Lincoln and Guba (1985), are simply translating or transporting conventional science concerns, regulations, or truth claims into a postpositivist frame (Scheurich, 1991; Smith, 1984). The previous allusion to the diaspora is apropos: emigrants often take their 'birthplace' culture (the conventional approach) with them to the new land (postpositivism). The result is usually a merging of old metaphors and new, as is readily apparent in much postpositivist research (Scheurich, 1991). The reason usually given, however, for why postpositivists use conventional science research criteria is that postpositivists initially had to survive in conventional science-dominated settings. One of the obvious ways to do this was for postpositivists to frame or justify their (usually qualitative) work within the traditional (usually quantitative) truth standards.

While this explanation may account for early postpositivist work, it does not seemingly account for other, more 'radical, conceptual recasting(s)' of validity that have arisen more recently (Mishler, 1990).

Successor Validity

New efforts by postpositivists, such as Mishler (*ibid*) or Lather (1986), have focused on developing modes of validation that do not arise out of the conventional approach to the social sciences. It would be more accurate to say that these new, successor validities arise in opposition to the conventional notions of how science has been understood and conducted in the social sciences. Using a concise but compelling range of citations, Mishler (1990), for instance, argues not only that conventional varieties of validity are inappropriate for postpositivist research but, further, that they are inappropriate for the actual, as opposed to the idealized, way that conventional scientific research is conducted. His goal is to locate issues of trustworthiness or validation 'within a community of scientists[3] as they come to share nonproblematic and useful ways of thinking about and solving problems' (p. 422). Validity, then, becomes an historically embedded social construction appropriated by a 'community of scientists' who decide that certain outstanding examples of research (i.e., 'shared exemplars', p. 422) will guide further work by the community in considering what is and is not trustworthy.

The result is that though validity is no longer related to establishing ahistorical truth warrants and though validity is now a social construction which 'may change with time' (*ibid*, p. 420), the idea that there must be a boundary line, a judgment criterion for deciding whose work is acceptable, is preserved. Throughout his discussion of validity, Mishler defines this line or judgment in terms of 'trustworthiness'. For example, he follows the sub-heading: 'Trustworthiness: Grounds for Belief and Action', with his reconstruction of:

> validation as the process(es) through which we make claims for and evaluate the
> '*trustworthiness*' (italics added) of reported observations, interpretations, and generalizations. The essential criterion for such judgments is the degree to which
> we can rely on the concepts, methods, and inferences of a study, or tradition of
> inquiry, as the basis for our own theorizing and empirical research. If our overall
> assessment of a study's *trustworthiness* (italics added) is high enough for us to act
> on it, we are granting the findings a sufficient degree of validity to invest our own
> time and energy, and to put at risk our reputations as competent investigators. As
> more and more investigators act on this assumption and find that it 'works', the
> findings take on the aura of objective fact; they become 'well-entrenched'. (p. 419)

Although Mishler has apparently departed from conventional social science validity criteria, he has retained what Foucault (1977) calls a 'regularity' (p. 199) — a regularity that is virtually the same as the regularity that 'originated' within the conventional approach to the social sciences. Validity, therefore, wears different epistemological masks, either that of the conventional approach to the social sciences or that of the more 'radical' postpositivist approach to the social sciences, but that which wears the masks, the regularity, is the same in both cases. In both, validity (as a regularity) is the deployment of an either/or criteria division between trustworthy and not trustworthy, a two-sided map which indicates what is considered acceptable (i.e. valid or trustworthy) and what is considered unacceptable (i.e. invalid or untrustworthy). That there is sometimes disagreement about whether a particular study is valid or trustworthy does not abrogate the fact that validity decisions as well as disagreements about trustworthiness assume this two-sided, either/or map.

Lather's 'Issues of validity in openly ideological research' (1986) is another 'radical conceptual recasting' of validity.[4] She wants validity to support 'research which both advances emancipatory theory-building and empowers the researched' (p. 64), but her chief anxiety about validity is similar to that of Mishler: 'My central concern is that new paradigm researchers must begin to be more systematic about establishing the *trustworthiness* (italics added) of data' (*ibid*, p. 65). She is worried that 'ignoring data credibility within openly value-based research programs will not improve the chances for the . . . legitimacy of the knowledge they produce' (*ibid*, p. 78). She offers four methods for obtaining this legitimacy — triangulation, construct validity, face validity, and catalytic validity. While her construct validity and face validity are defined in somewhat novel ways from a traditional viewpoint, it is her catalytic validity that 'is by far the most unorthodox' (*ibid*, p. 67).

Catalytic validity is described as 'the degree to which the research process reorients, focuses, and energizes participants in what Freire terms "conscientization", knowing reality in order to better transform it' (*ibid*, p. 67). More simply, catalytic validity is the degree to which research empowers and emancipates the research subjects. While the 'systematic' 'rigor' (words Lather frequently uses) necessary for accurate judgments of such degrees of emancipation is probably impossible to come by, her oft repeated and most fundamental concern is that 'openly ideological research' (*ibid*, p. 77) will be judged untrustworthy. Although Lather has clearly left conventional science's value-free stance far behind with her emancipatory-oriented epistemology, the use of validity as a criterion of judgment is retained. She too wants to draw a validity boundary line; she too wants to establish boundary criteria for legitimacy, acceptance, approval, or trustworthiness, even though the nomological net (the conventional perspective) out of which such criteria originated has been discarded; she too calls for a deployment of an 'either/or'; she too reinscribes the same bifurcated 'regularity'. Once again, it is intriguing that those 'more radical' postpositivists strongly reject conventional science, yet, they retain validity as a boundary for the two sides of a 'truth' map that divides the acceptable from the unacceptable.

Interrogated Validity

Unlike Mishler (1990) and Lather (1986), Cherryholmes (1988), interrogate validity rather than reproducing the same validity concerns within new paradigms, interrogates validity. Although his interrogation proceeds from multiple viewpoints, he arrives at ten statements that characterize 'a more mature view of construct validity' (p. 450). Several of these statements point in one direction: 'The discourses of construct validity are, in part, discourses of and about power' (*ibid*, p. 450).

If the validity discourses are 'of and about power', what implications does this have for why the same sort of orientation to validity traverses both conventional science and postpositivism? That is, how can validity, as power, function equally well in both a conventional orientation and a radical postpositivist orientation? The answer, as I have suggested throughout, is that the power function of validity serves as a boundary line or as a policing practice. Validity is the name of the policing practices that divide good research from bad (conventional social science: Kerlinger, Campbell and Stanley); separate acceptable (to a particular community) research from unacceptable research (postpositivism: Mishler); split emancipatory research from oppressive research (critical theory/feminism: Lather); and so on, given one's epistemological biases. If a research paradigm has a boundary line separating inclusion from exclusion (by whatever criteria), validity has become the name of that line. It continues to divide the research map into only two sides, a bifurcation. As such, it is a 'regularity' in the discursive practices called research, 'a fixing of norms for the elaboration of concepts and theories' (Foucault, 1977, p. 199) that transgresses the apparent differences or supposed incommensurability between conventional social science and even the 'more radical recastings' of postpositivism.

The typical justification, among all perspectives, for a validity judgment is to ensure quality, trustworthiness, and legitimacy. Without such a boundary, it is argued, there would be no way to prevent the acceptance of poor quality, untrustworthy, or illegitimate work. The fear is the same for both conventional science and for more radical recastings; without the appropriate validity, there is apparently no way to differentiate between the valid and the invalid, the trustworthy and the untrustworthy, the emancipated and the oppressed. Historically, however, boundaries also exclude that which questions or attacks the paradigmatic status quo as well as views outside the understanding available to that status quo. In other words, validity boundaries are always already ideological power alignments. They always create insiders and outsiders.

For example, qualitative research was originally marginalized by conventional scientists as useful merely for exploratory studies, thus, not valid in the same substantive sense that quantitative research was (see, for example, Campbell and Stanley, 1966). Feminist standpoint epistemologies continue to be considered as invalid by many within the academy (Harding, 1986). But even these more radical positions have experienced the same problem: white feminists, for example, have been accused of totalizing white feminist positions and concerns at the expense of women of color (Collins, 1991; Huggins, 1991).

To recognize, then, that validity is but a mask for a boundary or policing function across both conventional approaches and more radical versions of postpositivism raises unsettling questions. What is this sameness, this singularity of purpose, circulating throughout the apparently different research paradigms? Why are Campbell and Stanley, Lincoln and Guba, Lather, and Mishler more alike than they seem to realize? What is this singularity that wears the masks of validity?

Imperial Validity

Any epistemological or 'truth' map which separates, in a two-sided fashion, the true or the accepted from the not true or the unaccepted or the not yet accepted establishes internally a territory of the *Same* and externally a territory of the *Other* (Minh-ha, 1989; Taylor, 1986). That which is inside the boundary is congruent with itself according to its paradigmatic criteria (the Same); that which is outside the boundary is rejected or untheorized, unappropriated difference (the Other). As Spivak (1988) says, by 'explaining (through valid research), we exclude the possibility of the *radically* heterogeneous (the Other)' (p. 105). In the case of Mishler (1990), the exemplars recognized by a particular community of scholars set a pattern of sameness or similarity. In the case of Lather (1986), although the pattern of sameness differs — research as empowerment rather than research exemplars — the primary effect is equivalent. That which is allowed inside the boundary is a replication or reproduction of the Same; that which is outside the boundary is different, heterogeneous, the Other.

In fact, the Same/Other power binary appears to be endemic to virtually all constructions of validity. Because this binary — valid/invalid, Same/Other — underlies these seemingly different epistemological projects, it appears that this power relationship is intrinsic to the Western knowledge project itself. As a problematic, this two-sided 'truth' map, and its enforcement through the various practices of validity, transgresses the limits of each single paradigm. At the same time that it marks a disturbing sameness across the multiple paradigms, thus dissolving the much discussed polyvocality of multiple paradigms into the monotone of the Same/Other binary. In Taylor's (1986) words:

> From its inception in Greece, Western philosophy has, for the most part, privileged oneness and unity (the Same) at the expense of manyness and plurality (the Other). Accordingly, the Western philosophical project can be understood as the repeated effort to overcome plurality and establish unity by reducing the many to the one. (p. 4)

The heart of the Western knowledge project, which includes both conventional and postpositivist orientations, is research. The purpose of research is to study the world (the Other), organize that world through a theory (reform or reshape the Other into the Same), and produce a written text communicating the victory of the Same over the Other. As Spivak (1988) asserts, 'the desire to explain (through research is) . . . a symptom of the desire to have a self (the researcher) that can control knowledge and a world that can be known (i.e., converted to the Same)' (p. 104).

Validity is the determination of whether the Other has been acceptably converted into the Same, according to a particular epistemology. The world is the raw, untamed Other, as in raw data and as in rejected, invalid research. It must be cooked into a valid research-based theory so as to be visible and knowable; the coarse, untheorized, polyvocal Other is considered to be insufficient unto itself. It must be given meaning and appropriate form. It cannot be accepted as knowledge in its raw or rejected form; it must be re-formed (reformed) by valid theory so that

it can acceptably exist within the boundary line drawn by particular validity criteria. This research-based theorization of the raw Other transforms the Other into the
Same. What was once raw, polyvocal, and, above all, different (Other) becomes
through the research/theory process cooked, unified, and, above all, the Same.
Valid theory predicts and controls (i.e., dominates) the Other. Research-based theory
is the residence of the sovereign. The raw Other, through theorization, becomes the
subject of the sovereign. As with any relation of dominance, the one who dominates
(the Same) controls and reforms the one who is dominated by transforming the
dominated into the Same of the dominator. As Benjamin (1988) says, 'If I completely control the (O)ther, then the (O)ther ceases to exist' (p. 53). In such a
relationship, one side (the Same) maintains its boundaries (i.e., its validity); while
the Other (the raw untheorized world) must, to gain acceptance and legitimacy, lose
itself within the Same — must convert to and, thus, become the Same (*ibid*, p. 64).

But the Same is never satisfied with what it already is or what it has already
appropriated into the Same. The Same relentlessly seeks to capture and theorize
more data. This is why Nietzsche called the Western knowledge project the 'will
to power' — 'the so-called drive for knowledge can be traced back to a drive to
appropriate and conquer' (Spivak, 1976, p. xxii; see also Gardiner, 1992, pp. 99–
101). Lubiano (1991) labels the Western knowledge project as the 'Euro-American
territorial and cultural will to power' (p. 181). Spivak (1976) asserts that 'the will
to power is a process of "incessant deciphering" — figurating, interpreting, signifying (of the Other) through apparent identification (with the Same)' (p. xxiii). The
knowledge project, therefore, is not about increasing knowledge; it is about the
Same appropriating the Other, what hooks (1992) calls 'Eating the Other' (p. 21).
Nietzsche, according to Foucault (1977), contends that 'the historical analysis of
this rancorous will to knowledge reveals that all knowledge rests upon injustice . . .
and that the instinct for knowledge is malicious' (p. 163). Poster (1984) asserts that:

> What Foucault finds objectionable in standard social science is the unacknow-
> ledged implication of the claim of knowledge, that is, the will to power . . . Foucault
> argues that systematic social science, especially careful theoretical elaboration,
> contains within itself an element of domination. (p. 149)

Cixous (in Young R., 1990) has suggested that:

> The mode of knowledge as a politics of arrogation pivots at a theoretical level on
> the dialectic of the (S)ame and the (O)ther. Such knowledge is always centred in
> a self even though it is outward looking, searching for power and control of what
> is (O)ther to it. (pp. 3–4)

Robert Young (1990) argues that 'the appropriation of the (O)ther as a form of
knowledge within a totalizing system' (the Western knowledge project itself) can
be seen as the academic version of Western imperialism (pp. 3–4).

Drawing on Levinas, Young contends that this 'totalizing system' is based on
the 'implicit violence' of the Western knowledge project itself, 'in which the (S)ame

constitutes itself through a form of negativity in relation to the (O)ther, producing all knowledge by appropriating and sublating the (O)ther within itself' (*ibid*, p. 13). He continues that 'in Western philosophy, when knowledge or theory comprehends the (O)ther, then the alterity of the latter vanishes as it becomes part of the (S)ame' (*ibid*, p. 13). This is what Levinas calls 'ontological imperialism' (*ibid*, p. 13) or the 'imperialism of the (S)ame' (*ibid*, p. 14).

> In all cases the (O)ther is neutralized as a means of encompassing it: (Western) ontology amounts to a philosophy of power, an egotism in which the relation with the (O)ther is accomplished through its assimilation into the self (the Same). (*ibid*, p. 13)

Minh-ha (1989) contends that the Western knowledge project is the attempt 'to annihilate the Other through a false incorporation' (p. 66) by the Same.

My contention, then, is that the various kinds of validity, across both conventional and postpositivist paradigms, are a civilizational project, an imperial project. Wearing many different masks, validity is a social practice drawn from the heart of Western darkness. It is an either/or bifurcation line that divides the privileged Same from the as yet untheorized Other, that establishes the 'valid' domination of the Same over the Other, that delineates the conditions under which the Other can be validly incorporated into the Same. This does not mean, however, that conventional or postpositivist researchers consciously intend to enact this imperial project. It has little to do with individual conscious intentions. As Foucault (1977) says:

> These principles of exclusion and choice (validity in this case), whose presence is manifold, whose effectiveness is embodied in (validity) practices, and whose transformations are relatively autonomous, *are not based on an agent of knowledge (historical or transcendental)* (italics added) who successively invents them or places them on an original footing; rather, they designate a will to knowledge that is anonymous, polymorphous, susceptible to regular transformations, and determined by the play of identifiable dependencies. (pp. 200–1)

Validity practices, then, are a result of a largely unconscious or 'anonymous' Western preconceptual, interpretive grid that judges 'truth' as fundamentally dualistic (hooks, 1990; Johnson, 1981; Minh-ha, 1989). Validity practices are unconscious instantiations of a Western philosophical (or even theological) dualism, but the violence of this dualism, which is embodied in validity practices, is that it both represents 'reality' as exclusively either/or (Same/Other) and reproduces the domination of one (the Same) over the Other.

Both conventional and postpositivist validity practices (unconsciously) inscribe a two-sided 'truth' or 'trustworthiness' map; they both enact the same two-sided 'regularity'. In addition, the first side of the map (the valid or the trustworthy) is privileged over or is superior to the second side — the Other. In a critical and significant sense, then, both conventional and postpositivist views of validity, including so-called radical versions of the latter, reproduce the same Western preconceptual presumption (or map) — something is only either warranted (trustworthy) or not warranted (untrustworthy).[5] That this two-sided map may be highly problematic or may even be a violent imposition on a world of multiple, substantive differences — epistemological, racial, gender, or sexual-orientation-wise, to name but a few important differences — is surely troubling.

If, instead, our desire is to problematize and undermine this dualism and its appropriation and marginalization of the Other (the multiple differences), we need new imaginaries of validity. Such imaginaries suggest a doubled strategy. On one hand, these new imaginaries of validity need to unmask and undermine the dualistic regularity that unknowingly shapes our validity practices across the different paradigms. On the other hand, these new imaginaries need to highlight, support, celebrate polyphony, multiplicity, difference(s), the play of the Other. These new imaginaries need to reconstruct 'validity' or 'truth' as many sided or multiply perspectival, as shifting and complex.

Toward New Imaginaries: Validity as the Play of Difference

Developing new imaginaries of validity, however, is difficult. To simply lay out such imaginaries is, in an important sense, to reproduce practices of the Same. That is, for me to prescribe validities for/of the Other, in the sense of traditionally marginalized groups or in the sense of the as yet untheorized Other (the 'wild profusion', as Foucault [1973, p. xv] would say), is a redeployment of the Same. As a researcher, then, how can I engage or interact with 'the otherness of the other without transforming (her or) him into purely one's own (i.e., the Same) (Bakhtin, 1986, p. 71)? To imagine, instead, validity practices that are respectful and appreciative of the Other, validity practices that do not have, as Toni Morrison (1992) says, 'the mandate for conquest' (p. 3) requires a 'difference' approach.

One possible alternative is that this difference can be achieved through dialogue and collaboration between the researcher and the Other. Ellsworth (1989), however, has significantly problematized this approach. She has shown that the dialogic or collaborative option can be but another mask of the Same. The central problem appears to be that any non-local, prescriptive meta-narrative, any non-local prescribing of the right way or the proper approach, is but a new Same arrogating the Other to its truth regime. Ellsworth argues for local knowing, local validity, and local choices. It is in the particularities (the differences) of the local moment where the appropriate direction or choice may be conflict rather than collaboration, separation rather than unity, unknowing rather than knowing.

White (1991), drawing on such feminist work as Gilligan's and Ruddick's, suggests another alternative: a posture, an attitude, or, even, an epistemology of 'attentive care':

> (attentive) care requires a much stronger 'injunction to listen' to the (O)ther, a willingness to hold open an intersubjective space in which difference (the Other) can unfold in its particularity. This willingness entails a hesitancy to 'place' the other quickly and firmly within habitual interpretive molds (the Same). 'If difference

is to emerge there must first be silence, a willing suspension of habitual speech (and thought)' (Ruddick (1987) quoted in White). (pp. 99–100)

The 'willingness to hold open an intersubjective space in which difference can unfold in its particularity' evokes both Ellsworth's stance of local particularities, local choices, and a refusal to invoke the practices of the Same. One excellent example of this kind of openness would be Zora Neale Hurston's *Mules and Men* (1935/1990). hooks (1990) argues that even though Hurston was formally trained within the Western anthropological tradition, she saw through that tradition and redirected, reconstituted it to allow for the open, unmediated play of difference. However, I am apprehensive that in many cases this strategy of holding open a space of difference, while arresting, underestimates the persistent, anonymous, invidious proliferation of the Same/Other binary both within our practices and within our very subjectivities (including our thoughts, desires, needs, feelings, dreams, hopes).[6] A civilizational project is so preconceptually embedded in all that we do and think that altering it is disturbingly difficult.

A third alternative that has been proposed is Lather's (1993) 'Validity after poststructuralism'. She suggests four kinds of validity: 'ironic validity', 'paralogical validity', 'rhizomatic validity', and 'voluptuous validity', all of which she subsumes under the label 'transgressive validity' and all of which are informed by her feminist poststructural orientation. She provides descriptions of each of these four types and one example of a research study that exemplifies each type. While each of the four types is applicable to different research situations, it is the broader category, 'transgressive validity', that is central to Lather's reconstruction of validity.

She has, in my opinion, three general foci — a critical focus, a postmodern focus, and an ethical/political focus — for her four types of transgressive validity. First, Lather wants to unsettle truth regimes, implode 'controlling codes', and 'work against constraints of authority' (*ibid*, p. 686) — her critical focus. Second, she wants to foreground 'the insufficiencies of language and the production of meaning-effects', foster 'differences and heterogeneity', exceed 'the stable and permanent', put 'conventional discursive procedures under erasure', and embody 'a situated, partial, positioned, explicit tentativeness' (*ibid*, p. 685) — her postmodern focus. Third, she wants to anticipate 'a politics that desires both justice and the unknown', generate 'new locally determined norms of understanding', 'proliferate open-ended and context-sensitive criteria', support 'multiple openings, networks', enact 'practices of engagement and self-reflexivity', and bring 'ethics and epistemology together' (*ibid*, p. 685) — her ethical/political focus. Her basic project, then, is to offer or 'incite' validity practices that simultaneously critique the dominance of the Same, undermine the metaphysical dualism of the Same and the Other, proliferate and appreciate difference (the Other), and invent, out of her own ethical/political yearnings, a transformative space in which a non-dualistic multiplicity (difference) is cultivated.

Lather's transgressive validity practices evoke the kind of doubled strategy already discussed. She is both subversive toward the Same/Other regime and supportive of the play of differences. Though I ought to be satisfied, I am not. I am deeply apprehensive about the resourcefulness of the Same to reappear with new masks that only seem to be Other. I am deeply troubled by the anonymous imperial violence that slips quietly and invisibly into our (my) best intentions and practices and, even, into our (my) transformational yearnings. I fear our restless civilizational immodesty; I fear the arrogance we enact 'unknowingly'; I fear my seeming lack of fear in proposing new imaginaries of validity, even transgressive ones. Perhaps, instead, we (I) ought to be stunned into silence — literally, into silence, into a space of emptiness, into the clarity of unknowing that appropriates no one or no thing to its sameness, that 'which can neither be acquired nor lost' (Minh-ha, 1989, p. 76).

Failing that (fearing that?), I am most sanguine (less fearful) about the accelerating proliferation of marginalized voices — feminists of many kinds, the voices of people of color, lesbians and gays, and numerous Others whose bodies and minds continue to experience daily the prejudice and the violence of the inequitable binarial maps of the Western knowledge project. These voices, this multiplicity, is in the best historical position to undermine and move against bifurcated maps of validity, within which one side is better than the Other, within which the ineffable play of differences is subsumed by the Same, and within which the innumerable voices of difference are prevented from equitably participating together (both collaboratively and conflictually) in the conversation of humankind. What is called for here, then, in the absence (fear) of silence, is a Bakhtinian dialogic carnival,[7] a loud clamor of a polyphonic, open, tumultuous, subversive conversation on validity as the wild, uncontrollable play of difference.

Notes

1 For the purposes of this article, I label research that uses the traditional scientific method in the social sciences, from positivist or scientific realist to naive realist, as the 'conventional' approach. I label research that avowedly opposes the unproblematic application of the scientific method to the social sciences, including that research that is called interpretivist, constructivist, feminist, critical theorist, and race-based, as 'postpositivist'.

2 Postmodernists such as Foucault, Derrida, and Spivak have questioned the very idea of origins. According to them there are no true origins. Each origin upon examination is itself derivative. As Foucault indicates in *The Archaeology of Knowledge* (1972), the search for origins is 'the *never-ending* (my emphasis) tracing-back to the original precursors' (p. 4). In her translator's 'Preface' to Derrida's *of Grammatology* (1976), Spivak simply says 'all origins are similarly unoriginal' (p. xiii). My use, then, of the term 'originary' in reference to the 'home' of validity in conventional social science is meant to be ironic.

3 While Mishler readily admits that there may be conflict and disagreement within 'the community of scientists', I think he, along with T.S. Kuhn, in *The Structure of Scientific Revolutions* from whom Mishler draws the phrase 'community of scientists', underestimates the hegemonic implications of the idea of a 'community'. Use of the word 'community' seems to imply that all members and groups of the community have equal voice. Typically, however, there are complex tangles of power inequities that deeply infect

virtually all communities. Communites, when closely examined, are often composed of many smaller 'communities', some of which have more power to draw resources and choose 'exemplars' for research than others. The increasing use of the idea of community as the appropriate safe haven once we have given up on the idea of objective, neutral, ahistorical truth needs considerable critical discussion (see Iris Marian Young, 1990, pp. 300–23, as one excellent example of this kind of discussion).

4   Although it is apparent in Lather's (1993) more recent work — 'Fertile obsession: Validity after poststructuralism', (which I discuss later) — that she has substantially altered her conceptions of validity, her 1986 discussion of validity that is critiqued in this chapter has been frequently cited by other scholars. In fact, Michael Apple (1990–91 Vice-President of Division B of the American Educational Research Association [AERA]), cited Lather's 'catalytic validity' in a discussion about a code of ethics for AERA during a meeting of AERA's Governing Council (3 April 1991). Therefore, while she may have changed positions, some scholars continue to use her earlier formulations of validity.

5   Arguments that this 'validity' decision is often difficult, contestable, or 'fuzzy' begs the question; the map is still assumed to be two-sided.

6   For example of the sheer, but typically unnoticed, depth of these proliferations Harris (1993) persuasively argues that white supremacy is still embedded in our legal definitions of property and in governmental interventions like affirmative action, which are built on those legal definitions. For another example, see Stanfield's (1994) argument that even relatively radical efforts to develop African-American centered epistemologies reproduce Euro-American centered ones.

7   ' "Carnival" is Bakhtin's term for a bewildering constellation of rituals, games, symbols, and various excesses which together constitute an alternative "social space" of freedom, abundance, and equality', according to Gardiner (1992, p. 45).

References

ALLEN, M.J. and YEN, M.W. (1979) *Introduction to Measurement Theory*, Monterey, CA, Brooks/Cole Publishing Co.

BAKHTIN, M.M. (1986) *Speech Genres and Other Late Essays* (V.W. McGee, trans.), Austin, Texas, University of Texas Press.

BARONE, T.E. (1990) *'Subjectivity'*, paper presented at the annual meeting of the American Educational Research Association, Boston, April.

BENJAMIN, J. (1988) *The Bonds of Love: Psychoanalysis, Feminism, and the Problem of Domination*, New York, Pantheon Books.

BHASKAR, R. (1986) *Scientific Realism and Human Emancipation*, London, Verso.

BHASKAR, R. (1989) *Reclaiming Reality*, London, Verso.

CAMPBELL, D.T. and STANLEY, J.C. (1966) *Experimental and Quasi-experimental Designs for Research*, Skokie, IL, Rand McNally.

CHERRYHOLMES, C.H. (1988) 'Construct validity and the discourses of research', *American Journal of Education*, **96**, 3, pp. 421–57.

COLLINS, P.H. (1991) *Black Feminist Thought: Knowledge, Consciousness, and the Politics of Empowerment*, New York, Routledge.

COOK, T.D. and CAMPBELL, D.T. (1979) *Qusai-experimentation: Design and Analysis Issues for Field Settings*, Boston, MA, Houghton Mifflin.

EISNER, E. (1990) *'Objectivity'*, paper presented at the annual meeting of the American Educational Research Association, Boston, April.

ELLSWORTH, E. (1989) 'Why doesn't this feel empowering? Working through the repressive myths of critical pedagogy', *Harvard Educational Review*, **59**, 3, pp. 297–325.

FOUCAULT, M. (1972) *The Archaeology of Knowledge* (A.M. Sheridan Smith, trans.), New York, Pantheon Books.

FOUCAULT, M. (1973) *The Order of Things: An Archaeology of the Human Sciences*, New York, Vintage.

FOUCAULT, M. (1977) *Language, Counter-memory, Practice* (D.F. Bouchard, trans.), Ithaca, NY, Cornell University Press.

GARDINER, M. (1992) *The Dialogics of Critique: M.M. Bakhtin and the Theory of Ideology*, London, Routledge.

GUBA, E.G. (1990) '*Relativism*', paper presented at the annual meeting of the American Educational Research Association, Boston, April.

HARDING, S. (1986) *The Science Question in Feminism*, Ithaca, NY, Cornell University Press.

HARRIS, C.I. (1993) 'Whiteness as property', *Harvard Law Review*, **106**, 8, pp. 1710–91.

hooks, b. (1990) *Yearning: Race, Gender, and Cultural Politics*, Boston, MA, South End Press.

hooks, b. (1992) *Black Looks: Race and Representation*, Boston, MA, South End Press.

HOWE, K. and EISENHART, M. (1990) 'Standards for qualitative (and quantitative) research: A prolegomenon', *Educational Researcher*, **19**, 4, pp. 2–9.

HUGGINS, J. (1991) 'Black women and women's liberation' in GUNEW, S. (Ed) *A Reader in Feminist Knowledge*, London, Routledge, pp. 6–12.

HURSTON, Z.N. (1935/1990) *Mules and Men*, New York, Harper and Row.

JOHNSON, B. (1981) 'Translator's preface' in DERRIDA, J. (Ed) *Dissemination*, London, Athlone Press, pp. vii–xxxiii.

KERLINGER, F.N. (1986) *Foundations of Behavioral Research* (3rd ed), New York, Holt, Rinehart and Winston.

KUHN, T.S. (1970) *The Structure of Scientific Revolutions* (2nd ed), Chicago, IL, University of Chicago Press.

LATHER, P. (1986) 'Issues of validity in openly ideological research: Between a rock and a soft place', *Interchange*, **17**, 4, pp. 63–84.

LATHER, P. (1993) 'Fertile obsession: Validity after poststructuralism', *The Sociological Quarterly*, **34**, 4, pp. 673–93.

LINCOLN, Y.S. and GUBA, E.G. (1985) *Naturalistic Inquiry*, Beverly Hills, CA, Sage.

LUBIANO, W. (1991) 'Shuckin' off the African-American native other: What's "po-mo" got to do with it?', *Cultural Critique*, **20**, Winter, pp. 149–86.

MAXWELL, J.A. (1992) 'Understanding and validity in qualitative research', *Harvard Educational Review*, **62**, 3, pp. 279–300.

MILES, M.B. and HUBERMAN, A.M. (1984) 'Drawing valid meaning from qualitative data: Toward a shared craft', *Educational Researcher*, **13**, 5, pp. 20–30.

MINH-HA, T.T. (1989) *Woman Native Other*, Bloomington, IN, Indiana University Press.

MISHLER, E.G. (1990) 'Validation in inquiry-guided research: The role of exemplars in narrative studies', *Harvard Educational Review*, **60**, 4, pp. 415–41.

MORRISON, T. (1992) *Playing in the Dark: Whiteness and the Literary Imagination*, Cambridge, MA, Harvard University Press.

PHILLIPS, D.C. (1983) 'After the wake: Postpositivistic educational thought', *Educational Researcher*, **12**, 5, pp. 4–12.

POLKINGHORNE, D. (1983) *Methodology for the Human Sciences: Systems of Inquiry*, Albany, NY, State University of New York Press.

POSTER, M. (1984) *Foucault, Marxism and History*, Cambridge, Polity Press.

SALNER, M. (1989) 'Validity in human science research' in KVALE, S. (Ed) *Issues of Validity in Qualitative Research*, Sweden, Studentlitteratur, pp. 47–71.

SCHEURICH, J.J. (1991) 'Old metaphors and new', *Review Journal of Philosophy and Social Science*, **16**, 1&2, pp. 9–30.

SCHEURICH, J.J. (1994) 'Social relativism: A postmodernist epistemology for educational administration' in MAXCY, S.J. (Ed) *Postmodern School Leadership: Meeting the Crises in Educational Administration*, Westport, CT, Praeger, pp. 17–46.

SMITH, J.K. (1984) 'The problem of criteria for judging interpretive inquiry', *Educational Evaluation and Policy Analysis*, **6**, 4, pp. 379–91.

SPIVAK, G.C. (1976) 'Translator's preface' in DERRIDA, J. (Ed) *Of Grammatology*, Baltimore, MD, Johns Hopkins University Press, pp. ix–xc.

SPIVAK, G.C. (1988) *In Other Worlds: Essays in Cultural Politics*, New York, Routledge.

STANFIELD, J.H. II. (1994) 'Ethnic modeling in qualitative research' in DENZIAN, N.K. and LINCOLN, Y.S. (Eds) *Handbook of Qualitative Research*, Thousand Oaks, CA, Sage, pp. 175–88.

TAYLOR, M.C. (1986) 'Introduction: System . . . structure . . . difference . . . other' in TAYLOR, M.C. (Ed) *Deconstruction in Context: Literature and Philosophy*, Chicago, IL, University of Chicago Press, pp. 1–34.

WHITE, S.K. (1991) *Political Theory and Postmodernism*, Cambridge, Cambridge University Press.

WOLCOTT, H.F. (1990) 'On seeking — and rejecting — validity in qualitative research' in EISNER, E.W. and PESHKIN, A. (Eds) *Qualitative Inquiry in Education: The Continuing Debate*, New York, Teachers College Press, pp. 121–52.

YOUNG, I.M. (1990) 'The ideal of community and the politics of difference' in NICHOLSON, L.J. (Ed) *Feminism/Postmodernism*, New York, Routledge, pp. 300–23.

YOUNG, R. (1990) *White Mythologies: Writing History and the West*, London, Routledge.

5   Policy Archaeology: A New Policy Studies Methodology

> But, then, what is philosophy today — philosophical activity, I mean — if it is not the critical work that thought brings to bear on itself? In what does it consist, if not in the endeavor to know how and to what extent it might be possible to think differently, instead of legitimating what is already known. (Foucault, 1985, p. 9)

Although new issues or questions continue to emerge on a regular basis within policy studies, the territory or problematic that policy studies and its attendant research methodologies encompass has become relatively well defined. Even the more recent emergence of interpretivist or postpositivist approaches to policy studies and the efforts to develop methodologies that are congruent with these newer epistemologies (for example, Hawkesworth, 1988 or Kelly and Maynard-Moody, 1993) do not, for the most part, change the boundaries and borders of that defined territory. In contrast, what I propose here is a radically different approach to policy studies, one that opens up an entirely new territory, one that establishes a new problematic, and, thus, one that substantially alters and expands the policy studies arena. In addition, this new problematic critically interrogates both conventional policy studies and the new interpretivist-postpositivist approaches within the present historical moment. I call this new approach 'policy archaeology'.

Policy archaeology is drawn from my interactions with the early works of Foucault (1972, 1973, 1979 and 1988) and with three of his articles that were published in 1991 (1991a–c).[1] The emphasis, however, should be on 'my interactions' rather than on 'Foucault'. I do not pretend to have correctly 'interpreted' Foucault, but it is from my repeated readings of these works that I developed this new way of thinking about social and education policies and the social and education problems[2] that the policies are meant to solve or alleviate. In addition, while I openly acknowledge my significant debt to Foucault, I do not want to be captured by his work; I do not want to be held in thrall, as I have sometimes been, by the formidable power of his social theory.

In the first section of this article, I will critique conventional and interpretivist-postpositivist orientations (hereafter referred to as 'postpositivist' only) to policy studies and lay out the four arenas of study for this new policy studies methodology. In the following section, I will provide a short discussion on how this method could be applied to an education policy that is currently receiving considerable attention in the United States, the linkage of school, health, and social services. In the final section, I will make some concluding remarks about this new methodology. This chapter, however, is not an attempt to fully explicate policy archaeology;

such an effort would require more space than is possible here. Instead it is but an initial discussion of policy archaeology.

Policy Archaeology

Traditional and Postpositivist Policy Studies

Both traditional policy researchers and those who use the newer postpositivist approaches[3] assume that a social problem, for which a policy solution is needed, is like a disease. While there may be, in their view, *a priori* conditions (like poverty or dysfunctional families) that can be said to be the 'cause' of the disease (the social problem), at some point the disease requires either a real (the conventional approach) or a symbolic (the postpositivist approach) treatment, i.e., a policy solution. In a crucial sense, the emergence of the disease (social problem) is seen as 'natural' and 'real' (an empirical given), much like the natural emergence of the symptoms of a disease. While these policy researchers may think that in the best of all possible worlds society would not produce such problems, they see nothing unnatural or socially constructed about what comes to be labeled or identified as a social problem.

Given this traditional policy studies problematic, policy studies typically encompass one or more of four areas: (i) descriptions of social problems; (ii) discussions of competing policy solutions; (iii) considerations of general implementation problems; and (iv) evaluations of particular policy implementations. For example, Cornbleth and Waugh (1993), in their characterization of policy studies, largely verify the four areas I have described above (p. 31). Within the first of these four areas of policy studies, traditional policy researchers compile descriptions of social problems and discuss probable causes for the problems. For example, policy researchers might report on the demographic and attitudinal characteristics of students failing in school for the purpose of indicating some of the dimensions or 'causes' of the problem of failing students. Within the second area of traditional policy studies, policy researchers discuss the relative merits of different policy solutions. For example, policy researchers might compare the merits of intervening solely with the failing students with the merits of intervening with both the students and their families.

Within the third area, policy researchers study policies that have already been implemented in order to consider possible problems in implementation. For example, it may be found that an intervention with both failing students and their families may be difficult to arrange given the lack of availability of the family members, but this may not be apparent until the intervention is actually undertaken. Within the fourth area, policy researchers evaluate the effectiveness of the policy implementation. For example, policy researchers might evaluate whether or not a program intervening with both failing students and their families actually decreases the failure rate of such students.

Postpositivist policy researchers argue that they approach policy studies differently. For example, Kelly and Maynard-Moody (1993) contend that in contrast to the conventional approach (which they call the 'positivist' approach), postpositivist approaches 'now conceive of policies as symbolic and interpretive rather than as efficient solutions designed to solve society's ills' (p. 135). They see 'the policy process ... as a struggle over symbols. ... (, and) policies themselves are now considered as largely symbolic, a way to give voice to latent public concerns' (*ibid*, p. 135). Thus, policy solutions are no longer 'real' solutions or efforts to solve social or education problems; policies are now symbolic solutions to 'latent public concerns'. Nonetheless, there is no effort within this newer orientation to question or critique the 'natural' emergence of social problems. In fact, Kelly and Maynard-Moody (*ibid*) use the same medical metaphor that suffuses the conventional characterization of policy studies when they label social problems as 'society's ills'. They are, consequently, accepting the same empirically given status of social problems that the conventional approach accepts; the postpositivist deviation from the conventional approach is that policy activities are primarily symbolic performances rather than efforts at developing rational solutions to social problems.

That the new postpositivist orientation actually deviates little from the traditional one is even more evident in Hawkesworth's (1988) respected 'post-positivist' work, *Theoretical Issues in Policy Analysis*. She contends that: '. . . post-positivist policy analysis derives its justificatory force from its capacity to illuminate the contentious dimensions of policy questions, to explain the intractability of policy debates, to demonstrate the deficiencies of alternative policy proposals, to identify the defects of supporting arguments, and to elucidate the political implications of contending prescriptions' (p. 191).

These capacities are not different from those claimed by traditional (positivist) policy analysts; in fact, I fail to see any difference whatsoever between this postpositivist description of the problematic of policy studies and a positivist description.

While traditional and postpositivist policy analysts, at least, claim to conceptualize policy studies differently, they both accept or presume a commitment to the larger liberal worldview in which they exist. In that worldview, modern (or postmodern) free-enterprise democracies are the best, though not perfect, societies. Within the conventional approach, policy studies as a problematic, as an arena of inquiry, arises within liberal democratic societies for the purpose of improving the social order — analyzing and understanding its problems and discovering and devising the best solutions or, at least, ameliorizations. Policy analysts of the conventional orientation see themselves as potentially important contributors to the improvement of education and society. Within the postpositivist approach, policy studies as a problematic arises in order to symbolize 'latent public concerns' for the implicit purpose of maintaining or re-stabilizing the social order that might have eventually been threatened if the 'latent concerns' were not given voice through policies. Therefore, policy analysts of the postpositivist orientation also see themselves as potentially important contributors to the maintenance of education and society. Traditional policy studies, like medical studies, are the study of social diseases (social problems) for the purpose of curing the patient (the social body) or, at least, controlling the disease so the larger social body is preserved; postpositivist policy studies perform a similar function except they focus on the level of a symbolic performance. The question of whether substantial social problems are an indication that the liberal social order itself should be questioned is not typically addressed within either traditional or postpositivist approaches. Policy archaeology, however, takes a radically different approach to policy studies in virtually all its aspects, including definitions of problems and problem groups, discussions of policies and policy alternatives, and presumptions about the function of policy studies within the larger social order.

Policy Archaeology

I divide this new policy studies methodology into four arenas of study or focus:

Arena I.   The education/social problem arena: the study of the social construction of specific education and social problems.

Arena II.   The social regularities arena: the identification of the network of social regularities across education and social problems.

Arena III.   The policy solution arena: the study of the social construction of the range of acceptable policy solutions.

Arena IV.   The policy studies arena: the study of the social functions of policy studies itself.

The First Arena of Policy Archaeology

Instead of accepting a social problem as an empirical given, this arena questions or brackets this givenness. Paraphrasing Foucault (1972), '(t)he tranquility with which . . . (social problems) are accepted must be disturbed' (p. 25).[4] Policy archaeology, refusing the acceptance of social problems as natural occurrences, examines closely and skeptically the emergence of the particular problem. By what process did a particular problem emerge, or, better, how did a particular problem come to be seen as a problem? What makes the emergence of a particular problem possible? Why do some 'problems' become identified as social problems and other 'problems' do not achieve that level of identification? By what process does a social problem gain the 'gaze' of the state, of the society, and, thus, emerge from a kind of social invisibility into visibility? As Foucault said, 'how is it that one particular (discursive) statement (i.e., social problem in this case) appeared rather than another' (*ibid*, p. 27); 'what made it (a social problem) at the time it appeared' (*ibid*, p. 179). Policy archaeology posits that social problems are social constructions,[5] and it critically examines the social construction process — how the social problem was made 'manifest, nameable, and describable' (*ibid*, p. 41). Consequently, the territory of policy archaeology, contrary to that of traditional and postpositivist approaches, begins prior to the emergence and social identification of a 'problem' as a problem (though there must be a social identification of the problem before its antecedents may be studied). Policy archaeology studies the numerous, complex strands and traces of social problems prior to their naming as social problems. It examines the naming process, the process by which problems enter the gaze of the state and policy researchers. It critically probes why and how these strands and traces congeal (become visible) into what is thereafter labeled as a particular social problem.

But policy archaeology is not the study of the history of the emergence of a social problem. Archaeology is what Mahon (1992) has called the investigation of 'the historical a priori' (p. 60).[6] As Foucault (1989) said, 'I first used the word (archaeology) . . . in order to designate a form of analysis that wouldn't at all be a history (in the sense that one recounts the history of inventions or of ideas)' (p. 45). Foucault's comment does not mean, however, that historical artifacts or events are not part of policy archaeology as a method. One of the prominent features of Foucault's archaeology has been the retrieval and presentation of previously ignored but provocative historical documents that he then used as 'evidence' in the arguments he made. But the history of a particular social problem is not the focus of policy archaeology. Instead, the focus is to investigate the intersection or, better, the constitutive grid of conditions, assumptions, forces which make the emergence of a social problem, and its strands and traces, possible — to investigate how a social problem becomes visible as a social problem. Policy archaeology, according to my adaptation of Foucault (1972), investigates

> the conditions necessary for the appearance of a . . . (social problem), the historical conditions required if one is to 'say anything' about it, the conditions necessary if it (the social problem) is to exist in relation to other objects . . . (p. 44)

Consequently, a social problem

> does not wait in limbo the order that will free it and enable it to become embodied in a visible and prolix objectivity; it does not pre-exist itself, held back by some obstacle at the first edge of light. It (a social problem) exists under the positive conditions of a complex group of relations. (*ibid*, p. 45)

Policy archaeology 'tries to establish the rules of formation (of social problems and policy choices, in this case), in order to define the conditions of their realization' (*ibid*, p. 207). Policy archaeology tries to describe the 'complex group of relations' that make social problems and policy choices possible.

The Second Arena of Policy Archaeology

This arena of policy archaeology suggests that there are powerful 'grids' or networks of regularities (a kind of grammar or economy similar to Foucault's 'complex group of relations') that are constitutive of the emergence or social construction of a particular problem as a social problem, regularities that constitute what is labeled as a problem and what is not labeled as a problem. These grids, also, constitute the range of acceptable policy choices. This second arena of policy archaeology, however, is a complex one. It is based on the assumption that social problems do not achieve their visibility or recognition or status as social problems in an idiosyncratic or random or 'natural' fashion, but that visibility is not primarily a function of the interactive intentions and actions of consciously involved social agents or groups. Nor is the range of policies that get considered to 'solve' a social problem primarily the function of the same intentions and actions. Instead, policy archaeology suggests that there is a grid of social regularities that constitutes what becomes socially visible as a social problem and what becomes socially visible as a range of credible policy solutions. Policy archaeology as a methodology proposes that it can identify this grid or network of social regularities.

Understanding what I mean by 'social regularities', then, is critical to under-standing policy archaeology as a methodology. Foucault (1973) asserted that

> unknown to themselves, naturalists, economists, and grammarians (of the Classical age) employed the same rules to define the objects proper to their own study, to form their concepts, to build their theories. It is these rules of formation which were never formulated in their own right, but are to be found only in widely differing theories, concepts, and objects of study, that I have tried to reveal, by isolating, as their specific locus, a level that I have called, somewhat arbitrar-ily, *archaeological* (emphasis added) . . . I have tried to determine the basis or *archaeological system* (emphasis added) common to a whole series of scientific 'representations' or 'products' dispersed throughout the natural history, economics, and philosophy of the Classical period. (pp. xi–xii)

According to Foucault, scientists of various sorts define their objects, form their concepts, build their theories in seemingly different fields unconsciously using the same 'rules of formation', and he proposed that archaeology as a method could identify these 'rules of formation'. Similarly, I am arguing that widely different social and education problems and policy solutions are, in fact, constituted by the same grid of social regularities and that policy archaeology can identify these regularities. It is, therefore, the identification of these regularities that is the second arena of policy archaeology.

Four additional points need to be made about these regularities. (I am, thus, making four points about the second arena of policy archaeology.) The first point about the second arena of policy archaeology is that the regularities are not inten-tional; that is, no particular individual or group consciously created them. This does not mean, however, that no individual or group may not benefit from the regular-ities. Just as no individual or group has conscious control of the creation of the discursive regularities that provided the basis for the emergence of the human sciences (Foucault, 1972), no individual or group has conscious control of the creation of the social regularities that policy archaeology seeks to identify. Social regularities are positively[7] productive and reproductive without the need for con-scious or intentional agency or a fully self-aware subjectivity that controls or man-ages those productive and reproductive processes; social orders are continuously re-established or reproduced by the network of social regularities without the need for a controlling agency. In fact, as Foucault (1973) and other postmodernists have pointed out, agency or subjectivity, 'the already "encoded" eye' (p. xxi) is itself but another one of the inscriptions or productions/reproductions of the implicate social order. 'It must now be recognized that it is neither by recourse to a transcendental subject nor by recourse to a psychological subjectivity that . . . (social regularities, in this case) should be defined' (Foucault, 1972, p. 55).[8] Daily human micropractices (at home, at work, at play) are, thus, instantiations of these social regularities, but the 'sovereignty of the subject' of the liberal social order is rejected. For the policymaker or policy analyst, for example, these social regularities exist as a kind of a 'positive unconscious . . . a level (within the individual but shared across individuals) that eludes the consciousness of the scientist (policymaker and policy analyst) and yet is part of the scientific (or policy) discourse' (Foucault, 1973, p. xi).[9] Social regularities, then, constitute both categories of thought and ways of thinking.

The second point about the second arena of policy archaeology is that social regularities do not determine social problems or policy solutions as if from the outside or as if the regularities are an outside force; instead 'they constitute rather the set of conditions in accordance with which a practice is exercised (with which a social problem emerges)' (Foucault, 1972, p. 208). Social regularities are constitutive of social problems and of policy solutions. One reason such regularities are not a kind of deterministic mechanism is that social systems are incredibly complex with uncountable macro- and micro-interactions occurring on an hourly basis. Weather prediction is a somewhat useful example. The interactions are so complex over such a large territory that only overall tendencies and very short-term forecasts are possible. But I would suggest that human societies with their physical, social, and psychological interactions make planet-sized weather systems look fairly simple. Complex social systems can virtually never be totalized under any kind of regime; in fact, difference, as many poststructuralists have argued, is inherent in any unity. Another reason that this account of social regularities does not establish a determinism is that while these regularities are constitutive of dominant categories of thought and ways of thinking, other categories of thought and ways of thinking do exist. The latter, however, which are typically produced in communities of difference and marginalization of various sorts, do not achieve prominent social visibility. For example, critical race theorists or feminists often hold views of the social order in the United States that are very different than those views held by governmental agents and professionals, but the former views do not typically achieve the social credibility of the views of the latter. Policy archaeology suggests that social regularities are 'productive' and 'reproductive' in the sense that the regularities constitute what is socially visible or credible, but the regularities do not literally create material reality. Instead, they constitute what is socially selected and verified as 'real'. In the case of social problems and policy solutions, the network of regularities constitute what is socially legitimized (constructed) as a social problem and what is socially legitimized as the proper range of policy solutions.

The third point about these regularities is that they are historical. Regularities change and disappear, and new ones emerge. Just as Foucault (1979 and 1988) has delineated shifts in the epistemic level within Western history (as with madness or crime and punishment), policy archaeology posits that it can not only identify the regularities but also delineate shifts in such regularities that shape the emergence of social problems and policy solutions. In other words, this poststructuralist approach, unlike structuralist approaches, assumes that the regularities (what the structuralists would call 'deep structures' [White, 1978, p. 231]), that are being identified are not the same throughout all time or all societies. All social regularities are particular to particular time periods within individual societies. Historical shifts may lead to shifts in the grid of regularities that shape the emergence or visibility of particular social problems and policy solutions. In addition, policy archaeology, as a method for identifying social regularities, is itself emergent within a particular historical period; consequently, historical changes may lead to the decline and disappearance of policy archaeology as a relevant methodology.[10] However, particular social regularities need not change or disappear with the rise and fall of identified periods within a particular society or civilization. For example, male supremacy is one social regularity that has remained, though in different forms, throughout the entire history of Western civilization. The mutation of the particular forms of male supremacy, though, is of crucial importance: for instance, male supremacy prior to the emergence of the capitalist class structure is, in many ways, both similar and different to current forms of male supremacy.

The fourth point about the second arena of policy archaeology is that a poststructuralist approach moves against, though not entirely against, the distorting structuralist metaphor of 'depth' or 'deep structure'.[11] The structuralists — like Marx, Freud, and Levi-Strauss — have employed, implicitly or explicitly, a metaphor of architectural structures. The structuralists posited deep structures which were opposed to the superficial or the surface. The reason that this metaphor is distortive for the poststructuralist is that 'deep structural phenomena' and 'surface phenomena' both occur at the level of daily human micro-practices. As Foucault has said, all is surface, meaning not that everything is superficial but that everything happens at the surface, i.e., within the context of human activity. Thus, archaeology '(i)nstead of outlining a horizon that rises from the depths of history and maintains itself through history . . . is . . . at the most "superficial" level' (Foucault, 1972, p. 62). Again, however, the contention that everything happens at the 'surface', within human actions, does not require the assumption that these social agents are self-consciously aware of the social regularities shaping their subjectivities and their practices. Typically, social agents are not aware in this fashion.

The Third Arena of Policy Archaeology

This arena involves the study of how the range of possible policy choices is shaped by the grid of social regularities. Just as social problems are constituted by the grid of regularities, the range of acceptable policy solutions is similarly constituted. But again this shaping is not an intentional or conscious activity. The conscious activity of policy analysts or policy makers, for example, is not the issue. The grid of regularities is like a preconceptual field that constitutes some policy choices as relevant and others as virtually invisible; it privileges some choices over others. This arena, then, is the study of how the grid of social regularities generates the range of possible and 'impossible' policy solutions.

The Fourth Arena of Policy Archaeology

This arena is the examination of the function of conventional and postpositivist policy studies within the larger liberal social order.[12] Policy archaeology suggests that conventional and postpositivist policy studies themselves are, like social problems and policy solutions, constituted by social regularities. If this is so, then it is important to query what this function is, how it occurs, and what its effects are. For example, this kind of study might begin with questions like: Why have both conventional and postpositivist policy studies not questioned or examined the social problem emergence issue? Why have both approaches not studied the constructedness of social problems? Eventually, however, the study should lead to larger and more fundamental questions about the social-order function of conventional and postpositivist policy studies.

It should be understood, however, even though I have divided policy archaeology into four separate arenas, all of which have permeable boundaries, that the policy archaeology process is recursive or iterative; work on any particular problem-policy axis repeatedly passes through all four arenas, and, thus, work in any one arena may refashion or alter what has already been done in another arena. The 'end point' of the research occurs when the research effort is no longer producing any material that significantly refashions or alters any of the four arenas. Also, the (I–IV) order that I have given the four arenas is not meant to imply that this is the order in which a policy archaeologist should proceed; any ordering is possible. In fact, in the next section I start my application of policy archaeology to a specific education problem-policy solution axis with the second arena.

I now turn to a brief discussion of how policy archaeology might be applied to an education problem, the school failure of urban children, and a policy solution, the linkage of school, health, and social services — or 'school-linked children's services' (Kirst, 1992), that is currently receiving much attention in policy studies circles in the United States and elsewhere (see, for example, *The 1993 Politics of Education Association Yearbook*). I will not, however, present a fully developed policy archaeology of this problem-policy axis in this chapter.

Policy Archaeology Applied

As attention to previously ignored groups of students, groups like children of color, and attention to the generally negative conditions within which a significant proportion of American children live has grown, efforts to assist these children in order to increase their chances of success in school have coalesced around the idea that linking or integrating social, health, and school services which are already provided by many different governmental agencies is a reasonably good policy measure. In this particular case, while the policy solution — linked or coordinated children's services — is fairly straightforward conceptually, the problem that this policy is meant to address is messy, complex, and large. The descriptive litany is formidable: poverty, lack of health care, single-parent families, homelessness, and child abuse and neglect (see, for example, Adler, 1993, pp. 9–10; Capper and Hammiller, 1993, p. 2; Crowson and Boyd, 1993, p. 144; Dry-foos, 1991, pp. 121–3; Kirst, 1992, pp. 300–2; Koppich, 1993; pp. 52–3; Mawhinney, 1993, p. 34, among many others). Koppich (1993) concluded that 'plenty (of US children) face desperate existences' (p. 52), that '(m)any (children) are . . . poor or in fragile health or lacking sufficient family support, (and that) (c)hildren's problems often are severe' (*ibid*, p. 53). What brings all of this to the schoolhouse door, however, is the failure in school of those with the above life circumstances.

While I cannot at this point delineate all of the regularities which shape the social construction of this particular problem and this particular policy solution, I will suggest what some of those regularities (the second arena of policy archaeology) are, discuss how they shape the social construction of the problem — the failure of a particular group of school children (the first arena of policy archaeology), examine how these regularities constitute the range of policy solutions (the third arena), and address what the function of conventional and postpositivist policy studies is in relation to this particular problem-policy axis (the fourth arena). As I mentioned previously, I will apply each of the four arenas of policy archaeology to the problem-policy axis of linked school services, but I will do so in the following order: II, I, III, and, finally, IV.

Policy Archaeology Applied: Arena II

I would posit that there are five regularities (among others) that are necessary to the constitution or emergence or construction of the problem of failing school children. These are gender, race, class, governmentality, and professionalization. The complex grid-like intersection of these five regularities (and others as yet unidentified) makes it possible for this particular problem to emerge as a problem, constructs this problem, constitutes the problem as an 'object' of social visibility. But it is not sufficient simply to identify the regularities. While certain features of these particular regularities are readily visible to social agents, the positive proliferation of these regularities throughout social forms and practices are often not easily visible. While there is not space here for an extended discussion of all five of the regularities I have named, I will discuss race as a regularity, especially in terms of its 'invisibility' at the surface of human actions, and then briefly touch on the other four.

Racial differentiation is an old regularity in Western civilization, having assumed many different forms over different historical periods. But to label this regularity as 'race' or 'racial differentiation' is inadequate. The more appropriate label is 'white supremacy'.[13] The west in general and the United States in particular have a long history of white racial dominance. Today, however, in the United States it is frequently thought that white supremacy largely resides in the past, and it is certainly true that social struggles in the US have made illegal many white supremacist practices that were once accepted as 'natural' by most whites. During this earlier historical period, white supremacist beliefs and acts were socially 'invisible' (as racist beliefs and acts) to whites, and, now, many of these same beliefs and acts are socially 'visible' to whites as racist beliefs and acts. While these new visibilities are a valuable result of civil rights struggles, they leave much of the propagation of white supremacy, as a social regularity, unmarked or unseen. Social regularities are positively reproduced through the production of social life forms and practices. These regularities themselves, however, are not necessarily visible to social agents even though they exist at the surface of human practices. One example will illustrate this.

In an article entitled 'Whiteness as property', Harris (1993) persuasively argues that, to a significant extent, United States definitions of property arose historically in relation to the legal enshrinement of African-Americans as property and to the seizure of Native American lands. She cites numerous key legal cases in which the definition of property is 'contingent on, intertwined with, and conflated with race' (p. 1714) with the result being the legalization (legitimation) of the domination of African-Americans and Native Americans by whites (i.e., white supremacy). Indeed, she argues that 'whiteness' was a central concept that was used in the legal construction of the definition of property. In contrast, however, to arguments that the cited legal cases are of the dead past, Harris contends that '(a)fter legalized segregation was overturned, whiteness as property evolved into a more modern form through the law's ratification of the settled expectations of relative white privilege as a legitimate and natural baseline' (*ibid*, p. 1714). She asserts that this 'more modern form' reinstitutes racial subordination

> through modern conceptions of race and identity embraced in law. Whiteness as property has taken on more subtle forms, but retains it core characteristic — the legal legitimation of expectations of power and control that enshrine the (white dominant) status quo as a neutral baseline, while masking the maintenance of white privilege and domination . . . , (including) as the unspoken center of current polarities around the issue of affirmative action. (*ibid*, pp. 1714–15)

In short, property as whiteness has changed its form, but its 'core characteristic', white supremacy, is retained.

I suggest that this example illustrates how social regularities evolve and proliferate but still retain their 'core characteristic'. The grid of fundamental social regularities is the field necessary to the constitution of the forms or practices or 'objects' of social life, and these forms, in turn, reproduce the social regularities. The social regularities are like preconceptual glasses or frames through which human actions and categories, including social problems and policy solutions, become socially defined. While in the present or during some period of the past a particular regularity may be reinforced by conscious or intended human actions, regularities, operating like powerfully embedded preconceptual frames, generate throughout social forms in ways that are not necessarily visible to social agents. What Stanfield (1993a and 1993b) identifies as white ethnocentric modes of thinking about social life and categories of thought are privileged as common sense or natural or the best or are just assumed. In contrast, Native American conceptions of property, for example, disappear or, better, never appear within dominant social discourses because they are incongruent with the dominant social order. The invisibility of these alternative conceptions belies their continued presence as socially invisible parameters of socially visible, acceptable definitions of property. Such alternative definitions may not be socially seen, but they continue to be embedded in legal and popular definitions of property.

In an important sense, social regularities are constitutive both epistemologically and ontologically. They constitute our frames of knowing (epistemologies) and our 'nature of reality' categories (ontologies). What Foucault (1972) says about discourse can similarly be said about social regularities: social regularities 'do not identify objects, they constitute them and in the practice of doing so conceal their own invention' (p. 49) because the social order would be delegitimized if it were readily apparent that inequalities, for instance, were merely historical social constructions or that supposedly dead regularities like white supremacy continued to generatively multiply throughout the social order, including through the emergence and identification of social problems, problem groups, and policy solutions.

Gender and class, as regularities, operate similarly to race (though of course there are important differences) so I will not use any space here to discuss them or their complex interactions. Governmentality and professionalization, the other two regularities I have identified, are not so accessible. Governmentality is a word that Foucault (1991a) used to denote the emergence of a kind of governance mentality that expands its reach into all aspects of the lives of its citizens; it is the kind of governance that counts, describes, defines, that brings everything under its gaze (a Panopticon-type of governmentality), whereas in past times, according to Foucault, government had little concern for most aspects of the lives of its citizenry. As Gordon (1991) said:

> Computerization and administrative rationality begin to make possible for the first time (though, for Foucault, this mentality emerges prior to computers and coextensive with the emergence of the social sciences) a 'real' government of population which, by co-ordinating appropriate forms of expertise and assessment, is capable of identifying all those individual members of society who can be deemed, by manifesting some combination of a specified range of 'factors', to present a significant, albeit involuntary, risk to themselves or to the community (i.e., problem groups). (p. 45)

Governmentality is a kind of governmental rationality that equates the well-being or happiness or productiveness of individuals with behaviors that reinforce the social order. It is an insatiable management of social spaces, social practices and forms. It is like a monster, without a conscious master, a headless monster, that must consume everything, that must bring all social reality within its taxonomical or descriptive regime, that 'must bring under management those zones of social life which have hitherto remained formless' (Procacci, 1991, p. 164). Though individual governmental agents apply this mentality to their areas of responsibility, they typically are not conscious that they are proliferating a social regularity. Their individual actions are commonsensical given the grid of social regularities that is constituting social life. These individual agents do not have bad intentions; they are, instead, inscripted by and, in turn, inscripting governmentality. (Policy making and policy analysis are, of course, an integral part of this regime, but that will be discussed as a part of arena IV.)

Professionalization works closely in tandem with governmentality. Professionalization is the proliferation of professions to treat and manage the citizenry, i.e., produce disciplined, productive citizens, though, again, the larger implications of this goal are not evident to professionals themselves. Professionals, like government agents, typically operate with the best of intentions; indeed, good intentions are typically one facet of their professional socialization. Consequently, while professionals function within a mindset that legitimizes the need for and positive value of their therapeutic or transformational or management theories, the theories are instantiational ideologies, the regulational purpose of which is to fashion productive citizens according to the norms of the current social order, i.e., to normalize citizens. Just as sanity is a socially functional category constituted so as to be congruent with a particular historical period, as Foucault (1988) has argued, theories of management, schooling, and policy are the same. They accord with the regularities that constitute them. 'Appropriate' management of schools becomes that management which produces social-order-congruent citizens, i.e., productive[14] citizens. 'Appropriate' student behavior is that behavior which is obedient to, or congruent with, current conceptions of productive citizenry. Just as citizens are taught what sanity is by the marking, defining, excluding, and confining of the 'insane', productive students are disciplined not through the marking, defining, excluding, and confining of their bodies but by the public application of these processes to the bodies of unproductive students. Productive citizens continually relearn 'right behavior' by the public display of 'wrong behavior', especially through the social process of identifying social problems, problem groups, and policy solutions.

These five — race, gender, class, governmentality, and professionalization — are but five of the social regularities that comprise the dominant liberal social order, that constitute that which becomes visible and acceptable within that order. They operate like a grid that generates what may be seen and talked about, while occluding grid-incongruent alternative possibilities. Other societies or this society at other times might have or had different regularities. In fact, some of the ones I have named — race (white supremacy) and gender (male supremacy) — are very old, whereas professionalization has arisen primarily in the past 100 years. But, as was pointed out before, these are not the only social regularities operant in the contemporary world. I have discussed these five because I think they have par-ticular relevance for the school failure of children (the problem group) and the policy of school-linked services. The regularities of race, class, and gender are especially important to the social construction of the problem group (predominantly lower-class children, children of color, and children from female head-of-household fam-ilies), and the regularities of governmentality and professionalization are critical to the naming, describing, and treating of the problem and the problem group, though it is the complex interaction of the five regularities that constitutes the problem, the problem group, and the policy solution.

Policy Archaeology Applied: Arena I

The target or 'problem' population of the school-linked services policy is largely lower-class children (poverty, lack of health care, homelessness), children of single-parent families (which is, of course, gender related), and children of color (Adler, 1993; Capper and Hammiller, 1993; Crowson and Boyd, 1993; Dryfoos, 1991; Kirst, 1992; Koppich, 1993; Mawhinney, 1993). We have, therefore, a target population that accords well with the social regularities of class, gender, and race. This is a population that is not 'succeeding' in school, is not properly productive within the school setting and, thus, is not being properly prepared to be productive consumers/workers. Governmental agents (including policy analysts) point out, describe, and label the group (governmentality), and school, health, and social welfare professionals are linked together to treat the problem (professionalization).

According to policy archaeology, the grid of social regularities produce or construct this problem population. Social regularities 'arrange' the 'seeing' of this target group, the seeing of it as a problem group. This targeting, naming, labeling is the reproductive work of the grid of regularities; the grid both attunes its listeners to hear (see) a particular frequency (the problem group) and constitutes the fre-quency (the problem group) itself. The grid, thus, is both epistemological and ontological; it constitutes both who the problem group is and how the group is seen or known as a problem.

Social problems, like the failure in school of poor children of color, are, then, not aberrations but a necessary facet of the dominant social order, the grid of all social regularities operant in any particular period. The social order produces in complex ways both the failure in school of single-parent, poor, children of color and the identification of this group as a problem group. The labeling of the targeted group as a social problem is critical to the maintenance of the social order. The labeling of problem groups via social agents, particularly by socially legitimated social agents like professionals and policy analysts, positively disciplines produc-tive citizens by defining what a proper productive citizen is and by reaffirming the productive citizens' goodness or correctness. More simplistically, the social order and its attendant regularities reproduces by repeatedly producing 'bad' groups who are publicly identified as such (labeled, studied, treated) so that the productive behavior of 'good' citizens is repeatedly reinforced.

Another way to approach this is to see that other possible problem groups do not become socially visible as a problem group. For example, it could reasonably be argued that overwhelmingly white suburban schools (substantially born of white flight from people of color) are training grounds for white supremacy, not in the South African or Fascist sense, but in the sense that the social order privileges whites and that suburban schools inscribe the white supremacy regularity within the subjectivity of their white students. Through such schools the social order is constituting its privileged members — how to behave and how to think. But the social order will not constitute this privileged group as a problem group. The social order will not construct this white suburban student group as a problem group; it will not label, describe, study, and treat this group as a problem. It would be at odds with the regularity of white supremacy to identify this white group as a problem.

While race, gender, and class regularities are key to the social construction of the problem group, governmentality plays a critical role in the public identification of the group. The describing, numbering, and naming processes of governmentality (which includes policy processes) provide a description of the problem group that can be infinitely circulated in both academic media and the public media. As newspapers and television programs repeatedly display (make socially visible) this problem group, and academics, including policy analysts, legitimate the group's designation as a problem through journal articles, books, and conferences dedicated to this problem (as was the 1993 University Council on Educational Administration's — UCEA — annual conference), the problem group is made 'real'. Consequently, the doctors of social diseases, professionals of all sorts including educators, social workers, health workers, and psychologists, are called forth to treat the problem group with the chosen policy intervention. These professionals then use their 'knowledge' (knowledge that is congruent with and reproductive of the social order) to adjust or transform the social group. That fundamental social problems, like poverty or homelessness or racial prejudice, are never really 'solved' is generally not taken as a negative judgment on professionals or on professionalization. The public performance of the treatment of the problem group by the professionals, even if it fails, as it typically does, satisfies society that it is doing its best.

This discussion of the first arena of policy archaeology, the social construction of the problem, is, of course, inadequate. The full archaeology of the naming of the problem and the problem group needs extensive additional work. For example, four additional issues need to be addressed. One of these is why has this problem-solution axis emerged and been accepted so rapidly and widely (Crowson and Boyd, 1993).[15] Another is what has been the involvement of the Danforth Foundation in the production of this problem as a problem. A third question is: why do policy analysts report few conversations or research interviews with the target population itself; why is all of the policy commentary so curiously distant? A fourth question is: why do descriptions of the target population consume such a small part of policy discussions of this particular problem-policy axis? These, however, are but a few of the incitements that a more comprehensive application of the second arena of policy archaeology to this axis would address. I now turn, then, to a brief application of the third arena of policy archaeology, the study of policy choices.

Policy Archaeology Applied: Arena III

As the grid of social regularities constitutes the problem (and the problem group) and its identification through various public performances both popular and academic, it also constrains the choice of policy 'solutions' or treatments. Because of the 'before conscious thinking' preconceptual frame produced by the grid of social regularities and embodied throughout the social order, certain solutions (and not others) are seeable and knowable by social agents. Policy solutions that are radically at variance with the grid of regularities are not seeable or credible, especially solutions that question or undermine the order itself, like ones that would treat white racism as an important cause of the school failure of poor, urban, single-parent children of color. Only policy solutions that accord with that order will emerge as salient, probable possibilities.

The policy of 'linked school services', for example, is so obviously a creature of the grid of regularities that it is almost a caricature. On one hand, policy analysts argue that the problem group is very large — 20 per cent of all American children live in poverty; 32 per cent of African-American children (in California) live in poverty; 34 per cent of Hispanic children live in poverty; half of single-women with children live in poverty (Kirst 1992). On the other hand, descriptions of the problem group in scholarly policy commentary occupy such a small percentage of the printed space of their chapters and articles. For example, Koppich's (1993) comprehensive article in the special Politics of Education Association (PEA) edition of the *Journal of Educational Policy* has slightly over one page of eleven on the description of the problem (pp. 52–3). In fact, the edition has no comprehensive discussion of the problem or the problem group; the problem is simply assumed to be 'known'. It is only the solution that requires extended discussion. The 'true' nature of the problem and the problem group is of such little consequence in the analysts' policy commentary that the 'performance' nature of that work is highlighted. The minimal space in policy commentary that is devoted to a discussion of the nature of the problem and the problem group is almost a direct signal or code that the function of the policy work has little to do with really addressing the problem.

Another way that this policy solution is almost a caricature is that, on one hand, the analysts say that this large, terrible problem exists, but, on the other hand, the solution that has spread so quickly, that has garnered so much policy discussion, that has dominated such prestigious organization as PEA and UCEA, is simply the linking or coordinating of services that already exist. Does it not seem highly questionable that a large, terrible social problem affecting one-fifth of the nation's children and one-third or more of particular groups of children requires something as simple as linking existing governmental and professional arrangements? It is like the emperor with no clothes. Who could really believe, after reflecting on it, that such a formidable problem is solvable by merely adding a few extra linkages among current social arrangements? If present social, health, and schooling services have to date not been able to significantly 'solve' this large social problem, it is difficult to believe that linking them together would seriously impact a problem as sizeable as this one. Surely, if the problem is so large, it would call for a major restructuring of social, health, and schooling services or, even, some questions about the social order itself. The 'smallness' of the policy solution in relation to the 'largeness' of the problem, again, highlights the 'performance' nature of this policy solution.

Policy archaeology, however, does not suggest that other policies besides linking services will not be considered by policy analysts, but it does suggest that the range of policy choices will accord with the grid of regularities. In fact, there are many policies already present in the schools and in other settings that address this same problem and problem group, i.e., at-risk student programs, drop-out prevention programs, etc. These efforts, however, do accord with the grid of regularities. For example, the very label 'at-risk' tends to blame the students, their parents, and their cultures or, more rarely, the school, the teachers, and the administrators, but even blaming the latter three, which some critical theorists do, leaves invisible the workings of the implicate social order. Policy solutions which contradict or question that order do not emerge or, when they do emerge among the socially marginalized, do not achieve any credibility among the governmental and policy agents who serve as the legitimacy gatekeepers of the policy discourse. Consequently, that which can be construed as an appropriate policy solution is severely constrained by the social order and its complex workings through its constitution of the subjectivities, epistemologies, and ontologies of its members. Because, however, policy archaeology identifies the social regularities that create that order, it can critically highlight the constrained social construction of possible policy solutions. Why conventional and postpositivist policy studies cannot produce a similar analysis will be discussed in the next section.

Policy Archaeology Applied: Arena IV

Arena IV is the study of the social functions of policy studies themselves. Policy studies as a problematic, like education and social problems and policy solutions, is itself constituted by the grid of social regularities. Policy studies is but one governmental apparatus that produces grid-congruent problems, problem groups, and policy solutions. Policy analysts count, label, and describe problems and problem groups; they are, thus, key in the construction of such problems and groups; and, because of their 'expertise', they legitimate these constructions. In addition, their discussions and debates about possible policy solutions are similarly key to constraining the range of possible policy choices. As Frazer (1989) said:

> ... the functioning ... (social regularities, in this case) essentially involves forms of social constraint. Such constraints and the manner of their application vary. ... Typically, however, they include such phenomena as the valorization of some statement forms and the concomitant devaluation of others; the institutional licensing of some persons (like policy analysts) as authorized to offer authoritative knowledge claims and the concomitant exclusion of others; procedures for the

extraction of information from and about (counting, describing, labeling) persons (problem groups) involving various forms of coercion; and the proliferation of discourse orient to the objects of inquiry that are, at the same time, targets for the application of social policy. (p. 20 (see, also, White, 1991 for a similar discussion)

Postpositivist policy analysts, in general, think they see policy somewhat differently than conventional policy analysts, but they, too, do not question the social order. They even understand the performance nature of policymaking and policy studies, but they suggest that the function of the performance is to bring into the public arena 'latent public concerns' (Kelly and Maynard-Moody, 1993, p. 135). I would suggest they even imply that maintenance of the social order is a central function of such public performances, but they do not question that order, and they certainly do not suggest the order itself might be the problem. Postpositivist policy analysts are, thus, able to position themselves as epistemologically superior to conventional policy analysts, while they remain comfortably in accord with the social order. This reminds me of the changes in definitions of property, which Harris (1993) discussed, that leave the 'core characteristics' intact. Postpositivist policy analysts can argue, as Kelly and Maynard-Moody (1993) do, that they have left the conventional (positivist) orientation behind, but they cannot argue, in my view, that they are functioning any differently, vis-a-vis the social order, than conventional policy analysts. They have, thus, retained the 'core characteristics' of the network of social regularities. Both postpositivist policy analysts and conventional policy analysts make the problem and the problem group visible through sanctioned performances, and they both discuss only those policy solutions which sanction that order. The emergence, then, of postpositivist policy analysts can, therefore, be seen as but another production of the grid of social regularities.

Both conventional and postpositivist policy studies, then, are a key facet of the social construction of problems, problem groups, and the narrowly constrained range of policy solutions. More importantly, rather than solving or ameliorating social and education problems, both approaches to policy studies are constituted by the grid of social regularities and reproduce that grid. They are a singularly important way in which problems, problem groups, and solutions are made socially visible and in which the narrow range of policy solutions is legitimated. Even when policy analysts repeatedly conclude that a particular policy has not worked, as they often do, this judgment rarely leads to a larger critique of policy studies themselves or of the social order itself.

However, making problem groups visible and legitimizing the acceptable range of policy solutions are not the most important functions that policy analysts perform. The most important social function of policy analyses is the normalizing or disciplining of the population. Problems and problem groups are social constructions. The primary function of these constructions is not for the purpose of solving the problems or disciplining and normalizing the problem groups. Instead, the primary function of these social constructions is to provide a definition of correct, productive behavior to citizens who are already acting in concert with the social order. As public definitions and discussions of insanity teach and reteach the sane what insanity is, public definitions and discussions of social and education problems and problem groups teach and reteach the rest of the citizenry to remain in concert with the grid of social regularities. Socialization to a social order, then, is constantly repeated in social life. That such performances are conducted on the bodies, minds, and souls of the most vulnerable groups within society (such as one-fifth of all children and one-third of African-American and Hispanic-American children) is but one aspect of the violence of these productive processes within the highly inequitable United States social order. These vulnerable groups are simply a medium through which the larger population is continually renormalized to be in accord with the social order. Therefore, the primary function of policy studies is not, as is typically assumed, the solution of social problems (the conventional approach) or the symbolic performance of 'latent concerns'; it is the disciplining and normalizing of productive citizens.

In the case of linked school, health, and social services, policy analysts are an integral part of the public presentation of the problem and the problem group. Simultaneously, because of their role as experts, they legitimate that presentation and exclude others that do not accord with the dominant social order. Policy studies, thus, are a social performance (as the postpositivists would agree) that reassures the citizenry and affirms the commitment to 'do something' about social and education problems, even though such 'doing' typically has little effect on the more substantive social and education problems. However, the primary function of such social performances is the disciplining and normalizing of productive students: the performances repeatedly show students and their parents what unproductivity looks like, what being a 'bad' student looks like. Possible policy performances that would stage suburban white schools and their white students as 'bad' are simply not 'visible' to policy analysts and, thus, to the public. Consequently, policy studies as an area of scholarly work is not a scientific or 'neutral' enterprise that attempts to bring to public visibility and 'understanding' social and education problems; policy studies is itself a production of the grid of social regularities, and it carries out critically important reproductive work of that order.

Conclusion

I fear, by this point, that, rather than having established a new policy studies methodology, I have primarily alienated policy analysts and drawn a forbidding characterization of a monstrosity called the grid of social regularities whose anonymous activity imperviously subsumes individual agency. That, however, has not been my intent. While we seem to have great difficulty questioning free will and agency in our own present, we have little difficulty recognizing that members of societies long past operated in accord with the social orders of their times. For example, Romans during the height of the Roman Empire, no matter what their station in life, acted and thought in a manner congruent with that social order and with, I would say, the network of social regularities that comprised that dominant order. Why then refuse a similar reflectivity about ourselves within our social order? Surely we are no less constituted by our moment than they were by theirs.

But even if this reflectivity is accepted, my characterization could seem monstrously impersonal, as if our lives are being conducted through us and not by us. Consider, however, the problematic of policy studies. Policy analysts readily admit that the United States has large, serious social and education problems, the experience of which leads to desperate lives for a large proportion of our children. Indeed, many of our citizens, especially children, live in horrendously destructive conditions. This, however, is not new; it is not a predicament that has only emerged in the last five or ten years; it has been with us, to a greater or lesser degree, for at least 100 years, if not longer. This historical period also encompasses the emergence of the social sciences, among whose originating goals was the use of science to improve social life and the related emergence of the professions that were to utilize the knowledge developed by those sciences. This period also encompasses the explosive growth of public media that has brought the wide disparities of social life into everyone's living room. Why, then, have the social sciences, including the policy sciences, and the professions failed so disastrously? Why do those who are not experiencing desperate lives so readily ignore those who are, even when that desperation can be seen daily on television? As Henry Louis Gates has said, 'That nearly half of African-American children live in poverty is one scandal; another is simply that this fact has become an acceptable feature of our social landscape, as unremarkable as crab grass' (p. A16). Why are the most vulnerable groups seen as a social problem and the most powerful groups not seen as a problem within dominant public and academic discourses? What has brought us to this circumstance? What is it about our society that has produced this monstrous result?

I find inadequate the answers to these questions that rely on the individual political and moral agency of supposedly self-aware and free-choosing subjects of liberal and critical thought. Although it flies in the face of popular conceptions of free will and moral agency, conceptions which are constituted by and reproduce the liberal social order, it makes little sense to me to say that people simply do not care or that they are consciously racist or sexist or classist. If our society is one or all of these, how does it work? How is male supremacy reproduced? How is white supremacy reproduced? How can white supremacy fade as a conscious orientation among whites while so many African-Americans continue to experience white supremicist one?

Answers to these questions that are founded on structuralist assumptions, like those of Marx or critical theorists, I also find flawed in ways that I have argued throughout this chapter. Based on my intersection with Foucaultian poststructuralism, I have tried to develop a new methodological frame for policy studies, a frame which I have called policy archaeology, which provides a different approach to the questions I have raised in this conclusion. Through the problematic of policy studies I have tried to develop a different way of thinking about ourselves, our social and education problems, our efforts to solve them, and a different way of thinking about policy studies as one possible medium for this new thinking. In addition, I have tried to briefly explore how this methodology might be applied to one problem-policy axis. I am aware, however, that policy archaeology and its attendant assumptions are complex and sometimes ambiguous; I am similarly aware I have left loose ends and confusing contradictions. I think policy archaeology arenas 'I', 'III', and 'IV' are fairly clear, but arena 'II', the grid of social regularities and the one the other three arenas are so dependent upon, is based on complex, difficult concepts. The concept of 'social regularities' is a somewhat mobile metaphor that requires more scrutiny and thought. Nonetheless, I think I have initiated a new policy studies problematic. Whether my effort will incite critique or utilization of this problematic I do not know. I hope that it will provoke both.

Notes

1 I also should point out that my understanding and interpretation of Foucault has been particularly influenced by Frazer (1989), though I disagree with some of her criticisms. For Example, Frazer, like other critical theorists and feminists, privileges individual agency more than Foucault does or more than I do, as will become apparent as the reader proceeds through this chapter.

2 Social problems and education problems typically can only be artificially separated; for the most part I do not attempt such separation. For example, the violence being experienced in American schools is not separable from the violence being experienced throughout American society. Furthermore, policy archaeology as a policy studies methodology is equally applicable whether the focus is social or education problems and policies.

3 I do not here discuss the differences and similarities between policy archaeology and critical theoretical approaches, although many of these differences and similarities will be apparent as this chapter proceeds. For example, most critical approaches give center stage to the conscious actions of social agents, whereas my Foucaultian poststructuralism has little focus on this. For example, Simon (1989), who uses a critical approach, has said, 'What actually happens (to improve a particular situation) depends on *human* (emphasis in original) action' (p. 40). Still, my debt to critical theory should be abundantly obvious throughout this chapter. (For other examples of critical approaches to policy issues, see, for example, Ball, 1990; Dale, 1989; and Wallace, 1993. For one example of a discussion of neo-Marxist views of agency in relation to Foucault's views of agency, see Gordon, 1991.)

4 Occasionally I use quotes from Foucault in which I make substitutions in brackets which apply Foucault's statements to my subjects. For example, in the statement just cited I have substituted 'social regularities', my concept, for Foucault's concept, 'preexisting forms of continuity'. This substitution obviously changes the particular meaning of Foucault's statement, but I do not, however, think I change the more general meaning as it might be applied to my topic.

5 When I say that 'social problems are social constructions', I do not mean to imply that social problems do not exist or exist only in the perceptions of human agents. What I mean is that how social problems are named, defined, and discussed is a social process and that the social visibility of some 'problems' as social problems and the invisibility of other 'problems' as social problems, all of which will be discussed later in the article, is also part of this process of social construction. However, the issue of what is 'real' (social problems or whatever) is not as simple as common sense realism would have it; this issue is epistemologically an exceedingly complex one.

6   Although Mahon (1992) suggests, as others have, that Foucault drops archaeology in favor of genealogy because he found archaeology to be inadequate, I found Mahon's work to be particularly provocative for my own thinking about this article. I would, thus, recommend it not as some excellent interpretation of Foucault, though it may be that, but as a valuable incitement or a provocation.

7   I repeatedly use the word 'positive' in relation to the constitutive or productive/repro-ductive nature of social regularities. I have taken this from Foucault. He used the word 'positive' in relation to power to mean that the micro-circulation of power were gen-erative rather than constraining or controlling as the effects of power are commonly thought to be. Similiarly, I mean that the constituting of social regularities is generative. For a good discussion of Foucault's view of power, see Frazer (1989).

8   For other discussions of this issue, see Foucault (1973, pp. xiv or xxiii, or 1991, pp. 58–9). See also White (1978).

9   Hoy (1986) called this process 'subliminal socialization' (p. 15), which produced what Margolis (1993) has called 'a habit of mind' (p. 45).

10   One issue I do not discuss in this chapter, though it is certainly an important one, is that the grid of social regularities constitutes policy archaeology as a policy studies methodology just as this grid constitutes social problems, policy solutions, and con-ventional and interpretivist policy studies orientations. I hope to discuss this in some future piece.

11   Poststructuralists like Derrida and Foucault have held that it is impossible simply to move outside a particular regime of truth within a society. They argue that one can never entirely escape such regimes. There is inevitably, then, much structuralism in my 'poststructuralism', just as there is much structuralism in Foucault's works; such struc-turalism is currently inescapable. For example, Margolis (1993) says that, according to Foucault, 'we cannot abandon (the order within which we live), even where we would attack it' (p. 58).

12   By this point, some readers may have concluded that I think the social order is some totalized, determinative monster within which only unity and congruence exists, what Frazer (1989) calls 'a single, monolithic "symbolic order"' (p. 10). Although I have certainly emphasized the importance of the social order (the grid of social regularities taken as a whole), I do not see the social order as such a totalization. Social orders are historically shifting, complex, dispersed systems comprised of unities and differences, continuities and discontinuities. But, since there are always, in complex systems, poten-tial and incipient but marginalized and suppressed alternatives, there is a grid or net-work of social regularities which produces and reproduces a dominant order. One of the reasons that this order must perpetually reengage, retrain, renormalize and rediscipline its productive members is that difference is a constant turbulence, an impending threat to that order.

13   There seems to be a general, informal sanction against the labels 'white supremacy' or 'white racism'. Although there are some exceptions (for example, Scheurich, 1993 or Rains, 1994), most of the public and academic discourse on racial differentiation, dis-crimination, and inequity uses the term 'racism'. I would argue, however, that this informal sanction is but one example of the productive work of white supremacy as a regularity. In other words, the reluctance to use this particular label is a typical example of the effects of a social regularity. On the one hand, even I am reluctant to use this label because I know that many white readers I want to reach may close their minds, albeit unconsciously, to the issues I raise. On the other hand, I think it is dishonest not to use 'white supremacy' as the better descriptor.

14 'Productive' is a code for congruence with the larger social order. Productive citizens play a positive role — do not break rules, are not disobedient, go to work on time, are not disruptive — on a daily basis. Being a productive citizen means one is aligned 'in thought and deed' with the social order. Being unproductive calls forth various disciplinary apparatuses within schools, government, and private enterprise, though the true focus of such disciplinary practices is the continued normalization of the productive citizens and not so much the disciplining of the unproductive. Of course, no system is capable of totalization. Few individuals are completely congruent with the social order, and the system is sufficiently large, complex, and loose so as to absorb with little disruption some minor incongruencies.

15 For examples of the spread and acceptance of this problem-policy axis at different levels of governmental activity, see *Together We Can: A Guide for Crafting a Profamily System of Education and Human Services* (1993), which was produced by the US Department of Education and the US Department of Health and Human Services, and *Forces of Change: Shaping the Future of Texas* (1994), produced by John Sharp, the Texas Comptroller of Public Accounts.

References

ADLER, L. (1993) 'Introduction and overview', *Journal of Education Policy (Special Edition: The 1993 Politics of Education Association Yearbook)*, **8**, 5 and 6, pp. 1–16.

BALL, S. (1990) *Politics and Policy in Education*, London, Routledge.

CAPPER, C. and HAMMILLER, R.E. (1993) '*Intersections of "difference" in community-based interagency collaboration*', paper presented at the annual meeting of the American Educational Research Association, Atlanta, April.

CORNBLETH, C. and WAUGH, D. (1993) 'The great speckled bird: Education policy-in-the-making', *Educational Researcher*, **22**, pp. 31–7.

CROWSON, R.L. and BOYD, W.L. (1993) 'Coordinated services for children: Designing arks for storms and seas unknown', *American Journal of Education*, **101**, pp. 140–179.

DALE, R. (1989) *The State and Education Policy*, Milton, Keynes, Open University Press.

DRYFOOS, J.G. (1991) 'School-based social and health services for at-risk students', *Urban Education*, **26**, 11, pp. 118–37.

FOUCAULT, M. (1972) *The Archaeology of Knowledge and the Discourse on Language*, New York, Pantheon.

FOUCAULT, M. (1973) *The Order of Things: An Archaeology of the Human Sciences*, New York, Vintage.

FOUCAULT, M. (1979) *Discipline and Punish: The Birth of the Prison*, New York, Vintage.

FOUCAULT, M. (1985) *The Uses of Pleasure*, New York, Pantheon.

FOUCAULT, M. (1988) *Madness and Civilization: A History of Insanity in the Age of Reason*, New York, Vintage.

FOUCAULT, M. (1989) *Foucault Live (interviews 1966–84)*, New York, Simiotexte.

FOUCAULT, M. (1991a) 'Governmentality' in BURCHELL, G., GORDON, C. and MILLER, P. (Eds) *The Foucault Effect: Studies in Governmentality*, Chicago, IL, University of Chicago Press, pp. 87–104.

FOUCAULT, M. (1991b) 'Politics and the study of discourse' in BURCHELL, G., GORDON, C. and MILLER, P. (Eds) *The Foucault Effect: Studies in Governmentality*, Chicago, IL, University of Chicago Press, pp. 53–72.

FOUCAULT, M. (1991c) 'Questions of method' in BURCHELL, G., GORDON, C. and MILLER, P. (Eds) *The Foucault Effect: Studies in Governmentality*, Chicago, IL, University of Chicago Press, pp. 73–86.

FRAZER, N. (1989) *Unruly Practices: Power, Discourse and Gender in Contemporary Social Theory*, Minneapolis, MN, University of Minnesota Press.

GATES, H.L. (1994) 'A liberalism of heart and spine', *New York Times*, 27 March.

GORDON, C. (1991) 'Governmental rationality' in BURCHELL, G., GORDON, C. and MILLER, P. (Eds) *The Foucault Effect: Studies in Gvernmentality*, Chicago, IL, University of Chicago Press, pp. 1–51.

HARRIS, C.I. (1993) 'Whiteness as property', *Harvard Law Review*, **106**, 8, pp. 1710–91.

HAWKESWORTH, M.E. (1988) *Theoretical Issues in Policy Analysis*, Albany, NY, State University of New York Press.

HOY, D.C. (1986) 'Introduction' in HOY, D.C. (Ed) *Foucault: A Critical Reader*, New York, Basil Blackwell, pp. 1–25.

KELLEY, M. and MAYNARD-MOODY, S. (1993) 'Policy analysis in the post-positivist era: Engaging stakeholders in evaluating the economic development districts program', *Public Administration Review*, **53**, 2, pp. 135–42.

KIRST, M.W. (1992) 'Supporting school-linked children's services' in ODDEN, A.R. (Ed) *Rethinking School Finance: An Agenda for the 1990s*, San Francisco, CA, Jossey Bass.

KOPPICH, J.E. (1993) 'The politics of policy making for children', *Journal of Education Policy (Special Edition: The 1993 Politics of Education Association Yearbook)*, **8**, 5 and 6, pp. 51–62.

LATHER, P. (1991) *Getting Smart: Feminist Research and Pedagogy With/In the Postmodern*, New York, Routledge.

LINCOLN, Y.S. and DENZIN, N.K. (1994) 'The fifth moment' in DENZIN, N.K. and LINCOLN, Y.S. (Eds) *Handbook of Qualitative Research*, Thousand Oaks, CA, Sage, pp. 575–86.

MAHON, M. (1992) *Foucault's Nietzschean Geneaology: Truth, Power, and the Subject*, New York, State University Press.

MARGOLIS, J. (1993) 'Redeeming Foucault' in CAPUTO, J. and YOUNT, M. (Eds) *Foucault and the Critique of Institutions*, University Park, PA, Pennsylvania State University Press, 41–59.

MAWHINNEY, H.B. (1993) 'Discovering shared values: Ecological models to support interagency collaboration', *Journal of Education Policy (Special Edition: The 1993 Politics of Education Association Yearbook)*, **8**, 5 and 6, pp. 33–47.

PROCACCI, G. (1991) 'Social economy and the government of economy' in BURCHELL, G., GORDON, C. and MILLER, P. (Eds) *The Foucault Effect: Studies in Governmentality*, Chicago, IL, University of Chicago Press, pp. 151–68.

RAINS, F.V. (1994) *'Daring to see with different eyes: An exploration of white skin privilege'*, paper presented at the annual meeting of the American Educational Research Association Annual Meeting, New Orleans, April.

SCHEURICH, J.J. (1993) 'Toward a white discourse on white racism', *Educational Researcher*, **22**, 8, pp. 5–10.

SCHEURICH, J.J. (1995) 'A postmodernist critique of research interviewing', *International Journal of Qualitative Studies in Education*, **8**, 3, pp. 239–52.

SHARP, J. (1994) *Forces of Change: Shaping the Future of Texas*, Austin, TX, Texas Comptroller of Public Accounts.

SIMON, B. (1989) 'Education and the social order: The contemporary scene' in HARGREAVES, A. and REYNOLDS, D. (Eds) *Education Policies: Controversies and Critiques*, London, Falmer Press.

STANFIELD II, J.H. (1993a) 'Epistemological considerations' in STANFIELD, J.H. II and DENNIS, R.M. (Eds) *Race and Ethnicity in Research Methods*, Newbury Park, CA, Sage, pp. 16–36.

STANFIELD II, J.H. (1993b) 'Methodological reflections: An introduction' in STANFIELD, J.H. II and DENNIS, R.M. (Eds) *Race and Ethnicity in Research Methods*, Newbury Park, CA, Sage, pp. 3–15.

US DEPARTMENT OF EDUCATION AND US DEPARTMENT OF HEALTH AND HUMAN SERVICES (1993) *Together We Can: A Guide for Crafting a Profamily System of Education and Human Services*, Washington, DC, US Government Printing Office.

WALLACE, M. (1993) 'Discourse of derision: The role of the mass media within the education policy process', *Journal of Education Policy*, **8**, 4, pp. 321–37.

WHITE, H. (1978) *Tropics of discourse: Essays in Cultural Criticism*, Baltimore, MD, Johns Hopkins University Press.

WHITE, S. (1991) *Political Theory and Postmodernism*, Cambridge, Cambridge University Press.

6   Toward A White Discourse on White Racism: (An Early Attempt at an Archaeological Approach)

We are deeply concerned about the increasing incidence of racial and ethnic tensions in our country and the lack of focused attention being paid to this issue. (Civil Rights Panel, 1991)

My intention in this chapter is to 'talk' as a white academic with other white academics about racism. In my opinion, this is an unusual kind of effort. There is a considerable amount of work by people of color[1] that addresses racism and its numerous collateral topics, such as equity, multiculturalism, and affirmative action policies. There is also work by whites that addresses these same issues. I have read extensively in both of these domains, but what I have not found are efforts by white academics to talk among ourselves about our own racism, even though prominent academics of color, such as Hooks (1990) and Spivak (1988), have repeatedly said that one of the most important efforts white people could undertake to address racism would be to examine self-reflectively how white racism works.

Few educators will disagree that racism is one of the major social problems in this country. DuBois, perhaps the most widely and deeply respected Afro-American intellectual (West, 1989, p. 138) concluded that 'the problem of the twentieth century is the problem of the color-line' (*ibid*, p. 29) and that 'the white man, as well as the negro, is bound and barred by the color-line' (*ibid*, p. 129). Unfortunately, Dubois' conclusion continues to be as accurate at the end of the twentieth century as it was at the beginning. For example, Pine and Hilliard (1990) recently wrote:

Every time we are almost convinced that the nation is rising above the muck of racism, there come reminders of how little headway we have made — even at eliminating the most vulgar and conspicuous manifestations of the disease. Blatant, crude, egregious, and overt racism has come out of the closet again and into our schools. (p. 593)

The recent candidacy of David Duke for Governor in Louisiana, the Clarence Thomas hearings, the numerous episodes of racism on university campuses and in our neighborhoods and schools are but a few examples of the continuing hold that racism has on our society.

The Issue of Racism in the Academy

In over twenty years of experience with the academy, I have known very few white professors in education who would disagree that racism continues to be a deep and serious social problem. All of those with whom I have become familiar were against racism. Many of them even became visibly saddened when the topic was raised, as if they had just been reminded of an ongoing tragedy they had temporarily forgotten.

This picture of the white professoriate, though, is not meant to dispute contentions by people of color and by some whites that the academy is racially biased. In fact, I have had Afro-American friends who provided specifics of racist behavior by the very same white faculty who expressed anti-racist sentiments to me. Even more importantly, I have had Afro-American friends point out my own racist thoughts and behaviors. So I do not mean to give the impression that white faculty's opposition to racism means that they are not racist or that my own opposition to racism means that I am not racist. In fact, it is this contradiction between the conscious anti-racism of white faculty and the judgment of some people of color and of some whites that the academy is racist that is the central issue of this chapter.[2]

This contradiction creates a confusing and difficult dilemma. One side of this dilemma, the conscious anti-racism of white faculty, is founded solely on my own experience and my judgments of that experience. It is not based on a random sample of respondents to a survey, nor is it based on conclusions drawn from an experiment. It is founded only on my interactions with my own colleagues. Yet, I feel reasonably confident that a high percentage of white faculty, even under conditions that would erase social desirability response effects, would judge that they themselves do not support racism and are, for the most part, not racist. I would even go so far to say that white faculty, in education at least, would say that they themselves are strongly opposed to racism in any form.

The other side of the dilemma is the contention by many people of color and by some whites that the academy is racist. For example, Frierson (1990) asserts that 'the presence of racism in the institution(s of higher education) should be acknowledged as a reality' (p. 16). Reyes and Halcon (1988) claim that

> Discriminatory policies and manifestations of racism in educational institutions have changed little over the years . . . Chicano academics today are generally experiencing many of the same kinds of racial prejudices experienced by those who preceded them into the academy a generation ago. (pp. 310–1)

While I could cite numerous authors with similar viewpoints who are widely respected and write extensively about complexities of racism,[3] it would also be possible to find individual people of color who have had prolonged interactions with institutions of higher learning and who think that white faculty as individuals or as a group are not racist. For instance, I am a somewhat more than casual friend with one Afro-American student who has said to me that he has never experienced racism from white faculty. So I do not want to give the impression that people of color monolithically think the academy is racist.

The question embedded, however, in the contradiction between academic whites who think they are not racist and others who think the white academy is racist is how can we determine whether a person or group is racist or not? There is, of course, an extensive body of legislation and case law that confronts this problem from many different angles, most of which are based upon following overt effects, such as the percentage of Afro-Americans hired in relation to Afro-American applicants, back to overt and covert causes.[4] While this approach has been anywhere from fruitful to fruitless, depending on the commentator, I am not interested in working with this literature here. Instead I would like to explore a different approach.

How People of Color and Whites Define Racism

In my estimation, people of color, and those whites who have concluded that white academics are racially biased, are correct, but this does not primarily mean what white academics may think it means. Highly educated whites usually think of racism in terms of the overt behaviors of individuals that can readily be identified and labeled.[5] A person who does not behave in these identified ways is not considered to be a racist. Within this perspective, racism is a label for individuals but is not for social groups. In fact, Kluegel and Smith (1986) found that educated whites see racism as an individual issue and not as a racial group issue.

People of color, on the other hand, usually experience racism differently. DuBois (1989) speaks of the 'double consciousness' of Afro-Americans. Because of this double consciousness, which evolves as a coping response to racism, people of color grow up learning to look at themselves not through their own eyes nor through the eyes of their own race but through the eyes of whites:

> (T)he negro is a sort of seventh son, born with a veil, and gifted with second-sight in this American world, — a world which yields him no true self-consciousness, but only lets him see himself through the revelation of the other (white) world. It is a peculiar sensation, this double-consciousness, this sense of always looking at one's self through the eyes of others, of measuring one's soul by the tape of a world that looks on in amused contempt and pity. One ever feels his twoness, — an American, a negro; two souls, two thoughts, two unreconciled strivings; two warring ideals in one dark body, whose dogged strength alone keeps it from being torn asunder. (p. 3)

Dubois' self concept is not rooted in his individual self, nor is it solely rooted in his own race; his self-concept is rooted in a 'double', composed of both black and white. But in this double, the white view is privileged over the black view: 'this American world . . . yields him no true self-consciousness, but only lets him (the Afro-American) see himself through the revelation of the other (white) world' (*ibid*, p. 3).[6]

While many things have changed in this country regarding racial issues since DuBois' statement was published nearly ninety years ago, I maintain that he has captured a feature of the lives of people of color in this society that is still relevant.[7]

Because of racism, because 'they are constantly reminded by words, deeds, and unconscious gestures that they are out-group members' (Stanfield, 1985, p. 400), because they experience themselves collectively and historically as being treated differently based on their skin color, people of color learn to see themselves as a racialized people, as a social group defined by skin color.

Because of racism people of color are not only treated as a social group; they come to see themselves as defined by that group. As Kramer (1970) says, 'Members of minority groups have no choice about the status that is imposed upon them' (p. vii). In addition, because racism is imposed by whites upon people of color, the racialized group sense that people of color have does not originate in their own group. It originates in the actions and attitudes of the white race, that is, 'through the revelation of the other (white) world' (DuBois, 1989, p. 3).

We whites, however, experience ourselves as non-racialized individuals (Kluegel and Smith, 1986; Ogbu, 1978). We do not experience ourselves as defined by our skin color. We especially do not experience ourselves as defined by another race's actions and attitudes toward us because of our skin color. As Stanfield (1985) asserts, whites do 'not even . . . notice they are white' (p. 400).

This difference in how whites and people of color experience themselves is, I think, crucial to understanding why whites misunderstand judgments that they are racist. When people of color assert that the academy is racist, individual whites in the academy, who do not see themselves as racist, are offended or think the judgment does not apply to them. People of color see this unwillingness of whites to acknowledge their racism as one way that white academics protect their position of privilege. Neither whites nor people of color seem to understand that there is a clash here between a social group perspective, learned by people of color through the social experience of racism, and an individualized perspective, learned by whites through their racial socialization.

Individualism and Social Positionality

Among whites, the idea that each person is largely the source or origin of her/himself, that is individualism, is considered a natural facet of life.[8] Within the frame of this belief, individualism is seen as a naturally occurring, transhistorical, transcultural condition to which all humans naturally aspire. This belief, then, is deeply infused in white judgments about the way life works. For example, if a person does 'well' in life, it is seen as being largely due to her/his own individual choices; if she/he does 'badly' in life, it is also largely due to her/his choices. While it is thought that people have different capabilities, what a person does with her or his capabilities is considered to be more important than the capabilities themselves (Schuman, 1971), especially among more educated whites (Kluegel and Smith, 1986).

The problem with individualism, though, is that it hides the inequities in our social structures, especially racial inequities.[9] It also hides the fact that 'prejudice, discrimination, and racism do not require (individual) intention' (Pine and Hilliard,

1990, p. 595). People of all races are social beings, that is, 'human behavior is largely shaped by social/cultural experiences' (Gordon, Miller and Rollock, 1990). Boden, Giddens and Molotch (1990) make the same point in an article addressing the lack of sociological understanding in the academy: 'All too easily . . . academics define human actions as "psychologically" driven when they are, deeply and significantly, social in origin and orientation' (p. B2).

In different times and different places, people have acted, thought, and believed differently about virtually everything. Even in our own time, middle-class Cuban-Americans, to name just one group, have different codes of conduct than upper-class whites or lower-class Hispanics. For instance, Stanfield (1985) contends 'it is simply wrong to assume that everyone in the United States has the same cognitive style . . . The cognitive styles of classes, races, and ethnic groups differ; each of these social categories has different experiences, priorities, and ideas of what is relevant' (pp. 399–400). In fact, each of us is socially positioned or located by major sociological categories, such as race, class, and gender. Those in different positional intersections, like white, lower-class females or Asian, middle-class males, are socialized in different ways.

These positional intersections, however, are not equal in our society. There is instead a hierarchy of positions with upper-class white males at the top and lower-class males and females of color at the bottom. Resources and power — economic, intellectual, and emotional — are largely distributed according to this hierarchy (hooks, 1990; Ogbu, 1990; Ransford, 1977; Spivak, 1988; Stanfield, 1985; Weiler, 1988; Yetman and Steele, 1971, among many others). Whites as a group get more resources and power than people of color. The upper class as a group gets more resources and power than the middle class as a group, which gets more resources and power than the lower class. Men as a group get more resources and power than women.[10]

This inequitable distribution of resources and power by social group, however, is concealed by middle- and upper-income white people's investment in the idea of individualism. In contrast, because of racism's grouping effect and the double consciousness it produces, people of color are not as seduced by the idea of individualism. People of color, through their socially positioned experience, know that they are a racialized group rather than simply separate individuals.

Although we live in a culture that distributes its resources most disproportionately to middle- and upper-class, white males, this does not mean that there are not exceptions to this arrangement nor that other groups do not persistently resist the inequitable distribution. Middle- and upper-class, white males, nonetheless, consistently reap the most benefits and have done so for a very long time within Western culture. The result of this historical dominance is that the styles of thinking, acting, speaking, and behaving of the dominant group have become the socially correct or privileged ways of thinking, acting, speaking, and behaving (Kovel, 1970 [cited in Pettigrew and Martin, 1987]; Kramer, 1970; Stanfield, 1985; Weiler, 1988).

One of the main ways this happens is that the ways of the dominant group become universalized as measures of merit, hiring criteria, grading standards, predictors of success, correct grammar, appropriate behavior, and so forth, all of which are said to be distributed as differences in individual effort, ability, or intelligence. Membership in a social group and the group-related, inequitable distribution of resources and power, thus, disappear under the guise of individualism.

Social Success and Social Awards

The best way, then, to succeed, that is, receive rewards, recognition, promotions, salary increases, material resources, and so forth, is to learn and reproduce the ways of the dominant group. This learning and reproduction is easiest for those who grow up socialized into these dominant ways. Thus the children of middle- and upper-class whites are the ones that are most likely to succeed because they have been raised (socialized) in the ways of the dominant group. Some children of the dominant group, of course, fail and some children from lower social groups succeed, but on average, the chances of success are substantially better if she/he is raised within a dominant group family.

Members of non-dominant groups and their children have a chance to succeed if they learn the ways of the dominant groups and if they are socially or economically closer to the top of the hierarchy. But, contrary to the popular idea that anyone can succeed, there are limits no matter how well one learns the ways of the dominant group. If a person is low enough in the social hierarchy of groups, no matter how well that person learns to internalize the ways of the dominant group — will never attain the level of success that comes much more easily to one who grows up within a dominant group family.[11]

Although each individual is to some extent different, and thus there is some contribution that is due to an individual's particular constellation of skills and abilities, the rewards each person receives are to a considerable extent an effect of the inequitable distribution of resources and power by race, class, and gender. However, the socially reinforced belief in individualism allows those at the higher reaches of the social hierarchy (which, in my opinion, includes white academics) to believe that they receive more rewards because they are special individually, because they have more skills, more talents, more intelligence, and so forth. They do not 'see' how these rewards as related to their group position within the social hierarchy.

In a very real sense the cream is skimmed off the social milk and fed to those in the higher groups as if they were individual rather than social rewards, while those at the very bottom of the hierarchy drink a milk so diluted as to be hardly distinguishable from water. Those in the upper levels of the social hierarchy become addicted to the seductive connection of various rewards with the idea that they receive these rewards because of their uniqueness as an individual.

Individualism is Addictive

This process occurs within the academy as well as virtually everywhere else within our society. I have experienced it myself. While I grew up within a working class family and have had to train myself to behave like a upper-middle class person, I did grow up white and male. Although my working class origins placed some hurdles along the way, I was aided by the fact that I am male and white and that I have been able and willing to learn upper-middle class ways. Such accommodations (or compromises, if you will) have allowed me to be fairly successful in terms of garnering social rewards, mostly within the academy.

I can personally say that this process is highly addictive, very difficult to resist. All of the rewards are offered in terms of the idea that I am receiving them because of my special, individual talents, abilities, and efforts. It is very easy, then, to convince myself that this individual specialness is true and to become deeply committed to a kind of personal egotism or arrogance. While it is surely true that individual differences play some significant role in the distribution of social rewards, it is very easy to forget, even in the face of the kind of commitment I have tried to express in this chapter, that the rewards I receive are deeply connected to my race, class, and gender, that is, to my membership in a highly favored social group.

According to Bledstein (1978), this cult of the individual is an integral part of academic life. There is a special emphasis on the freedom of professors, once they are tenured, to be highly individualistic and thus not defined by any social group categories. Bledstein in his book on higher education in this country, has said:

> The culture of professionalism (Bledstein's referent for the academy) emancipated the active ego of a sovereign person as he performed organized activities within comprehensive spaces. The culture of professionalism incarnated the radical idea of the independent democrat, a liberated person seeking to free the power of nature within every worldly sphere, a self-governing individual exercising his trained judgment in an open society . . . (This) professional person strove to achieve a level of autonomous individualism, a position of unchallenged authority heretofore unknown in American life. (*ibid*, pp. 87–8)

The culture of the academy not only emphasizes the individual standing of each professor but also inculcates a rationalization of individualism as a positive virtue.

The price we white academics pay for this orientation is that we lose sight of the multiple effects of our membership in a favored social group. We lose sight of how much we and, more importantly, our intellectual productions (books, articles, presentations, symposia) are, at least to a significant extent, enacted by our race, gender, and class. Our intellectual products, which play an important part in how our society knows and reproduces itself, are marketed as if they are individual products, unrelated to or reproductive of social group membership. Our social positionality simply disappears from the conscious surface of our products. For example, a book I might write would be seen solely as the work of my individual self; it would not be seen as a white, upper-middle-class male production.

This perspective returns us to the earlier point that white academics tend to misunderstand judgments that white professors are racist. As I said before, we white academics tend to see this as a judgment of our individual behaviors rather than as a judgment of our membership in a social group. People of color, on the other hand, because of the 'double consciousness' forced upon them by racism, see both themselves and whites as enacted by their racial categories. When people of color contend that we white academics are racist, they are not primarily judging our individual behavior (though certainly they sometimes are); they are, most importantly, judging our membership in a racial group that has produced and maintained skin color as a socially enforced category of difference within a hierarchy of social groups.

In addition, people of color are saying, correctly I think, that we whites operate as if we are oblivious of our racial positionality and its effects in terms of the inequitable distribution of resources and power within our society. Because of this lack of awareness, we white academics learn to act as if our social rewards — salary, position, recognitions, and so on — are solely the product of our special, idiosyncratic individuality. We thus ignore the inequitable distribution of such awards by social group and the impact of this inequitable distribution on ourselves and our intellectual products. More critically, we ignore the fact that the inequitable distribution of resources and power is, in a very important sense, constitutive of who we are as upper-middle-class academic whites.

We Whites are in this Problem Together

Recognizing our social group position raises another important point for us whites. Virtually all academic whites occupy, as whites, the same general social position no matter what each individual's opinions about racism may be. Even if a white academic strongly opposes racism in her or his intellectual work, she/he still benefits as a white from the inequitable social distribution of power and resources. There is no individual escape from one's racial group. We whites, because of our social group membership, are socially bound together, just as people of color are, in terms of addressing racism. This social group membership orientation is particularly relevant to efforts by whites to confront white racism. Unfortunately, many whites who have made a commitment to addressing racism also consider themselves superior to those whites who have not made the same commitment. This division into 'good' whites who address racism and 'bad' whites who do not is implicit in the writings of many anti-racist whites. It is also implicit, albeit in a much more complex fashion, in such philosophical orientations as those versions of Marxism that locate racism as a phenomenon secondary to the class hierarchy (McCarthy, 1988; Young, 1990).

A full recognition of the advantages we gain as a result of our racial positionality means that all of us whites are in the struggle against white racism together. None of us gets an individual dispensation that releases us from our racial position, from its inequitably derived rewards, or from white racism. Our positionality requires that we whites must work together to address this situation; otherwise, we are assuming we can escape our social group membership and its effects through claims for special status for individual anti-racist whites.

I do not make this last point lightly. I know from my own personal experience that it is very easy to divide those who are 'politically correct' from those who are not. I often fall into this myself. The indirect claim of superiority, because I am focusing on white racism when others are not, is highly seductive. It is very easy for me to think that I have done my part because I am on the 'politically correct' side.

What arises out of this is a way of talking or writing (through tone or word choice, for instance) that implicitly communicates my ideological or political superiority. Not only does this approach alienate those I need to communicate with, but it falsely represents me as if I am less affected by my racial group membership than those whites who do not address white racism. In my opinion, no matter how much I individually confront the issue of white racism, I cannot escape being white. I cannot escape the inequitable distribution by race and its effects on me. As West (1990) says of those in my position, I am both 'progressive and coopted' (p. 94). Since I cannot individually escape my racial group and its position within the inequitable social hierarchy, no matter how much I individually detest racism, I am compelled to work inclusively with other members of my racial group to address white racism.

Two Suggestions

I would, thus, make two suggestions to facilitate a white discourse on white racism within the academy. We white academics need, first, to begin to understand and make conscious, especially within our intellectual work, the fact that in our society all people are racialized persons, that is, all people are socially influenced in significant ways by their membership in a racial group. We whites need to study and report how being white affects our thinking, our behaviors, our attitudes, and our decisions from the micro, personal level to the macro, social level. We need to make white racism a central, self-reflective topic of inquiry within the academy. We need to become aware of our racial positionality as it affects our intellectual products and then infuse this reflexivity into those products.

Second, we need to undertake this effort in a way that does not attempt to separate 'good' whites, willing to confront white racism, from 'bad' whites, unwilling to confront white racism. While this non-divisive approach makes good, practical, political sense, it is even more important to understand that as long as the discourse on white racism divides 'good' whites from 'bad' whites, it misses the central argument advanced in this essay. That is, in our society everyone is racially located and experiences the inequitable distribution of resources and power by racial group, even though a belief in individualism conceals this inequitable distribution. It does not matter whether we are a 'good' white or a 'bad' white; all whites are socially positioned as whites and receive social advantages because of this positionality. No individual white gets to be an exception because of his or her antiracism.

Virtually no one would dispute that racism is one of the chief social problems in this society and in many other societies. It is certainly not surprising that no consensus exists on how to solve the problem. In this chapter, following the advice of the victims of racism, I have tried to start from where I am. Since I am a white, male academic, I have tried to start from there. I have attempted to consider how we white academics participate in the reproduction of racial inequity. I have attempted, at least to some extent, to be candid about my own participation in that reproductive process, to talk, for instance, about my own experience of the seductions of individualism. I have made suggestions about what we white academics need to do and how we need to do it. It is not my intention, however, that this chapter be a definitive consideration of white racism in the academy. It is neither the first word nor the last. It is only an attempt to discuss my thoughts about white racism in the academy and to provoke additional conversation, in agreement or disagreement (both are helpful, useful, and important). While none of us can escape the innumerable, intricate, large and small ways that our society daily advantages or disadvantages each of us racially, I do not believe we are fatally condemned to continue the present inequities. The key question is, how do we end this tragedy? I suggest that we white academics begin with a white discourse on white racism. I hope this chapter facilitates that conversation.

Notes

1   I will use the phrase 'people of color' to denote the collective of all non-white races in the United States. I do not wish, though, to imply, in some totalized fashion, that the different non-white races are all somehow the same in general or in regards to racism. Each race has had different historical experiences in this country that are constitutive of its racial culture. Ogbu (1978 and 1990), for instance, has written that, because of the historical effects of slavery, the contemporary position of Afro-Americans is different from that of other races, such as those that freely immigrated to this country. In addition, throughout this chapter, I do not mean to imply that each race is monolithic in its viewpoints about anything, especially racism; there are, as West (1990) says, 'differences (class, gender, region, sexual orientation)' among all peoples of color (p. 103). In addition, McCarthy (1988) asserts that 'the characterization of minority groups in monolithic terms leads to unwarranted generalizations about the social, political, and cultural behavior of racially oppressed groups' (p. 272) (see also, Ransford, 1977, on this issue). Nonetheless, since the focus of this chapter is on whites and white racism, and not primarily on the experiences of people of color, I need a single, collective term for the other-than-white races. Other possible terms that have frequently been used are more problematic for various reasons. The term 'non-white' is lacking because it derives its meaning from whites rather than from people of color themselves, thus reinscribing a hegemonic relationship of whites over people of color. Sometimes, though, it is the only term that works grammatically; the term 'people of color' cannot be used as an adjective. The term 'minorities' is also inadequate because people of color are only minorities at the national level and within some other specific contexts: in the world as a whole and in many contexts people of color are the majority. For example, 'California is already a "majority" of "minorities" insofar as its schools are concerned' (Gutherie and Reed, 1991, p. 7). Finally, although the term 'people

of color' is also lacking because everyone is, strictly speaking, a person of (skin) color, this term is the one that is currently most frequently used by people of color that I read.

2   That a person of color in an institutional setting with whites is the only one to recoginze that there is racism in the setting is a common point made in the literature on racism. For example, Feagin (1991) says that it is typical for 'a black employee to perceive the subtle undercurrent of prejudice not perceived by white employees' (p. 86). Pettigrew and Martin (1987) contend that 'often the black is the only person in a position to draw the conclusion that prejudice is operating in the work situations' (p. 50).

3   See, for example, Baratz and Baratz (1970); Feagin (1991); Higham (1971); Pine and Hilliard (1990); and Reyes and Halcon (1988). For more philosophical treatments of the racism of the Western knowledge project, see Gordon, Miller and Rollock (1990); Hooks (1990); Minh-ha (1989); Said (1979); Spivak (1988); Stanfield (1985); and Young (1990).

4   See, for example, Pettigrew and Martin (1987) in the *Journal of Social Issues* which devoted one complete issue (volume 43, number 1) to the topic of racism and employment.

5   I would suggest that what many academic and other middle-class whites see as racism is the styles of racism historically common to working-class whites. Indeed, in much of the public, popular discourse on racism in the media (newspapers, television, radio, movies), racism is characterized almost solely in terms of white working-class racism. Pettigrew and Martin (1987) call this style of racism 'raw, overt bigotry' (p. 46) while Kovel (1970) calls it 'dominative racism' (quoted in Pettigrew and Martin, 1987, p. 46). While many middle-class whites find 'raw, overt bigotry' or 'dominative' examples of racism to be repugnant, they tend not to be aware of their own, more subtle styles of middle-class racism.

6   Pine and Hilliard (1990) make the same point about students of color: 'Students of color . . . experience conceptual separation from their roots: they are compelled to examine their own experiences and history through the assumptions, paradigms, constructs, and language of other people.' (p. 596).

7   The determination of which racial groups in the United States experience Dubois' 'double consciousness' would initiate a lively debate. I do not think, however, that the central purpose of this chapter requires that I take some stand on this issue. My unwillingness to engage this here does not mean that I think this debate is unimportant; it is very important. Neither does my unwillingness mean that I do not have a sense of where I would stand in such a debate; I simply think that to attempt to discuss this issue here would not only take too much additional space but, more importantly, would detract from the central point I am trying to make.

8   I do not mean to imply that people of color do not also value individualism. What I am saying is that people of color are much more aware of their racialized group status than whites are of their racial group status and that thus the influence of the idea of individualism on people of color is significantly less than on whites.

9   The idea of individualism as hindering white attention to racism does not originate with me. For example, Ogbu (1978) made this same point in his influential *Minority Education and Caste: The American System in Cross-Cultural Perspective*. I do, however, think that raising this issue within the context of white academics talking to other white academics is an important addition to the work of Ogbu and others.

10   Although I appear here to treat the social categories of race, class, and gender as if they operate independently from each other, I do this only to simplify the larger argument

that I am trying to develop. Actually each category intersects with the other categories in very complicated ways.

11 DuBois (1989) expressed awareness of this difference in life chances when, in speaking of a young Afro-American man, he said 'I had feared for Jim. With a cultured parentage and a social caste to uphold him, he might have made a venturesome merchant or a West Point cadet' (p. 49).

References

BARATZ, S.S. and BARATZ, J.C. (1970) 'Early childhood intervention: The base of institutional racism', *Harvard Educational Review*, **40**, pp. 29–50.

BLEDSTEIN, B.J. (1978) *The Culture of Professionalism: The Middle Class and the Development of Higher Education in America*, New York, W.W. Norton & Co.

BODEN, D., GIDDENS, A. and MOLOTCH, H.L. (1990) 'Sociology's role in addressing society's problems is undervalued and misunderstood in academe', *The Chronicle of Higher Education*, **36**, 23, pp. B1 and B3.

CIVIL RIGHTS PANEL TO STUDY ISSUE OF RACISM IN SCHOOLS, *Education Week*, **11**, 14, p. 22.

DUBOIS, W.E.B. (1989) *The Souls of Black Folks*, New York, Bantam Books. (original work published in 1903).

FEAGIN, J.R. (1991) 'Blacks still face the malevolent reality of white racism', *The Chronicle of Higher Education*, **38**, 14, p. A44.

FRIERSON, JR., H.T. (1990) 'The situation of black educational researchers: Continuation of a crises', *Educational Researcher*, **19**, 2, pp. 12–17.

GORDON, E.W., MILLER, F. and ROLLOCK, D. (1990) 'Coping with communicentric bias in knowledge production in the social sciences', *Educational Researcher*, **19**, 3, pp. 14–19.

GUTHERIE, J.W. and REED, R.J. (1991) *Educational Administration and Policy: Effective Leadership for American Education*, Boston, MA, Allyn & Bacon.

HIGHAM, J. (1971) 'Toward racism: The history of an idea' in YETMAN, N.R. and STEELE, C.H. (Eds) *Majority and Minority: The Dynamics of Racial and Ethnic Relations*, Boston, MA, Allyn & Bacon, pp. 230–52.

hooks, b. (1990) *Yearning: Race, Gender, and Cultural Politics*, Boston, MA, South End Press.

KLUEGEL, J.R. and SMITH, E.R. (1986) *Beliefs about Inequality: Americans' Views or What is and What Ought to Be*, New York, Aldine de Gruyter.

KOVEL, J. (1970) *White Racism: A Psychological History*, New York, Pantheon (quoted in Pettigrew and Martin, 1987.)

KRAMER, J.R. (1970) *The American Minority Community*, New York, Thomas Y. Crowell Co.

McCARTHY, C. (1988) 'Rethinking liberal and radical perspectives on racial inequality in schooling: Making the case for nonsynchrony', *Harvard Educational Review*, **58**, 3, pp. 265–79.

MINH-HA, T.T. (1989) *Woman Native Other*, Bloomington, IN, Indiana University Press.

OGBU, J.U. (1978) *Minority Education and Caste: The American System in Cross-cultural Perspective*, New York, Academic Press.

OGBU, J.U. (1990) 'Racial stratification and education' in THOMAS, G.E. (Ed) *US Race Relations in the 1980s and 1990s: Challenges and Alternatives*, New York, Hemisphere Publishing, pp. 3–34.

PETTIGREW, T.F. and MARTIN, J. (1987) 'Shaping the organizational context for Black American inclusion', *Journal of Social Issues*, **43**, 1, pp. 41–78.

PINE, G.J. and HILLIARD, III, A.G. (1990) 'Rx for racism: Imperatives for America's schools', *Phi Delta Kappan*, **71**, 8, pp. 593–600.

RANSFORD, H.E. (1977) *Race and Class in American Society: Black Chicano Anglo*, Cambridge, MA, Schenkman Publishing.

REYES, M.L. and HALCON, J.J. (1988) 'Racism in academia: The old wolf revisited', *Harvard Educational Review*, **58**, 3, pp. 299–314.

SAID, E.W. (1979) *Orientalism*, New York, Vintage Books.

SCHUMAN, H. (1971) 'Free will and determinism in public beliefs about race' in YETMAN, N.R. and STEELE, C.H. (Eds) *Majority and Minority: The Dynamics of Racial and Ethnic Relations*, Boston, MA, Allyn & Bacon. pp. 382–90.

SPIVAK, G.C. (1988) *In Other Worlds: Essays in Cultural Politics*, New York, Routledge.

STANFIELD, J.H. (1985) 'The ethnocentric basis of social science knowledge production', *Review of Research in Education*, **12**, pp. 387–415.

WEILER, K. (1988) *Women Teaching for Change: Geender, Class & Power*, New York, Bergen & Garvey.

WEST, C. (1989) *The American Evasion of Philosophy: A Genealogy of Pragmatism*, Madison, WI, University of Wisconsin Press.

WEST, C. (1990) 'The new cultural politics of difference', *October*, **53**, pp. 93–109.

YETMAN, N.R. and STEELE, C.H. (1971) 'Introduction' in YETMAN, N.R. and STEELE, C.H. (Eds) *Majority and Minority: The Dynamics of Racial and Ethnic Relations*, Boston, MA, Allyn & Bacon, pp. 3–15.

YOUNG, R. (1990) *White Mythologies: Writing History and the West*, London, Routledge.

7 Coloring Epistemologies: Are Our Research Ephistemologies Racially Biased? (An Example of an Archaeological Approach)

With Michelle D. Young

Respected scholars of color (for example, Stanfield, 1985, 1993a and 1994), have suggested, even within the pages of this journal (Banks, 1993 and 1995; Gordon, Miller and Rollock, 1990), that the epistemologies we typically use in educational research may be racially biased. They have argued that our epistemologies[1] — not our use of them, but the epistemologies themselves — are racially biased ways of knowing, implicitly proposing, thus, a new category of racism that could be labeled *epistemological racism*. There has been, however, a provocative lack of response — pro or con — to this race-oriented argument by leading educational methodologists in journals of education, including this one.[2] But this lack of response is in curious contrast to the lively and contentious debates on other epistemological issues, such as quantitative versus qualitative (for example, Cizek, 1995), objectivity versus subjectivity (for example, Heshusius, 1994), validity (for example, Lenzo, 1995; Moss, 1994), or paradigmatic issues in general (for example, Bereiter, 1994; Delandshere and Petrosky, 1994; Gage, 1989).

If we were among those raising this race-oriented issue, we would wonder why our efforts to argue that the epistemologies of educational research were racially biased provoked virtually no response, particularly among those who author the quantitative and qualitative research methods textbooks we all typically use. We would certainly wonder whether our argument was ignored because it raised the disquieting issue of race, because it was thought to be a weak or irrelevant argument, or because the argument was simply not understood. Unfortunately, we might also wonder whether this was just one more incidence of Ellison's (1952) 'invisible man' syndrome, of whites ignoring racial issues and people of color.

As researchers whose race is white and who have written and presented on both epistemological and racial issues (Scheurich, 1993 and 1994b; Young, 1995a and 1995b), we want to offer a substantive response to the argument of the scholars of color who have contended that our research epistemologies are racially biased. It will be our claim that the lack of response to date to the racial bias argument is not primarily a function of overt or covert racism, as some might argue, or of institutional or societal racism, as others might suggest. Instead, we will contend that this silence is a function of a different lack — a lack of understanding among researchers as to how race is a critically significant epistemological problem in educational research.

Our purpose then is to discuss how our range of research epistemologies — including positivism, postpositivisms, neo-realisms, interpretivisms, constructivisms, the critical tradition, and postmodernisms/poststructuralisms[3] — can be understood as racially biased in a way that will (i) facilitate an understanding of just what *epistemological racism*[4] is; (ii) ignite the kind of spirited debate that has occurred around other, arguably lesser, research issues; (iii) draw some of the prominent research epistemologists, especially those who author methods textbooks, into this debate; and, (iv) provoke additional efforts among scholars of all races to address this problem. We will pursue this purpose by discussing five categories of racism and their linkages to research, and we will conclude with some suggestions about what initially needs to be done to address *epistemological racism.*

The first two categories of racism we shall discuss — overt and covert racism — are typically defined as operating at the individual level; the next two are organizational and social categories — institutional and societal racism — and, in effect, create the social context for the prior two categories. The final one is a civilizational category, and it, we will contend, creates or constitutes the possibility for all of the prior four categories.[5] Further, it is the latter category that is the salient one for discussions regarding the racial bias of research epistemologies. Figure 1 illustrates and positions these categories; it also graphically depicts the structure of this chapter. The individual level, which includes both overt and covert racism, sits within the institutional level, which sits within the societal level. All of these four sit, in a hierarchy of smaller to larger and broader, inside the largest and broadest category, the civilizational level.[6]

Two Categories of Individual Racism: Overt and Covert

Racial bias or racism is typically understood in popular culture and in academia in terms of individual acts of overt prejudice that are racially based, i.e., *overt racism* (see, for example, Kluegel and Smith, 1986; Ogbu, 1978; Reyes and Halcon, 1988; Rizvi, 1993; Scheurich, 1993; Tatum, 1992). For example, if a college professor makes a racial slur during a class lecture, this is seen as overt racism. Overt racism, then, is a public, conscious, and intended act by a person or persons from one race with the intent of doing damage to a person or persons of another race chiefly because of the race of the second person or persons.[7] While there are many in the US who are overt racists, there is a general social consensus, at least at the public level,[8] that these behaviors are socially unacceptable (though verbalizations of overt racism are constitutionally protected in most cases).

A second kind of individual racism is *covert racism.* The only real differ-ence between overt and covert racism is that the latter is not explicitly public. For example, a superintendent may consciously not promote a Hispanic-American to

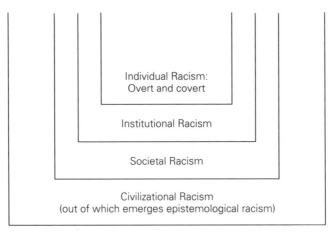

Individual Racism:
Overt and covert

Institutional Racism

Societal Racism

Civilizational Racism
(out of which emerges epistemological racism)

Figure 1

the principalship in a majority white geographical area, even though the Hispanic-American applicant may be the most qualified. While this superintendent may be consciously acting in a racist manner, she/he will publically provide a socially acceptable reason for her/his decision. Persons making covert, racially biased decisions do not explicitly broadcast their intentions; instead, they veil them or provide reasons which society will find more palatable. A public consensus, though perhaps not as strong as the one for overt racism, also exists with regards to covert acts of racism, and, in fact, many laws prohibit such acts, particularly in the area of employment practices.

Whether covert or overt, however, racism in the US is overwhelming seen as an individual phenomenon (Kluegel and Smith, 1986; Ogbu, 1978). And this is as much true in academia as in popular culture (Scheurich, 1993). If a person answers 'no' to the question of whether she/he is racist, the respondent typically means that she/he does not, as an individual, engage in conscious, intended racism or that she/he is not, as an individual, consciously racist. Researchers, just like other members of this society, typically judge their own lack of racism based on personal evaluations that they do not, as an individual, have a negative judgment of another person just because that person is a member of a particular race. While this individualized, conscious, moral or ethical commitment to anti-racism is a significant and meaningful individual and historical accomplishment, the fact that it restricts our understanding of racism to an individualized ethical arena is a barrier to a broader, more comprehensive understanding of racism — for society and for researchers.

Understanding that we need to get beyond issues of individual racism, whether overt or covert, is critical to initiating a consideration of whether our research epistemologies are racially biased. For example, if we, as researchers, were to read an article that argued that our research epistemologies were racially biased and if we disagreed with this argument because we did not consider ourselves, as individuals, to be consciously or intentionally racist, this judgment would indicate that we did not understand epistemological racism. The error here is that racial critiques of research epistemologies have virtually nothing to do with whether an individual researcher is overtly or covertly racist. A researcher could be adamantly anti-racist in thought and deed and still be using a research epistemology that, given our later discussion of epistemological racism, could be judged to be racially biased. Consequently, researchers considering the issue of epistemological racism need to get beyond the question of whether personally they are racists or not because this latter judgment is not related to judgments about epistemological racism.

Institutional Racism

Institutional racism exists when institutions or organizations, including educational ones, have standard operating procedures (intended or unintended) that hurt members of one or more races in relation to members of the dominant race (for further discussions of institutional racism, see Feagin and Vera, 1995; Hacker, 1992; Reyes and Halcon, 1988). Institutional racism also exists when institutional or organizational cultures, rules, habits, or symbols have the same biasing effect. For example, if an institution's procedures or culture favors whites for promotion, such as promotion to a full professorship or to a principalship, over persons of color, this is institutional racism. If a school's standard pedagogical method is culturally congruent with the culture of white students but not with the cultures of students of color (a widespread problem — see, for example, Cummins, 1986; Ladson-Billings, 1995; Hilliard, 1992; King, 1991; Lee, Lomotey and Shujaa, 1990, among many others), this is institutional racism.

One particularly important type of institutional racism that occurs in research communities arises when racially biased beliefs or assumptions are embedded within a research discipline or a particular community of researchers or within the variables, labels, or concepts of a discipline or community (Paredes, 1977; Stanfield, 1985, 1993a and 1993b). For example, if educational researchers commonly use, as they once typically did, a phrase like 'culturally disadvantaged' or 'cultural deprivation' to indicate why some students of color did not succeed in school, this is institutional racism (McCarthy, 1993). While not using this particular phrase ('institutional racism'), Gordon *et al.* (1990) have argued, within the pages of this journal, that this kind of racism is endemic to the social sciences: '*Much of the social science knowledge* (emphasis added) referable to Blacks, Latinos, and Native Americans ignores or demeans (members of these races and) . . . often presents distorted interpretations of minority conditions and potentials' (p. 14).

But Gordon *et al.* (1990) are not the only ones who have made this point about the endemic institutional racism of social science research. Banks (1995), Barakan (1992), and Shuey (1958), among many others spread across the different social science disciplines, have asserted that 'scientific' knowledge has commonly been based on racially biased assumptions, labels, perspectives, etc. From Linneaus' 1735 categorization that related race to psychological attributes and positioned the white race as having superior psychological attributes (Webster, 1992) and Caldwell's similar contentions in 1830 to *The Bell Curve* (Herrnstein and Murray, 1994) and the works of Shockley (1992) in the present era, scientists and social scientists have used racist ideas regarding inherited characteristics of different racial groups (Banks, 1995).

Unfortunately, educational researchers have been and continue to be key participants in this reproduction and elaboration of institutional racism. Examples of such racism by educational researchers in the past include the mental and intellectual measures taken from 'cranium estimates', 'theories of racial difference' taken from anthropology and biology, 'theories of race and intelligence' taken from genetics, and 'curriculum theories' that argued that 'Black families and Black communities . . . were "defective" and "dysfunctional"'' (McCarthy, 1993, p. 332; see, also, Gould, 1981). While the use of these racially oriented 'cranium estimates' or other such categories would now be considered unacceptable, label-based institutional racism continues to exist. For example, higher percentages of students of color are currently more likely to be labeled 'at-risk', 'learning disabled', or 'emotionally disturbed' (see, for example, Cuban, 1989; Mercer, 1988; Ortiz, 1986).

But, while institutional racism is more widespread than commonly realized (see Hacker, 1992; Feagin and Vera, 1995) and while expanding our understanding of it is critically important, institutional racism is not epistemological racism. For instance, one could use either racist or anti-racist concepts or labels within a positivist or a constructivist epistemology, but research epistemologies themselves are not necessarily a function of the concepts or labels with which they are used. (This could be argued to be not true for the critical tradition; many of its advocates would consider racist assumptions to be incongruent with its epistemology, but this will be addressed later.) Our point, similar to the point we have made about individual racism, is that researchers who think that epistemological racism is equal to institutional racism misunderstand the former.

Societal Racism

The second type of social racism is *societal racism*. Societal racism is similar to institutional racism, but it exists on a broader, society-wide scale, though societal racism has received even less attention than institutional racism. In fact, it usually takes major social conflicts, like those of the mid and late 1960s, or major social events, like the OJ Simpson trial, for societal racism to receive broad social attention, as, for example, in the *Report of The National Advisory Commission on Civil Disorders* (1968). This report is, of course, the one that used the often quoted statement that 'Our nation is moving toward two societies, one black, one white — separate and unequal' (*ibid*, p. 1). This report also argued that the 'most fundamental' (*ibid*, p. 5) cause of the inequitable bifurcation was a long-term national history of 'white racism' (*ibid*, p. 5) and that this racism deeply pervaded numerous facets of national life, from employment and housing to education and political representation.

Societal racism, then, can be said to exist when prevailing societal or cultural assumptions, norms, concepts, habits, expectations, etc. favor one race over one or more other races (Hacker, 1992; Feagin and Vera, 1995). For example, while it is certainly true that there is a complex range of definitions of what good leadership is within the mainstream of public life in the US, that range is actually relatively limited when compared to definitions of good leadership in other cultures, inside or outside the US. The widely respected anthropologist, James Clifford (1988), has demonstrated how mainstream definitions of leadership served as a disadvantage to a Native American tribe, known as the Mashpee. In a US trial held to determine the validity of the Mashpee's status as a tribe, the mainstream culture's definition of leadership was used to weaken the testimony of the Mashpee chief, especially in terms of proving whether the chief was a 'true' or 'real' leader. This 'proof' of a leadership deficiency was then used to undermine the legitimacy of the Mashpee's claim to be a tribe.

Similarly, if the socially promoted idea — through the media, through legal practices, through governmental programs — of what a good family is, is primarily drawn from the dominant culture's social, historical experience, that is societal racism. The privileging of one view over others, like the favoring of a white middle-class view of families over an African-American view[9] of families, results in social practices that have direct negative effects on families that deviate from the dominant norm (Billingsley, 1968; Hill, 1972; Littlejohn-Blake and Darling, 1993; Stanfield, 1985, p. 408; Willis, 1993). The idea that a Mashpee definition of leadership or an African-American definition of a family might be considered as equal to a mainstream definitions is typically not seen as reasonable or warranted in formal or informal social practices.

However, societal racism is, also, not epistemological racism. The latter is drawn from a more fundamental level than societal racism; epistemological racism comes from or emerges out of what we have labeled the civilizational level, the deepest, most primary level of a culture of people. The civilization level is the level that encompasses the deepest, most primary assumptions about the nature of reality (ontology), the ways of knowing that reality (epistemology), and the disputational contours of right and wrong or morality and values (axiology) — in short, presumptions about the the real, the true, and the good. But these presumptions emerge from a broader terrain than just the US; the presumptions to which we refer are fundamental to Euro-American modernism, the historical period within which the ontologies, epistemologies, and axiologies of contemporary Western Civilization have arisen (see, for example, Bernstein, 1992; or Lyotard, 1984). Our argument, then, is that epistemological racism is drawn from the civilizational level, and, thus, it is to the civilizational level that we must turn to engage directly the question of whether our research epistemologies are racially biased or not.

Civilizational Racism

The civilizational level is the level of broad civilizational assumptions, assumptions that, though they construct the nature of our world and our experience of it, are not typically conscious to most members of a civilization (Foucault, 1979 and 1988). These assumptions are deeply embedded in how those members think and in what they name 'the world' or 'the Real' through various categories or concepts (Said, 1979; Stanfield, 1985 and 1994). But these assumptions are different for different civilizations, such as the Hopi civilization (Loftin, 1991) or the Zuni civilization (Roscoe, 1991), and, thus, each civilization constructs the world differently for its inhabitants: 'Not all people (i.e., civilizations, in this case) "know" in the same way' (Stanfield, 1985, p. 396). In addition, large, complex civilizations often include a dominant culture and one or more subordinate cultures. In this context, subordinate cultures, races, and other groups often have different civilizational assumptions: 'Just as the material realities of the powerful and the dominated produce separate (social, historical experiences) . . . , each (racial or social group) may also have distinctive epistemologies or theories of knowledge' (Collins, 1991, p. 204). One consequence is that '(d)ominant racial group members and subordinate racial group members do not think and interpret realities in the same way because of their divergent structural positions, histories, and cultures' (Stanfield, 1985, p. 400).[10] For instance, 'What is considered theory in the dominant academic community is not necessarily what counts as theory for women-of-color' (Anzaldúa, 1990, p. xxv; see, also, Banks, 1993, pp. 7–8; Banks, 1995, p. 16; Cose, 1993; Collins, 1991).

The name for the Euro-American culture's construction of 'the world' or 'the Real', as was noted above, is modernism. Modernism is an epistemological, ontological, and axiological network or grid that 'makes' the world as the dominant Western culture knows and sees it (Foucault, 1972, 1973, 1979 and 1988; Frankenberg, 1993; Goldberg, 1993; Stanfield, 1985; West, 1993). Though this grid has evolved and changed to some degree, it has, nonetheless, maintained a kind of coherence and consistency, particularly in terms of some of its primary assumptions (that is, its civilizational level assumptions). One of these primary assumptions, the one we are addressing here, is *civilizational racism*.

Beginning with the modernist period, European colonial and territorial expansion was typically undertaken under the rationale of the supremacy of white civilization, along with other rationales, such as those about economics and religion. For instance, Hacker (1992) asserts that 'For at least half a dozen centuries, . . . "white" has implied a higher civilization based on superior inheritance' (p. 7) (see, also, Takaki, 1993). To the English attending the Globe Theater in order to see Shakespeare's *The Tempest*, 'Caliban (the character who epitomizes the native people of the "new" world) represented what Europeans had been when they were *lower* (emphasis added) on the scale of development' (*ibid*, p. 32), while Prospero (the character who depicts the English conqueror) declares that he came to the new world 'to be the lord on't' (Shakespeare, quoted in *ibid*, p. 35; see, also, Feagin and Vera, 1995; Frankenberg, 1993; Goldberg, 1993; Harris, 1993; Stanfield, 1985; Webster, 1992; West, 1993, pp. 3–32). Widely circulated racial hierarchies and exclusions, such as these, became then a central feature in the emergence of Western modernism and modernist thought and, consequently, white racism or white supremacy became interlaced or interwoven into the founding fabric of modernist

Western civilization (for an extended discussion of this point, see, Goldberg, 1993, but also see Stanfield, 1985).[11]

These racial rationales were, of course, central, along with other rationales, to the founding of the US. Taking land from and killing Native Americans was justified by the whites' definition of property as well as the supposed supremacy of white civilization — like that depicted in Thomas More's *Utopia* (Takaki, 1993, p. 35; see, also, Feagin and Vera, 1995; Hacker, 1992; Harris, 1993). Similar rationales were used in taking the Southwest from the Mexicans, whom Stephen F. Austin, one of the prominent political leaders of the 'Texas revolution', disparagingly called 'a mongrel Spanish-Indian and negro race' (De León, 1983, p. 12; see, also, Takaki, 1993). The enslavement of African-Americans and the 'subsequent decades of Jim Crow laws, peonage, tenancy, lynchings and second-class citizenship' (West, 1993, p. 256) were also justified in the same racially exclusionary terms (Feagin and Vera, 1995; Hacker, 1992; Harris, 1993; Takaki, 1993), though, of course, these justifications were not the only justifications driving slavery or the appropriation of Native American and Mexican-American land.

While this is an extremely brief summary of a complex argument about white racial supremacy and the fact that it was interlaced within the founding assumptions of Western civilization, our point can be made in a simpler way. The white race, what Stanfield (1985) has called 'a privileged subset of the population' (p. 389), has unquestionably dominated Western civilization during all of the modernist period (hundreds of years). When any group — within a large, complex civilization — significantly dominates other groups for hundreds of years, the ways of the dominant group (its epistemologies, its ontologies, its axiologies) not only become the dominant ways of that civilization, but also these ways become so deeply embedded that they typically are seen as 'natural' or appropriate norms rather than as historically evolved social constructions (*ibid*). To a large degree, the dominant group, whatever its composition, makes its own 'community the center of the universe and the conceptual frame that constrains all thought' (Gordon *et al.*, 1990, p. 15). Thus, the dominant group creates or constructs 'the world' or 'the Real' and does so in its own image, in terms of its ways, its social historical experiences (Banks, 1993; Collins, 1991; Minh-ha, 1989; Morrison, 1992; Stanfield, 1985 and 1994; West, 1993; see, especially, Said, 1979, for an entire volume that discusses how the West gave 'reality' to its construct of 'the Orient').

In this view, ontologies, epistemologies, and axiologies are not outside history or sociology; they are deeply interwoven within the social histories of particular civilizations and within particular groups within those civilizations. As Gordon *et al.* (1990) assert, 'Knowledge, technology, and the production of knowledge are cultural products . . . Knowledge production operates within communicentric (ontological and epistemological) frames of reference, which dominate and enable it' (p. 14). Similarly, Stanfield (1994) has said:

> The experiences that construct paradigms in sciences and humanities are derivatives of cultural baggage imported into intellectual enterprises by privileged residents

of historically specific societies and world systems. This is important to point out, because it is common for scholars to lapse into internal analyses while discussing paradigms and thus to ignore the rather commonsense fact that sciences and humanities are products of specific cultural and historical contexts that shape the character of intellectual work. (pp. 181–2)

Or, as Banks (1993) more simply states, 'all knowledge reflects the values and interests of its creators' (p. 4).

Consider who the major, influential philosophers, writers, politicians, corporate leaders, social scientists, educational leaders (for example, Kant, Flaubert, Churchill, Henry Ford, Weber, Dewey) have been over the course of Western modernism. They have virtually all been white. And, it is they who have constructed the world we live in — named it, discussed it, explained it. It is they who have developed the ontological and axiological categories or concepts, like individuality, truth, education, free enterprise, good conduct, social welfare, etc., that we use to think (that thinks us?) and that we use to socialize and educate children. This racially exclusive group has also developed the epistemologies, the legitimated ways of knowing (for example, positivism, neo-realisms, postpositivisms, interpretivisms, constructivisms, the critical tradition, and postmodernisms/poststructuralisms) that we use. And it is these epistemologies and their allied ontologies and axiologies, taken together as a lived web or fabric of social constructions, that makes or constructs the world or the Real (and that relegates other socially constructed 'worlds', like that of African-Americans or the Cherokee, to the 'margins' of our social life and to the margins in terms of legitimated research epistemologies).

These influential people and their 'world-making' or 'reality-making' activities or practices, however, are not separate from the social history within which they live: 'all knowledge is relative to the context in which it is generated' (Gordon *et al.*, 1990, p. 15). And, thus, 'when academics and public opinion leaders construct knowledge(,) . . . they are influenced by the ideas, assumptions, and norms of the cultures and subsocieties in which they are socialized' (Banks, 1995, p. 16). Just as Julius Caesar was 'constructed' by the social history of his particular group, saw and understood the world in terms of the social constructions of his people in their time and place, the influential authors of modernism have been constructed by their position, place, and time. Just as Caesar did not see the world from the point of view of other cultures that Rome dominated, these influential Western modernists did not see the world from within the epistemologies and ontologies of other races and cultures inside or outside of Western modernism. 'How we create, define, and validate social knowledge (and, thus, reality) is determined largely through our cultural context' (Stanfield, 1985, p. 388).[12]

Our argument, however, is not that these influential white individuals were involved in a racial conspiracy or moral bad faith, but that these individuals can only name and know from within the social context available to them, from within the social history in which they live. While we seem to have little trouble understanding that those far away in time existed in terms of their social contexts, i.e., Julius Caesar, we seem to resist understanding this about ourselves. We, as our predecessors did, live, understand, work, think, and act within a particular social history, within a particular social construction. We do not live, in some universal sense, above culture or history; we live inside a culture, inside a civilizational social construction; we live in the terms and ways of a particular social history.[13]

This, then, is our central argument about epistemological racism. Epistemologies, along with their related ontologies and epistemologies, arise out the social history of a particular social group. Different social groups, races, cultures, societies, or civilizations evolve different epistemologies, each of which reflects the social history of that group, race, culture, society, or civilization; that is, no epistemology is context-free. Yet, all of the epistemologies currently legitimated in education arise exclusively out of the social history of the dominant white race. They do not arise out of the social history of African-Americans, Hispanic-Americans, Native Americans, Asian-Americans, or other racial/cultural groups — social histories that are much different than that of the dominant race (a difference due at least partially to the historical experience of racism itself (see, for example, Collins, 1991)). Cornell West (1993) validates this judgment when he says 'social practices . . . (and research is a social practice) are best understood and explained . . . by situating them within . . . cultural traditions' (p. 267). It is, then, in this sense that scholars of color contend that the dominant research epistemologies are racially biased.[14]

By epistemological racism, then, we do not mean that the researchers using, say, positivism or postmodernism are overtly or covertly racist as individuals. Nor do we mean that epistemological racism is a conscious institutional or societal conspiracy in favor of whites (Gordon, 1993, p. 267). Epistemological racism means that our current range of research epistemologies — positivism to postmodernisms/poststructuralisms — arise out of the social history and culture of the dominant race, that these epistemologies logically reflect and reinforce that social history and that racial group (while excluding the epistemologies of other races/cultures), and that this has negative results for people of color in general and scholars of color in particular. In other words, our 'logics of inquiry' (Stanfield, 1993a) are the social products and practices of the social, historical experiences of whites, and, therefore, these products and practices carry forward the social history of that group and exclude the epistemologies of other social groups. But, again, the critical problem — for all of us, both whites and people of color — is that the resulting epistemological racism, besides unnecessarily restricting or excluding the range of possible epistemologies, creates profoundly negative consequences for those of other racial cultures with different epistemologies, ontologies, and axiologies.

The Negative Consequences of Epistemological Racism

First, epistemologies and research that arise out of other social histories, such as African-American social history or Cherokee social history, are not typically considered legitimate within the mainstream research community (see Anzaldúa, 1990; Collins, 1991; Gordon, 1990 and 1993; Minh-ha, 1985; Sarris, 1993; Stanfield, 1993a, 1993b and 1994; among many others). As Reyes and Halcon (1988) suggest, 'the traditional Euro-centric perspective used to evaluate their (scholars of color) scholarship disadvantages nontraditional (race-based) research because predominantly white male academics lack the appropriate cultural perspectives from which to judge its real merit' (p. 307). Similarly, Collins (1991) contends that '(w)hile black women can produce knowledge claims that contest those advanced by the white male community, this community does not grant that black women scholars have competing knowledge claims based in another (equally warranted) knowledge validation process' (p. 204) (see, also, Stanfield, 1994, p. 176). Or, as Sarris (1993) asks, 'Can Apache stories, songs, and so forth be read (or heard) and thus understood in terms of Euroamerican-specific expectations of language and narrative (i.e., Euro-American epistemologies)' (p. 427)?

Second, there has been a large chorus of scholars of color (including Anderson, 1993; Anzaldúa, 1990; Collins, 1991; Paredes, 1977; Sarris, 1993; Stanfield, 1994; among others) who have contended that dominant group epistemologies and methodologies — the epistemologies and methods themselves and not just 'bad' applications of these epistemologies and methodologies — tend to distort the lives of other racial groups. For example, Gordon *et al.* (1990) have asserted that

> Examination of the social and educational research knowledge bases relative to Afro-Americans indicated that these sciences have traditionally attempted to understand the life experiences of Afro-Americans from a narrow cultrocentric perspective and against equally narrow cultrocentric standards (i.e., epistemological racism). (p. 15)

Consequently, as Stanfield (1985) has said, mainstream '(s)ocial science knowledge production about racial minorities still dwells on the pathological and on the sensational' (p. 411). A result of this is that these negative distortions pass into the dominant culture as 'truth', thus becoming the basis of individual, group, and institutional attitudes, decisions, practices, and policies (i.e, institutional and societal racism). Another result is that these distortions are often encultured into those who are the victims of the distortions (hooks, 1990; Rebolledo, 1990), especially children who have less ability to resist (McCarthy, 1993; Stevenson and Ellsworth, 1993; Weinberg, 1993), necessitating 'painful struggle(s) of accepting and rejecting internalized negative and disenabling self-conceptions' (West, 1993, p. 270; see, also, Banks, 1993). A further result is that, frequently, 'minority scholar's time is consumed in efforts to refute or neutralize fallacious findings, questionable theories, and inappropriate interpretations' (Gordon *et al.*, 1990, p. 16) of mainstream research and scholarly commentary.

Third, the dominant research epistemologies — from positivism to postmodernisms — implicitly favor white people because they accord most easily with their social history (Banks, 1993; Gordon, 1993; Stanfield, 1985). Thus, even though it may be unintended, the 'clothes', that an epistemology could be said to be, fit better and are more comfortable to white researchers because white researchers themselves are a product of the social history of whites, just as the dominant epistemologies are a product of white social history. That is, the range of epistemologies that have arisen from the social history of whites 'fits' whites because they themselves, the nature of the university and of legitimated scholarship and knowledge, and the specifications of different research methodologies are all cultural products of white social history. While scholars of color have had to wear these 'white' clothes (be bicultural) so that they could succeed in research communities, however sociologically, historically, or culturally ill fitting those clothes might be, white scholars have virtually never had to think about wearing the epistemological clothes of people of color or even to consider the idea of such 'strange' apparel. The negative consequence for scholars of color, however, is that they must learn and become accomplished in epistemologies that arises out of a social history that has been profoundly hostile to their race and that ignores or excludes alternative race-based epistemologies because mainstream research communities have assumed that their epistemologies are not derived from any particular group's social history, i.e., are free of any specific history or culture. That scholars of color have successfully become epistemologically bicultural to survive as scholars is a testament to them — their strength, their courage, their perseverance, and their love of scholarship — rather than a testament to the race/culture-free nature of mainstream research epistemologies.

The critical tradition might argue, however, that it has not participated in the production of these negative consequences, that it has consistently opposed racism in all of its many aspects or forms (for examples of critical tradition-based, anti-racist work, see Scheurich and Imber, 1991; Scheurich and Laible, 1995; among many others). And to a significant extent this is true. Many white scholars have literally devoted their careers to anti-racism. In addition, the critical tradition has for many scholars of color been the only epistemologically friendly set of 'clothes' (West, 1993, pp. 78–9; Stanfield, 1994). Some scholars of color even contend that, to some extent, the 'new' epistemologies (to be discussed shortly) based on the sociocultural histories of people of color are derived from the critical tradition (for example, Gordon *et al.*, 1990, pp. 18–19). Consequently, it is important that the critical tradition be honored for its anti-racist work and insight and its willingness to question and oppose racism in environments that are often hostile to such efforts.

Nonetheless, the critical tradition, even if more favored by intellectuals of color, is itself almost exclusively drawn from white social history, from what Stanfield (1985) has called 'European-derived paradigms' (p. 399). The critical tradition's ontology, epistemology, and axiology are predominantly the creation of white scholars and their social context (for example, Gordon, 1993, or Stanfield, 1994). Cornell West (1993), one of the eminent scholars of the critical tradition, argues, therefore, that the dependency of intellectuals of color on the critical tradition may be 'debilitating for black intellectuals because the cathartic needs it (critical theory) satisfies tend to stifle the further development of black critical consciousness and attitudes' (p. 79). In addition, virtually all of the different critical approaches, including critical theory, feminism, lesbian/gay orientations and critical postmodernism, have been repeatedly cited for their racial biases (see, for example, Alarco'n, 1990; Bell, 1992; Frankenberg, 1993; hooks, 1990; Huggins, 1991; Minh-ha, 1989; Stanfield, 1994, pp. 179–81; Stevenson and Ellsworth, 1993; West, 1993). Consequently, as

Ellsworth (1989) as argued in a different context, while critical theory has been important to anti-racist efforts and perhaps important to the development of new race-based epistemologies, it is not necessarily the appropriate epistemological frame for all race-oriented emancipatory work. Advocates for the critical tradition, therefore, need to support the emergence and acceptance of other epistemologies that are derived from different racial or cultural social histories,[15] to which a brief introduction follows.

'New' Race-Based Epistemologies

One prominent example of an effort to develop, and apply, a 'new' race-based epistemology (some of them actually are historically 'old') is Patricia Hill Collins' *Black Feminist Thought* (1991). In this important work, she has a chapter entitled, 'Toward an Afrocentric feminist epistemology', in which she names and discusses the four 'contours' (p. 206) or characteristics of her race-based epistemology: 'concrete experience as a criterion of meaning' (pp. 208–12), 'the use of dialogue in assessing knowledge claims' (pp. 212–15), 'the ethic of caring' (pp. 215–17), and 'the ethic of personal accountability' (pp. 217–19). To develop this epistemology, she says she 'searched my own experience and those of African-American women I know for themes we thought were important', and she relied 'on the voices of black women from all walks of life' (p. 202), many of whom she cites and discusses in her explanation of the four 'contours'. Accordingly, her Afrocentric feminist epistemology, 'like all specialized thought (such as positivism to postmodernisms), reflects the interests and standpoint of its creators' (p. 201).

That this epistemology is respected by other black women is evidenced by the fact that Gloria Ladson-Billings (1995) recently published, in the *American Educational Research Journal*, results from a three-year research study[16] that uses Collins' Afrocentric feminist epistemology as her 'theoretical grounding' (p. 471).[17] Ladson-Billings, in her study of 'successful teachers of African-American children' (p. 471), after stating her choice of Collins' epistemology, briefly discusses each of Collins' four contours and her use of them to provide the epistemological grounding for her study of these successful teachers. Ladson-Billings' appropriate concern is to select an epistemology that reflects 'who I am, what I believe, what experiences I have had', given her 'membership in a marginalized racial/cultural group' (*ibid*, p. 470). That is, she chooses to use an epistemological frame that 'fits' her social history, that emerges out of her race/culture's social history, rather than an epistemological frame that has emerged out of the social history of the dominant race.

But Collins is not the only one who has developed a race-based epistemology, nor is she the first. Molefi Kete Asante has for some time advocated an Afrocentric epistemology that he has developed through a relatively large body of work (for example, 1987, 1988, 1990 and 1993), and this work, along with that of other African-American scholars advocating a similar perspective, has inspired or supported a wide range of scholarship, including that of Azibo (1990), Baldwin (1981), Banks (1992), Gordon (1990 and 1993), Kershaw (1989 and 1992), King (1990),

Taylor (1987), among numerous others (see, also, the entire issue of *The Journal of Negro Education*, volume 61, number 3, guest edited by Edmund W. Gordon). From Asante's viewpoint (1993), 'Afrocentricity is *a perspective which allows Africans to be subjects of (their own) historical experiences rather than objects* (author's emphasis) on the fringes of Europe (i.e., Western modernism)' (p. 2). Later in the same book, Asante, in a chapter entitled 'On Afrocentric metatheory', briefly discusses the 'cosmological issue' (pp. 106–7), the 'epistemological issue' (pp. 107–8), the 'axiological issue' (p. 108), and the 'aesthetic issue' (pp. 108–9), four issues that he sees as central to Afrocentricity. In 'Afrocentrism and the Afrocentric method', Kershaw (1992) discusses the steps of an 'Afrocentric emancipatory methodology', a method that includes qualitative methodology, analysis and description of the data collected, critical dialogue with those involved in the research, education, and action, all leading to the generation of Afrocentric knowledge. Kershaw cites John Gwaltney's *Drylongso: A Self Portrait of Black America* (1980) as 'an excellent example of Afrocentric generated practical knowledge' (p. 165).

More recently, another race-based epistemology has begun to gain the attention of 'progressive intellectuals of color' (West, 1995, p. xi). This epistemological perspective originated in legal studies. According to West,

> Critical race theorists have, for the first time, examined the entire edifice of contemporary legal thought and doctrine from the viewpoint of law's role in the construction and maintenance of social domination and subordination. In the process, they not only challenged the basic assumptions and presuppositions of the prevailing paradigms among mainstream liberals and conservatives in the legal academy, but also confronted the relative silence of legal radicals — namely critical legal studies writers — who 'deconstructed' liberalism, yet seldom addressed the role of deep-seated racism in American life. (*ibid*, p. xi)

However, this perspective has just begun to migrate from legal studies into the social sciences generally and into education specifically.[18] That this migration is occurring, though, is evidenced by a 'call for papers' on critical race theory for the *International Journal of Qualitative Studies in Education*, under the special issue editorship of Donna Deyhle, Laurence Parker, and Sofia Villenas of the Department of Educational Studies at the University of Utah.

Most white scholars are, however, unfamiliar with this race-based range of work because it often appears in explicitly race-oriented academic journals (like *The Journal of Negro Education*) or in books by race-oriented publishers (like Africa World Press) that have typically been started because of the lack of acceptance, in mainstream journals or by mainstream presses, of research on African-Americans by African-Americans using African-American perspectives. For example, Padilla (1994) suggests that the lack of research on African-Americans in six of the leading APA journals, may be 'because the peer-reviewing process serves the gatekeeping function of excluding research that does not conform to acceptable *paradigms* (emphasis added) or methodologies' (p. 250). Similarly, Gordon (1990) says,

> The number of Black Studies libraries at universities and at private and public collections around the country bears witness to an enormous body of literature written by African-American scholars, while the academy gives little credence or visibility to this work in preservice and inservice discussions. This curricular gap says as much about *the theories and paradigms* (emphasis added) embraced and disseminated by university faculty as do the resulting pedagogical practices and worldviews of teachers, principals, and school districts. (pp. 89–90)

In other words, the very existence of these journals is one of the consequences of the mainstream exclusion of race-based epistemologies and the research resulting from these perspectives; the problem, of course, for scholars of color is that for tenure and promotion these race-oriented journals are not as respected as the mainstream ones.

It is not our intention, however, to privilege some of the race-based epistemologies over others. The ones we have briefly introduced here are those we have become most familiar with and those that we increasingly see being used in educational research. There are other efforts to develop these new race-based epistemologies and extensive arguments among scholars of color about these epistemologies, but a comprehensive survey of these race-based epistemologies and current discussions of them would require an entire article (an article we would certainly like to read). Our point is that these new epistemologies exist and that they need to be understood, respected, and discussed, just as those epistemologies that have been produced by dominant race are understood, respected, and discussed.

What is to be Done?

> Research needs to be based on the reality of our (Hopi) existence as we experience it, not just from the narrow and limited view American universities carried over from the German research tradition. (Hopi Tribal Council Chairman Vernon Masayesva, quoted in Krupat, 1993, p. xix)

While there has been a powerful social tendency among whites and white society to define racism in individual terms or, at best, in limited institutional terms, such as in hiring or promotion, we do not think most white researchers consciously support racism in any terms — individual, institutional, societal, or civilizational. But this intention is not sufficient if our argument here is a persuasive one. In a very important sense, we white researchers are unconsciously promulgating racism on an epistemological level. As we teach and promote epistemologies like positivism to postmodernism, we are, at least implicitly, teaching and promoting the social history of the dominant race at the exclusion of people of color, scholars of color, and the possibility for research based on other race/culture epistemologies. We can, however, use our opposition to racism to consider the question of whether our dominant epistemologies are racially biased or not and, if they are, to begin to change this situation.[19]

The single, most important effort needed is to initiate a vigorous debate/dialogue among scholars of all races, including particularly those who write the commonly used methods textbooks. Of all the myriad issues crucial to educational research, surely this ought to be a hotly debated one. For instance, we know there are many scholars who would oppose our contention that epistemologies arise out of the social history of specific groups. Many traditional researchers or social scientists, for instance, argue that their epistemology reaches above history toward a context-free kind of truth. Let these scholars join the discussion. Let them lay out their arguments in public debate. Let us have a fierce row over this. If the possibility that our typical epistemologies are racially biased is not genuinely worth the price of a spirited intellectual conflict, what is?

Second, those of us who teach methods courses must begin to study, teach, and, thus, legitimate the research epistemologies that arise out of the social histories of people of color. Often 'students get the message either directly or indirectly that ethnic-related research is not something that they should engage in as part of their training or for their dissertation research' (Padilla, 1994, p. 24). As professors, we need to support an informed understanding and skillful use of these race-based epistemologies by interested students of color. (But we ought not to try to force them in this direction as most students of color typically know that race-oriented scholarship is more risky than mainstream-oriented scholarship.) As scholars, we need to add race-oriented journals to our own reading lists, and we need to increase our valuation of those journals during tenure and promotion proceedings. As dissertation chairs, we must support doctoral studies drawn from these new race-based epistemologies. As journal editors, editorial board members, and journal reviewers we must study and support the publication both of discussions of these epistemologies and of studies based on them, like that of Ladson-Billings (1995). Even better, we need to solicit this kind of work, including doing special editions of our journals. As editors and reviewers for publishing companies, we must insist on the inclusion of race-based perspectives in methods textbooks.

We know that efforts of these sorts are possible. We have taught research methods courses in which we cover other race/culture-based epistemologies (African-American, Hispanic-American, Native American, Asian American, among other racial designations), along with positivism to poststructuralisms. We have class members help find new materials, and the students of color are continuously educating us through their class discussions of the materials and through their written work. In addition, other professors at our university have become interested in this approach, and there is now serious discussion of a college-wide course of this sort. Furthermore, we know of professors at other universities who have been doing the same. In addition, as the new editor and managing editor of a respected academic journal, we support and promote the publication of scholarship discussing race-based epistemologies and research based on those perspectives.[20]

Obviously these suggestions are insufficient, but they are only intended as initial steps toward a crucially needed conversation that to-date, unfortunately, has largely been attended to only by scholars of color. But our hope is that other white researchers will join this conversation because we have been able, hopefully, to provide a useful discussion of just what *epistemological racism* is. We especially hope that those who write, or are considering writing, research methods textbooks will join this conversation.

Racism of any sort is heinous, most terribly for its victims but also for its perpetrators.[21] One of the worst racisms, though, for any generation or group is the one that we do not see, that is invisible to our lenses, the one we participate in without consciously knowing or intending it. Are we not seeing the biases of our time just like those a hundred years ago did not see the biases of their time? Will those who look back at us in time wonder why we resisted seeing our racism? The unfortunate truth is that we can be strongly anti-racist in our own minds but be promulgating racism in profound ways we do not understand (Pine and Hilliard, 1990, p. 595). As Cose (1993) says in *The Rage of a Privileged Class*, 'people do not have to be racist — or have any malicious intent — in order to make decisions that unfairly harm members of another race' (p. 4). It is our contention here, based on the seminal, ground-breaking work of scholars of color, that we educational researchers are unintentionally involved, at the epistemological heart of our research enterprises, in a racism — epistemological racism — that we generally do not see or understand. Once we see and understand it, though, we cannot continue in our old ways. To do so would be to betray our fundamental commitment as educators and as educational researchers.

Notes

1 Although the scholars of color, who address the issue of whether our epistemologies are racially biased, do not name all of the specific epistemologies to which they are applying this question, we argue that this judgment can justifiably be applied to a broad range of currently 'popular' epistemologies, including positivism, postpositivisms, neo-realisms, interpretivisms, constructivisms, the critical tradition, and postmodernisms/poststructuralisms (all of which are briefly defined in endnote #3).

2 Race, undeniably, is a tricky social construction: to use it is to reinforce it as really 'real', to naturalize it (Webster, 1992); to not use it is to act as if race were no longer a significant differentiating variable in social life (Wright, 1994) or in enducation and research (Webster, 1992). In some Southern states, in the past, to have but one drop of African-American blood was, according to law, to be an African-American, while today the race of a child of parents of two different races is problematic or, even, a personal choice on some official forms. Race, then, has always been a mobile construct. As Rizvi (1993) says, race as a construct 'is continually changing, being challenged, interrupted, and reconstructed, in the actual practices in which people engage' (p. 129) and in the discourses they employ (see, also, Toni Morrison's *Playing in the Dark: Whiteness and the Literary Imagination* (1992) for one discussion of this issue). By race, we mean historically and socially situated, race-based cultures that are tied both positively (i.e., cultural pride) and negatively (i.e., racism) to skin color (see, for instance, Lee, 1995). We understand, however, both that skin color within 'one' race can vary considerably and that the experience of a race-based culture by its members can also vary considerably. We also understand that the growing, though still relatively small, number of bi-racial or, even, tri-racial individuals significantly complicates what a particular race-based

culture is and who is a member. We would, nonetheless, argue that there are a range of 'positive' consistencies or features within a race-based culture that make it a culture, such as the Mexican-American one (though we would not say that all of those consistencies or features apply equally to all members). We would also argue that the 'negative' external force of persistent racism, past and present, against these race-based cultures is a significant factor in maintaining these cultures as more or less consistent entities that could be called a 'culture' (for a provocative discussion of these issues, see Appiah, 1992).

3   We define 'positivism' as the traditional application of the scientific method within the social sciences. We are aware, nonetheless, of the debates about whether this is the appropriate label or not and agree that strictly speaking it is not (Phillips, 1987), but language, as usual, is at least partially uncontrollable, and, thus, it seems that the meaning we give it is the one that has passed into common academic parlance. With 'postpositivisms', we concur with Guba and Lincoln (1994) that they represent 'efforts of the past few decades to respond in a limited way (that is, while remaining within essentially the same set of basic beliefs) to the most problematic criticisms of positivism' (p. 109). By 'neo-realisms', we mean that range of realisms, including scientific realism (for example, Bhaskar, 1986 and 1989) and coherentist realism (for example, Evers and Lakomski, 1991), that has sought, similarly to postpositivism, to address the strong criticisms of the scientific method that have emerged over the past few decades, while maintaining the basic validity of the scientific method. By 'interpretivisms' and 'constructivisms', we agree with Schwandt (1994) that they are 'a loosely coupled family of methodological and philosophical persuasions . . . that share the goal of understanding the complex world of lived experience from the point of view of those who live it' (p. 118). Within the 'critical tradition', we include critical theory, feminism, and lesbian/gay perspectives, all of which start from the experiences of a social group that has been excluded, marginalized, or oppressed over lengthy historical periods, which typically include a critique of social inequities related to those experiences, and which work toward, directly or indirectly, some sort of emancipatory social change for those groups. By postmodernisms/poststructuralisms, we include the work of the French theorists, like Foucault, Irigaray, and Derrida, that subjects the fundamental, civilizational assumptions of modernism itself to critique. But we also include in this category the work of many others, like that of Patti Lather (1991) or Judith Butler (1993), who have extensively appropriated this philosophy to their own interests.

4   While our focus is on 'epistemological racism', a similar argument to the one we have made here could be made about 'ontological racism' or 'axiological racism' all three of which, we say later, are aspects of the 'civilizational level'. Of course, none of these three can really be separated from each other; an epistemological position, an ontological position, and an axiological position are 'strongly' interdependent. However, we focus here on 'epistemological racism' because we are researchers and because research itself is the techniques or processes for 'producing knowledge' within a particular epistemology. In a certain sense, then, research, as techniques and processes, is 'housed' within epistemo' ʒₑy, rather than within ontology or axiology, though, as we said above, any particular epistemology is interdependent with a particular ontology or axiology. This is not to say, though, that ontological or axiological positions are not fundamental to research; in fact, we would hope someone would provide a discussion of axiological racism for researchers.

5   We do not mean to imply that these categories exhaust all types of racism, though we believe they are reasonably comprehensive. We also do not mean to imply that our

category schema is better than others, such as those of Dube (1985); virtually all cat-egory schema in the social sciences are heuristic devices, the utility of which must be evaluated within the discourse in which they are used. As Banks (1993) says of his knowledge categories, 'The . . . categories approximate, but do not describe, reality in its total complexity. The categories are useful conceptual tools. . . . (but) the relationship between the . . . categories of knowledge is dynamic and interactive rather than static' (p. 6).

6   For those familiar with the poststructuralist work of Foucault, we would argue that what we are here calling the 'civilizational' level is somewhat similar to an 'archaeological' level, the level, that is, at which the 'real' is constituted. In his genealogical period, however, Foucault would oppose the structuralist metaphor of levels (though his archae-ological works have been argued to be structuralist [see Gutting, 1989]); he would argue, in this later work, that all 'levels' occur at the level of human activity (*ibid*). While we agree with his latter or genealogical position, our diagram of the 'levels' of racism and our argument is based on a structuralist metaphor, one in which each subsequent level is deeper and broader than the prior one. We have done it this way because the struc-turalist bias is so deeply embedded in all of us that it is remarkably difficult to draw a readily understandable graphic that can portray multiple influences, some of which are more fundamental or more primary or more constitutional than others, while drawing them all at the same 'level'. We have, consequently, adopted a structuralist metaphor (graphic) in the interest of making our larger point about the racial bias of research epi-stemologies more accessible. However, our focus on the 'civilizational' level actually grows out of a larger project in which one of us (Scheurich) has drawn from the archae-ological work of Foucault (1972, 1973, 1979 and 1988) to formulate a poststructuralist approach to social theory and research methodology. For those interested in seeing the initial efforts to sketch the outlines of that project, see 'Policy archaeology: A new policy studies methodology' (Scheurich, 1994a).

7   The difference between white racism and the racism of people of color is a highly contentious issue. We strongly agree with Tatum (1992) who, in the context of an article about her personal experiences as teacher of a course entitled 'Group exploration of racism' and attended primarily by white students (who typically evaluate the course as one of their best college educational experiences) says, 'a distinction must be made between the negative racial attitudes held by individuals of color and white individuals, because it is only the attitudes of whites that routinely carry with them the social power inherent in the systematic cultural reinforcement and institutionalization of those racial prejudices. To distinguish the prejudices of students of color from the racism of white students is *not* (her emphasis) to say the former is acceptable and the latter is not; both are clearly problematic. The distinction is important, however, to identify the power differential between members of the dominant and subordinate groups' (p. 3). Similarly, Hacker (1992) says that 'Individuals who do not have power may hold racist views, but they seldom cause much harm' (p. 29; see, also, Feagin and Vera, 1995, pp. ix–x). Con-sequently, for individual racism, we have stated our definitions in race-neutral terms, though the tendency to define racism solely as individual is chiefly done by whites; for all of the other types of racism we discuss, our definitions are constructed in terms of the racism of the dominant group.

8   Numerous scholars of race argue that this social consensus is 'lip-service' opposition to racism and not a real commitment (see, for example, Howitt and Owusu-Bempah, 1990, for a discussion of this). Unhappily, our classroom experience with white students validates this. These students will readily support racial equality, but the distance between

that initial verbal support and a strong commitment to change racial inequalities is very large.

9 We are not suggesting that either of the two mentioned groups — Hopi or African-American — are completely homogeneous or would totally agree on what good leadership is. Nonetheless, if US society were seriously drawing on ideas of what good leadership is from these two or from the many other race/culture groups within this society, there is little doubt that the presidential campaign would be significantly altered. For instance, Hopi ideas of leadership are much different because for the traditional Hopi all acts are sacred acts (Loftin, 1991), an approach very foreign to US presidential campaigns. See Stanfield (1993a, pp. 19–25) for an insightful discussion of this issue.

10 This assumption that dominant culture and a non-dominant culture, both within the same society, can 'see' the same event in entirely different ways — through different cultural 'lenses' — is recently apparent with the OJ Simpson trial. Near the end of the trial but prior to the verdict, over 70 per cent of those in the dominant white culture believed Simpson was guilty, while over 60 per cent of those in the African-American culture believed Simpson was not guilty. Each group was seeing differently, in our opinion, because each was looking through the lens of a different social history.

11 Pre-modernist Europe typically was biased against 'barbarians', not races; at that time 'race' tended not to be a primary category of exclusion (Goldberg, 1993). West (1993) verifies this when he asserts that 'the first substantial racial division of humankind is found in the influential *Natural System*, (1735) of the preeminent naturalist of the eighteenth century, Carolus Linnaeus' (p. 262). Foucault (1980) also substantiates this view that race emerges as a critical exclusionary category in the modernist period when he says, in reference to the beginning of modernity, that 'the new concept of race tended to obliterate the aristocratic particularities of blood' (p. 148).

12 To argue that these people were influential because they, at least in part, saw beyond or were superior to their social circumstances does not work. WEB DuBois was easily one of the greatest intellectuals of his era or of any era. If anyone can be said to rise above or be superior to her or his time and place, DuBois was that person, but he had only limited influence on the social mainstream during his life and continues to be largely under-appreciated by intellectuals in general. The anti-racist discourse, which itself arose out of the cultural experience of African-Americans, that he 'spoke' was not significantly legitimated in his time and still is not in this one.

13 It is a modernist assumption, one which we disagree with, that subjectivities and discourses to individuals (agents) and their contexts can be separated. That is, modernism posits that an individual (an agent, a subjectivity) can act or think outside of the epistemological, ontological, and axiological web (context, discourses) within which the individual exists. However, we would suggest, following the French poststructuralists, that individualism (agency) or subjectivity itself is a production of the web, context, discourses. Consequently, when we cite influential philosophers, writers, etc., we do not intend to imply that epistemological racism is an individual production. It is not; it is a production of the Western Modernist web, and these influential individuals are 'spoken' by that web. Of course, alternative webs, discourses, contexts do exist. For example, anti-racist discourses do exist, even among a small proportion of whites (though we would argue that this white anti-racism is deeply dependent, for its existence and survival, upon cultures of color and their anti-racist efforts). However, these anti-racist discourses, whether asserted by people of color or whites, have been marginalized within Western Modernism because the anti-racist discourses do not fit the white culture's deeply embedded civilizational assumptions. Whether we are now at an historical moment

when anti-racist discourses might be more significantly influential in the modernist West (which would require a shift in civilizational level assumptions to something that might be called postmodernism), we do not know. We are equally hopeful and sceptical. That this chapter is getting published in a major outlet is hopeful; nonetheless, the central initiating point of this essay is that prior discussions of race-based epistemologies authored by scholars of color have largely been ignored by white research epistemologists and methodologists, a not hopeful fact.

14 A major implication of our argument is a new, and more fundamental, definition of what racism is; it is epistemological and ontological. It is woven at the deepest level into the construction of 'the Real'. That is, racism is primarily located in the founding civilizational categories — the ontology — and the epistemologies that dominate Western civilization. Remedies for racism, then, that focus only on the individual level or even only on the institutional or societal level will be insufficient. What is required is that the 'real' — its dominant ontology and epistemologies — be coconstructed in a relatively equal way by all races/cultures.

15 Race-based discussions of research epistemologies and methodologies by scholars of color in the US, like the many cited here, can provocatively be seen, by critical theorists, as a significant contribution to global postcolonial studies. In fact this US discussion can be seen as an 'internal' or 'domestic' postcolonial literature. A theme-oriented comparison between the literature cited here and that contained in collections like *The Post-Colonial Studies Reader* (1995) will make our point readily apparent.

16 See Ladson-Billings' book, *The Dreamkeepers: Successful Teaching for African-American Students* (1994) for a more comprehensive treatment of her study.

17 This is the first time that we know of that a specific race-based epistemology has been used in a study published in an AERA journal.

18 In our opinion, the best text to date on critical race theory is *Critical Race Theory: The Key Writings That Formed a Movement* (1995), edited by Crenshaw, Gotanda, Peller and Thomas.

19 John Hope Franklin, in an interview on his 80th birthday, recently said, 'I'm not very optimistic (about racism in the US), I really am not . . . just about the time you sit down or sit back and say, "Oh, yes, we're really moving", you get slapped back down' (Applebome, 1995, p. 37). Bell (1992) in *Faces at the Bottom of the Well: The Permanence of Racism* argues persuasively that racism is such a necessary part of white US culture, that it is, in effect, 'a permanent component of American life' (p. 13), but he also argues that this judgment should not stop us from working for racial equality in all aspects of our social life. While we are apprehensive that the first part of what he said is true, the second part is a necessity.

20 One of us, Scheurich, is the new editor of the *International Journal of Qualitative Studies in Education* and the other, Young, has been the managing editor of this journal.

21 For those who want to read about the negative effects of white racism on whites — what Wendell Berry (1990) has called 'the white misery of white racism' (p. 63) (see Feagin and Vera [1995] for a social account and Wendell Berry (1989) for a personal meditation on the effects of racism on whites).

References

ALARON, N. (1990) 'The theoretical subject(s) of this bridge called my back and Anglo-American feminism' in ANZALDÚA, G. (Ed) *Making Face, Making Soul Haciendo*

Caras: Creative and Critical Perspectives by Feminists of Color, San Francisco, CA, Aunt Lute Books, pp. 356–69.

ANDERSON, M.L. (1993) 'Studying across difference: Race, class, and gender in qualitative research' in STANFIELD, J.H. II and DENNIS, R.M. (Eds) *Race and Ethnicity in Research Methods*, Newbury Park, CA, Sage, pp. 39–52.

ANZALDÚA, G. (1990) 'Haciendo caras, una entrada' in ANZALDÚA, G. (Ed) *Making Face, Making Soul Haciendo Caras: Creative and Critical Perspectives by Feminists of Color*, San Francisco, CA, Aunt Lute Books, pp. xv–xxviii.

APPLEBOME, P. (1995) 'Keeping tabs on Jim Crow: John Hope Franklin', *The New York Times Magazine*, 23 April, pp. 34–7.

APPIAH, K.A. (1992) *In My Father's House: Africa in the Philosophy of Culture*, New York, Oxford University Press.

ASANTE, M.K. (1987) *The Afrocentric Idea*, Philadelphia, PA, Temple University Press.

ASANTE, M.K. (1988) *Afrocentricity*, Trenton, NJ, Africa World Press.

ASANTE, M.K. (1990) *Kismet, Afrocentricity, and Knowledge*, Trenton, NJ, Africa World Press.

ASANTE, M.K. (1993) *Malcolm X as Cultural Hero and Other Afrocentric Essays*, Trenton, NJ, Africa World Press.

ASHCROFT, B., GRIFFITHS, G. and TIFFIN, H. (Eds) (1995) *The Post-colonial Studies Reader*, London, Routledge.

AZIBO, D.A.Y. (1990) 'Personality, clinical, and social psychological research on Blacks: Appropriate and inappropriate research frameworks' in ANDERSON, T. (Ed) *Black Studies: Theory, Method, and Cultural Perspectives*, Pullman, WA, Washington State University Press, pp. 25–41.

BALDWIN, J.A. (1981) *Afrikan (Black) Personality: From an Africentric Framework*, Chicago, IL, Third World Press.

BANKS, J.A. (1993) 'The canon debate, knowledge construction, and multicultural education', *Educational Researcher*, **22**, 5, pp. 4–14.

BANKS, J.A. (1995) 'The historical reconstruction of knowledge about race: Implications for tranformative learning', *Educational Researcher*, **24**, 2, pp. 15–25.

BANKS, W.C. (1992) 'The theoretical and methodological crisis of the Afrocentric conception', *Journal of Negro Education*, **61**, 3, pp. 262–72.

BARAKAN, E. (1992) *The Retreat of Scientific Racism: Changing Concepts of Race in Britain and the United States Between the World Wars*, New York, Viking.

BELL, D. (1992) *Faces at the Bottom of the Well: The Permanence of Racism*, New York, Basic Books.

BEREITER, C. (1994) 'Constructivism, socioculturalism, and Popper's world 3', *Educational Researcher*, **23**, 7, pp. 21–3.

BERNSTEIN, R.J. (1992) *The New Constellation: The Ethical-political Horizons of Modernity/postmodernity*, Cambridge, MA, MIT Press.

BERRY, W. (1990) *The Hidden Wound*, San Francisco, CA, North Point Press.

BHASKAR, R. (1986) *Scientific Realism and Human Emancipation*, London, Verso.

BHASKAR, R. (1989) *Reclaiming Reality*, London, Verso.

BILLINGSLEY, A. (1968) *Black Families in White America*, Englewood Cliffs, NJ, Prentice-Hall Inc.

BUTLER, J. (1993) *Bodies that Matter: On the Discursive Limits of 'Sex'*, New York, Routledge.

CIZEK, G.J. (1995) 'Crunchy granola and the hegemony of the narrative', *Educational Researcher*, **24**, 2, pp. 15–17.

CLIFFORD, J. (1988) 'Identity in Mashpee', *The Predicament of Culture: Twentieth-Century Ethnography, Literature and Art*, Cambridge, MA, Harvard University Press, pp. 277–345.

COLLINS, P.H. (1991) *Black Feminist Thought: Knowledge, Consciousness, and the Politics of Empowerment*, New York, Routledge.

COSE, E. (1993) *The Rage of a Privileged Class*, New York, Harper Collins.

CRENSHAW, K., Gotanda, N. and THOMAS, K. (Eds) (1995) *Critical Race Theory: The Key Writings that Formed the Movement*, New York, New Press.

CUBAN, L. (1989) 'The "at-risk" label and the problem of urban school reform', *Phi Delta Kappan*, **70**, pp. 780–4 and pp. 799–801.

CUMMINS, J. (1986) 'Empowering minority students: A framework for intervention', *Harvard Educational Review*, **56**, 1, pp. 18–36.

DELANDSHERE, G. and PETROSKY, A.J. (1994) 'Capturing teachers' knowledge: Performance assessment', *Educational Researcher*, **23**, 5, pp. 11–18.

DE LEÓN, A. (1983) *They Called Them Greasers: Anglo Attitudes Toward Mexicans in Texas, 1821–1900*, Austin, Texas, University of Texas Press.

DUBE, E.F. (1985) 'The relationship between racism and education in South Africa', *Harvard Educational Review*, **55**, 1, pp. 86–91.

ELLISON, R. (1952) *Invisible Man*, New York, Vintage Books.

ELLSWORTH, E. (1989) 'Why doesn't this feel empowering? Working through the repressive myths of critical pedagogy', *Harvard Educational Review*, **59**, 3, pp. 297–325.

EVERS, C.W. and LAKOMSKI, G. (1991) *Knowing Educational Administration: Contemporary Methodological Controversies in Educational Administration Research*, Oxford, Pergamon Press.

FEAGIN, J.R. and VERA, H. (1995) *White Racism*, New York, Routledge.

FOUCAULT, M. (1972) *The Archaeology of Knowledge*, New York, Pantheon.

FOUCAULT, M. (1973) *The Order of Things: An Archaeology of the Human Sciences*, New York, Vintage.

FOUCAULT, M. (1979) *Discipline and Punish: The Birth of the Prison*, New York, Vintage.

FOUCAULT, M. (1980) *The History of Sexuality, Volume I: An Introduction*, New York, Vintage.

FOUCAULT, M. (1988) *Madness and Civilization: A History of Insanity in the Age of Reason*, New York, Vintage.

FRANKENBERG, R. (1993) *The Social Construction of Whiteness: White Women, Race Matters*, Minneapolis, MN, University of Minnesota Press.

GAGE, N.L. (1989) 'The paradigm wars and their aftermath: A historical sketch of research on teaching since 1989', *Educational Researcher*, **18**, 7, pp. 4–10.

GOLDBERG, D.T. (1993) *Racist Culture: Philosophy and the Politics of Meaning*, Oxford, Blackwell.

GORDON, B.M. (1990) 'The necessity of African-American epistemology for educational theory and practice', *Journal of Education*, **172**, 3, pp. 88–106.

GORDON, B.M. (1993) 'Toward emancipation in citizenship education: The case of African-American cultural knowledge' in CASTENELL, L.A., JR. and PINAR, W.F. (Eds) *Understanding Curriculum as Racial Text: Representations of Identity and Difference in Education*, Albany, NY, State University of New York Press, pp. 263–84.

GORDON, E.W. (Ed) (1992) 'Afrocentrism and multiculturalism: Conflict or consonance?', *Journal of Negro Education*, **61**, 3.

GORDON, E.W., MILLER, F. and ROLLOCK, D. (1990) 'Coping with communicentric bias in knowledge production in the social sciences', *Educational Researcher*, **19**, 3, pp. 14–19.

GOULD, S.J. (1981) *The Mismeasure of Man*, New York, W.W. Norton & Co.

GUBA, E.G. and LINCOLN, Y.S. (1994) 'Competing paradigms in qualitative research' in DENZIN, N.K. and LINCOLN, Y.S. (Eds) *Handbook of Qualitative Research*, Thousand Oaks, CA, Sage, pp. 105–17.

GUTTING, G. (1989) *Michel Foucault's Archaeology of Scientific Reason*, Cambridge, Cambridge University Press.

GWALTNEY, J. (1980) *Drylongso: A Self-portrait of Black America*, New York, Random House.

HACKER, A. (1992) *Two Nations: Black and White, Separate, Hostile, Unequal*, New York, Charles Scribner's Sons.

HARRIS, C. (1993) 'Whiteness as property', *Harvard Law Review*, **106**, 8, pp. 1707–91.

HERRNSTEIN, R.J. and MURRAY, C. (1994) *The Bell Curve: Intelligence and Class Structure in American life*, New York, Free Press.

HESHUSIUS, L. (1994) 'Freeing ourselves from objectivity: Managing subjectivity or turning toward a participatory mode of consciousness?', *Educational Researcher*, **23**, 3, pp. 15–22.

HILL, R.B. (1972) *The Strengths of Black Families*, New York, Emerson Hall Publishers, Inc.

HILLIARD, III, A.G. (1992) 'Behavioral style, culture, and teaching and leaning', *Journal of Negro Education*, **61**, 3, pp. 370–7.

hooks, b. (1990) *Yearning: Race, Gender, and Cultural Politics*, Boston, MA, South End Press.

HOWITT, D. and OWUSU-BEMPAH, J. (1990) 'The pragmatics of institutional racism: Beyond words', *Human Relations*, **43**, 9, pp. 885–99.

HUGGINS, J. (1991) 'Black women and women's liberation' in GUNEW, S. (Ed) *A Reader in Feminist Knowledge*, London, Routledge, pp. 6–12.

KERSHAW, T. (1989) 'The emerging paradigm in Black studies', *The Western Journal of Black Studies*, **13**, 1, pp. 45–51.

KERSHAW, T. (1992) 'Afrocentrism and the Afrocentric method', *The Western Journal of Black Studies*, **16**, 3, pp. 160–8.

KING, J.E. (1991) 'Dysconscious racism: Ideology, identity, and the miseducation of teachers', *Journal of Negro Education*, **60**, 2, pp. 133–46.

KING, W.M. (1990) 'Challenges across the curriculum: Broadening the bases of how knowledge is produced', *American Behavioral Scientist*, **34**, 2, pp. 165–80.

KLUEGEL, J.R. and SMITH, E.R. (1986) *Beliefs About Inequality: Americans' Views of What Is and What Ought To Be*, New York, de Gruyter.

KRUPAT, A. (1993) 'Introduction' in KRUPAT, A. (Ed) *New Voices in Native American Literary Criticism*, Washington, DC, Smithsonian Institution Press, pp. xvii–xxv.

LADSON-BILLINGS, G. (1994) *The Dreamkeepers: Successful Teachers of African American Children*, San Francisco, CA, Jossey-Bass.

LADSON-BILLINGS, G. (1995) 'Toward a theory of culturally relevant pedagogy', *American Educational Research Journal*, **32**, 3, pp. 465–91.

LATHER, P. (1991) *Getting Smart: Feminist Research and Pedagogy With/in the Postmodern*, New York, Routledge.

LEE, C.D., LOMOTEY, K. and SHUJAA, M. (1990) 'How shall we sing our sacred song in a strange land? The dilemma of double consciousness and the complexities of an African-centered pedagogy', *Journal of Education*, **172**, 2, pp. 45–61.

LEE, J.C.S. (1995) 'Navigating the topology of race' in CRENSHAW, K., GOTANDA, N. and THOMAS, K. (Eds) *Critical Race Theory: The Key Writings that Formed the Movement*, New York, New Press.

LENZO, K. (1995) 'Validity and self-reflexivity meet poststructuralism: Scientific ethos and the transgressive self', *Educational Researcher*, **24**, 4, pp. 17–23.

LITTLEJOHN-BLAKE, S.M. and DARLING, C. A. (1993) 'Understanding the strengths of African American families', *Journal of Black Studies*, **23**, 4, pp. 460–71.

LOFTIN, J.D. (1991) *Religion and Hopi Life in the Twentieth Century*, Bloomington, IN, Indiana University Press.

LYOTARD, J.F. (1984) *The Postmodern Condition: A Report on Knowledge* (G. Bennington and B. Massumi, trans.) Minneapolis, MN, University of Minnesota Press.

McCARTHY, C. (1993) 'Beyond the poverty of theory in race relations: Nonsynchrony and social difference in education' in WEIS, L. and FINE, M. (Eds) *Beyond Silenced Voices: Class, Race, and Gender in United States Schools*, New York, SUNY, pp. 325–46.

MERCER, C.D. (1988) *Students with Learning Disabilities*, Columbus, OH, Merrill.

MINH-HA, T.T. (1989) *Woman Native Other*, Bloomington, IN, Indiana University Press.

MORRISON, T. (1992) *Playing in the Dark: Whiteness and the Literary Imagination*, Cambridge, MA, Harvard University Press.

MOSS, P.A. (1994) 'Can there be validity without reliability?', *Educational Researcher*, **23**, 2, pp. 5–12.

NATIONAL ADVISORY COMMISSION ON CIVIL DISORDER (1968) *Report of the National Advisory Commission on Civil Disorders* (Publication No. 1968 O — 291–729), Washington, DC, US Government Printing Office, 1 March.

OGBU, J.U. (1978) *Minority Education and Caste: The American System in Cross-cultural Perspective*, New York, Academic Press.

ORTIZ, A. (1986) 'Characteristics of limited English proficient Hispanic students served in programs for the learning disabled: Implications for policy and practice (Part II)', *Bilingual Special Education Newsletter*, University of Texas at Austin, vol IV.

PADILLA, A.M. (1994) 'Ethnic minority scholars, research, and mentoring: Current and future issues', *Educational Researcher*, **23**, 4, pp. 24–7.

PAREDES, A. (1977) 'On ethnographic work among minority groups: A folklorist's perspective', *New Scholar*, **6**, pp. 1–32.

PHILLIPS, D.C. (1987) *Philosophy, Science, and Social Inquiry*, Oxford, Pergamon Press.

PINE, G.J. and HILLIARD, A.G., III. (1990) 'Rx for racism: Imperatives for America's schools', *Phi Delta Kappan*, **71**, pp. 593–600.

REBOLLEDO, D. (1990) 'The politics of poetics: Or, what am I, a critic doing in this text anyhow?' in ANZALDU'A, G. (Ed) *Making Face, Making Soul Haciendo Caras: Creative and Critical Perspectives by Feminists of Color*, San Francisco, CA, Aunt Lute Books, pp. 346–55.

REYES, M.L. and HALCON, J.J. (1988) 'Racism in academia: The old wolf revisited', *Harvard Educational Review*, **58**, 3, pp. 299–314.

RIZVI, F. (1993) 'Children and the grammar of popular racism' in McCARTHY, C. and CRICHLOW, W. (Eds) *Race Identity and Representation in Education*, New York, Routledge, pp. 126–39.

ROSCOE, W. (1991) *The Zuni Man-woman*, Albuquerque, NM, University of New Mexico Press.

SAID, E.W. (1979) *Orientalism*, New York, Vintage Books.

SARRIS, G. (1993) 'Hearing the old ones talk: Reading narrated American Indian lives in Elizabeth Colson's autobiographies of three Pomo women' in KRUPAT, A. (Ed) *New Voices in Native American Literary Criticism*, Washington, DC, Smithsonian Institution Press, pp. 419–52.

SCHEURICH, J.J. (1993) 'Toward a white discourse on white racism', *Educational Researcher*, **22**, 8, pp. 5–10.

SCHEURICH, J.J. (1994a) 'Policy archaeology: A new policy studies methodology', *Journal of Education Policy*, **9**, 4, pp. 297–316.

SCHEURICH, J.J. (1994b) 'Social relativism: A postmodernist epistemology for educational administration' in MAXCY, S.J. (Ed) *Postmodern School Leadership: Meeting the Crises in Educational Administration*, Westport, CT: Praeger, pp. 17–46.

SCHEURICH, J.J. and IMBER, M. (1991) 'Educational reforms can reproduce societal inequities: A case study', *Educational Administration Quarterly*, **27**, 3, pp. 297–320.

SCHEURICH, J.J. and LAIBLE, J. (1995) 'The buck stops here — in our preparation programs: Educative leadership for all children (no exceptions allowed)', *Educational Administration Quarterly*, **31**, 2, pp. 313–22.

SCHWANDT, T.A. (1994) 'Constructivist, interpretivist approaches to human inquiry' in DENZIN, N.K. and LINCOLN, Y.S. (Eds) *Handbook of Qualitative Research*, Thousand Oaks, CA, Sage, pp. 118–37.

SHOCKLEY, W. (1992) 'Society has a moral obligation to diagnose tragic racial IQ deficits' in PEARSON, R. (Ed) *Shockley on Eugenics and Race: The Application of Science to the Solution of Human Problems*, Washington, DC, Scott-Townsend.

SHUEY, A. (1958) *The Testing of Negro Intelligence*, Lynchburg, VA, Bell.

STANFIELD, II, J.H. (1985) 'The ethnocentric basis of social science knowledge production', *Review of Research in Education*, **12**, pp. 387–415.

STANFIELD, II, J.H. (1993a) 'Epistemological considerations' in STANFIELD, J.H. II and DENNIS, R.M. (Eds) *Race and Ethnicity in Research Methods*, Newbury Park, CA, Sage, pp. 16–36.

STANFIELD, II, J.H. (1993b) 'Methodological reflections' in STANFIELD, J.H. II and DENNIS, R.M. (Eds) *Race and Ethnicity in Research Methods*, Newbury Park, CA, Sage, pp. 3–15.

STANFIELD, II, J.H. (1994) 'Ethnic modeling in qualitative research' in DENZIN, N.K. and LINCOLN, Y.S. (Eds) *Handbook of Qualitative Inquiry*, Newbury Park, CA, Sage, pp. 175–88.

STEVENSON, R.B. and ELLSWORTH, J. (1993) 'Dropouts and the silencing of critical voices' in WEIS, L. and FINE, M. (Eds) *Beyond Silenced Voices: Class, Race, and Gender in United States Schools*, New York, SUNY, pp. 259–71.

TAKAKI, R. (1993) *A Different Mirror: A History of Multicultural America*, Boston, MA, Little, Brown.

TATUM, B.D. (1992) 'Talking about race, learning about racism: The application of racial identity development theory in the classroom', *Harvard Educational Review*, **62**, 1, pp. 1–24.

TAYLOR, R.L. (1987) 'The study of black people: A survey of empirical and theoretical models', *Urban Research Review*, **11**, 2, pp. 11–15.

WEBSTER, Y.O. (1992) *The Racialization of America*, New York, St. Martin's Press.

WEINBERG, R. (1993) 'IQ correlations in transracial adoptive families', *Intelligence*, **17**, 4, pp. 541–56.

WEST, C. (1993) *Keeping Faith: Philosophy and Race in America*, New York, Routledge.

WEST, C. (1995) 'Foreword' in CRENSHAW, K., GOTANDA, N. and THOMAS, K. (Eds) *Critical Race Theory: The Key Writings that Formed the Movement*, New York, The New Press.

WILLIE, C.V. (1993) 'Social theory and social policy derived from the black family experience', *Journal of Black Studies*, **23**, 4, pp. 451–9.

WRIGHT, L. (1994) 'One drop of blood', *The New Yorker*, 25 July, pp. 46–55.

YOUNG, M.D. (1995a) *'Diverse women: The ethics of cross-group feminist research'*, paper presented at the second annual Gender Studies Conference, Austin, May.

YOUNG, M.D. (1995b) *'Putting on paradigms and perspectives: Using multiple frames in our search for women'*, paper presented at the Southwest Conference on Gender Studies, San Antonio, November.

8   An Archaeological Perspective,
Or It Is Turtles All the Way Down

In this final chapter, I first briefly discuss realism, which I think is a useful label for the underlying philosophical frame out of which almost all researchers in education and the social sciences in general are doing their research, even though some of these researchers are claiming a variety of paradigmatic labels. In this first part, though, what I mostly do is to define what I mean by realism rather than to argue with its tenets. Secondly, I discuss what I mean by a postmodernist archaeological perspective. This discussion builds on, but significantly departs from, my previous considerations of archaeology in the chapter on 'Policy archaeology'. It also significantly departs from Foucault's archaeological work, though it was initially drawn from that work. Finally, the discussion in this last chapter should be seen as an initial effort to pursue certain lines of thought rather than as a more developed version of this pursuit. Nonetheless, it does continue the effort to breach the still heavily defended barricades protecting subject-centered perspectives by proposing one example of an orientation that strongly decenters subjectivity. This chapter ends with some concluding remarks for the book as a whole.

Speaking Realism

Virtually all of the research in education and the social sciences that I read is what I would call realist, even though the researchers often claim many different perspectives, from positivist or interpretivist to constructivist or criticalist. Indeed, I could easily say that realism is virtually the 'given' in both educational research and social scientific research. In my view, even though we think we have moved into an era of multiple paradigms, we shuffle the paradigmatic furniture in the structure called research while largely leaving the underlying realist architecture untouched.

However, before I discuss what I mean by 'realism', I need to say that I do not intend to set up one more binarial opposition, in this case one between realism and archaeology. Realism is the broad given; in fact, it is so 'natural', so pervasive, so commonplace that it is virtually invisible, and virtually all research methods courses and all research implicitly use realism no matter what the espoused epistemology is. However, realism, under various names (for example, positivism), is being questioned throughout the social sciences, in literature and literary criticism, and in philosophy. There are, thus, a plurality of voices, many of which are at odds with each other, critiquing and questioning realism; I see archaeology, then, not as a successor regime to realism but as a multiplicative possibility within the emerging endeavors to dissolve and disperse realism. I do not think, however, that it is yet possible to get totally outside of realism; it is still too deep, too embedded. Consequently, even my efforts to describe an archaeological position will inevitably be infected with realism. Futhermore, the archaeology I describe here is not Foucault's. While it has emerged out of my repeated reading of Foucault's archaeological work and while I have certainly appropriated or misappropriated portions of that work, I think, were he still with us, that he would agree that what I call archaeology is not what he intended. Nonetheless, I owe him a large debt for at least being a provocateur of my current thinking.

What, then, do I mean by realism? I do *not* mean more recent philosophical positions that use the label 'realism' as a part of their labels, like scientific realism, though these positions are obviously related to what I mean by realism. Nor do I mean the philosophical doctrine of logical positivism, though this, too, is related. Most researchers in education and the social sciences generally are not really trained to be so philosophically sophisticated as to be operating out of a well worked, coherent philosophical position like these. All but a few researchers in education, and I am being descriptive not demeaning, are trained to do research methods, like quantitative, statistical research or qualitative research or both, not philosophy, though there are some exceptions, such as Guba, Lather, Lincoln, Schwandt, and Denzin, who are unusually focused on underlying philosophical issues.

To say, however, that social science researchers are not trained to do philosophy, however, does not mean they are *not* operating out of a philosophical position. They *are* operating out of a philosophy, a taken-for-granted philosophy that I label 'realism'. What I mean by taken-for-granted is that realism is a set of interrelated assumptions about researchers, research, and reality that social science researchers act out of without understanding that they are doing so. It is like driving a car; most people use them, but few people understand or pay much attention to them. Therefore, one way that realism can be described is as the common, everyday way research is conceptualized and done. For instance, a researcher assumes that she or he is a relatively independent individual, i.e., subjectivity or agent, who has a fairly well researcher-trained 'mind' or consciousness that can independently choose to go out and, say, observe a classroom, see what is happening there, and write a report that gives the reader at least something of what is 'real' in that classroom. This is realism in action.[1]

For analytic purposes, I suggest that realism is composed of three interlinked aspects — an autonomous subjectivity (what Derrida [1981] calls 'the conscious and speaking subject' [p. 29]), a reasonable mind executing the practices of reason (research methodology), and valid or trustworthy representations or interpretations of the real or, at least, of real stories. What I mean by the first one, an autonomous subjectivity, is that the 'I', the subjectivity, or the agency of the researcher is primarily individual and autonomous, a kind of free singularity, capable of somewhat independent thought and action. In addition, it is assumed that this subjectivity is universal, the natural condition of all humanity. What I mean by the second, a reasonable mind executing the practices of reason, is that this subjectivity has or is capable of having a mind or consciousness that can be systematic, rigorous, reasonable (i.e., the mind of a trained researcher using research methods). What I mean by the third, trustworthy interpretations of the real, is that the researcher through systematic research can yield valid or trustworthy knowledge of the real or, at least, of real stories. But it must be emphasized that these three are interlinked; to call but one into question is not sufficient. For instance, to trouble or subvert representational practices without troubling or subverting subjectivity and research practices of reason, like coding, is insufficient, leaving, especially, the heart of realism, its privileged subject, in place. The reason, then, that I call most research realist is because it is said to yield what is really happening in reality or to yield the real stories being told by real people.

I know that some readers will object that if I am questioning the very existence of gross material reality, my questioning is highly suspect. In rebuttal, social science research, for the most part, does not address gross material reality; instead, research mainly addresses interpretations or constructions of 'reality'. When we conduct research, we are typically little concerned about just the sheer movement of bodies or the sheer existence of things; instead, we are mostly concerned with interpretations. In this regard, such words as 'at-risk' or 'achievement' may have some connection to something called material reality, but those connections are rarely simple and usually infused with complex and ambiguous issues of interpreted meaning. Consequently, realist research typically mixes a little material reality with a lot of interpreted meaning with little attention to the nature of the mixture.

In addition, even material objects are seen in an interpretive fashion; for example, a new school is a material object, but it may be seen by a taxpayer as a property tax increase, by a developer as a sure way to draw new home buyers, by a parent as a nearby place for a child to walk to school, or by a student as a boring place. Even the concept 'material reality' is itself a complex, interpreted term and, thus, cannot be assumed to have a transparent, easily definable meaning. Therefore, I think that those who assert that to question realism is to question material reality are raising a more problematic issue than they initially may think. In fact, this issue is an exceedingly complex philosophical one that continues to be a matter of much debate among different philosophical positions. Even if some highly respected philosophers feel the issue has been solved in one particular way, others, equally respected, strongly differ.

I know that other readers will object that they are very explicit about not being realists. This group will say that they are explicit about the fact that they can only tell their stories, not the one true story. They will say that they are telling partial stories, or they will say they are telling multiple stories. They may even decline any intentions to represent something called 'reality'. However, I would suggest that these efforts to create postrealist research are substantially inadequate; they are like a liberal realism that still basically maintains realism. In particular, few of these efforts have actualized any kind of research that de-centers subjectivity itself, nor have they proposed alternative methodologies that take the place of such systematic research practices, as audiotaping, systematic coding, and pattern analysis of the resulting codes, all of which are modernist practices of reason (which is the same 'reason' that qualitative researchers complain about in their characterizations of positivist, quantitative research).

Virtually the only aspect of realism, therefore, that this latter group has typically addressed is the representational practices of realism. But what has frequently been called 'the crisis of representation' is really a serious mischaracterization of the crisis. The crisis is more appropriately the crisis of realism itself, with representational practices as only one aspect of this crisis. To 'play' with various postrealist modes of representation, like partial accounts or multiple stories or disrupted research texts, rather than to address the entire interwoven set of realist assumptions is to leave the other key aspects of realism, particularly the nature of subjectivity and the research practices of reason, safely in place. While I applaud these efforts to develop postrealist approaches to research, it needs to be understood that the development of a postrealist perspective will require a much greater, more extensive philosophical shift, particularly in our basic assumptions about the ways research is conceived and practiced.

What I want to do, then, is offer one kind of postrealist alternative to a realist perspective. I want to offer an alternative that I cannot with confidence say is completely worked out, though I doubt any view can ever achieve that state. Indeed, I will readily admit that my attempt is a somewhat rough hewn one, perhaps even a cartoon. I find it hard to hold onto a postrealist perspective; I think I have it, and then I lose my sense of it. Consequently, what follows is like a rough carving that needs additional work on the details. I wish, of course, to blame all of this on the fact that to conceive of a postrealist perspective within the pervasiveness of realism is to attempt a formidable task; however, the problem may simply be that I do not think or write well enough or that I have not thought and wrote long enough on it. In addition, my description is highly abstract, but that I cannot blame on anything but my own inclinations and pleasures. Whatever your opinion is, what follows is my effort to offer an initial sketch of one postrealist perspective that attempts to address all three aspects of realism.

Writing Archaeology

I suggest that we metaphorically or cartoonistically think of a culture, a society, a civilization (I will usually use culture to stand for all three, though there are important differences in many instances) as a complex three-dimensional array of concepts or names or categories (I will hereafter use 'categories') — life, boat, love, individuality, highway, freedom, research, reality, etc., which are interconnected or dependently linked for meaning in intricate ways. In a particular culture, some of these, like individuality in the US, are generally seen as more important than others, like boat. So, we could think of a three-dimensional tinker toy construction,[2] in which the nodes are categories and the interconnections are meaning linkages connecting the categories. Some categories are nearer the bottom of this tinker toy construction because they are more important, more primary, more foundational to a particular culture. In addition, at the lowest level, typically outside the reflective consciousness of its members (sort of like a cultural unconscious), are the deepest rules, the deepest foundational assumptions for a particular culture, rules or assumptions that I call, following Foucault, 'social regularities', rules or assumptions that *constitute* the nature of reality, the ways to know reality, the nature of the subjectivity of the knower, etc.

It is this complex construction, then, that metaphorically is the culture, and, thus, different cultures would have more or less different constructions. For example, those that have some sort of spirituality as their primary focus, like Tibet of the 1200s, would have a different construction, especially at the lower levels, than those that have economics as their primary focus, like the contemporary US. Or, a culture that assumed individuals were the primary social unit would have a different construction than one that assumed that the family or the tribe was the primary social unit. Now, while using the metaphor or cartoon picture of the tinker toy construction is initially useful, it is all much more complex than this because the 'construction', the culture, is 'alive', is dynamic, is a virtual tumult of micro to macro activities or events. However, each culture still 'lives' *as* its array of categories, though over time these change and rearrange, more easily and rapidly at the top than at the bottom, however. Consequently, the lives of the members of a particular cultural construction take place within the terms (categories) of this complex, dynamic construction. To be a member of that culture is to live — think, act, talk, be — literally in the terms of its interlinked categories or nodes. I call this whole construction, an archaeology, and I call viewing a culture in this way an archaeological perspective.

In this archaeological view, then, *nothing* within a culture exists outside the cultural array of categories, and *everything* derives its meaning from the interdependent meaning linkages connecting the categories. For example, in the US the category of 'dollar', which sometimes refers to a green piece of paper, derives its meaning through interlinking with a web of other categories, such as 'money', 'work', 'value', 'worth', 'purchasing', 'owning', 'power', etc., each of which itself derives its meaning in complex ways through linkages with these and other categories, some of which are deeper and more fundamental than others, like, for example, 'capitalism'. To use a category, then, is implicitly to call forth, to call into play, to ignite, to turn on a vast array of other categories that meaning-wise hover silently in the background, but without which the specific category could not exist. Further, in some sense, to use any one category is to use the whole construction. (I think Wittgenstein, though I remember not where, said something to the effect that to use one word of a language was to use the whole language.) The numerous categories, thus, depend on one another, kind of like turning on a circuit of lights (the lights are nodes and the wires are meaning linkages) turns on all of the lights because they are all part of the same circuit. To repeat, then, all that a particular culture is, exists within this array of categories and meaning linkages, and the categories at the deepest level constitute what are the most fundamental assumptions or rules within a particular archaeology.

Though my metaphor of a tinker toy construction may seem a little odd, what I have said above does not really deviate that much from how many sociologists or anthropologists might view a culture. Humans are social beings living within cultural contexts within which they define who they are, what is relevant, what has meaning, etc., and there are considerable differences among the many different cultural contexts that currently exist or have existed historically. However, I do not mean to imply a Levi-Strauss type of anthropological or sociological structuralism in the sense that there is some universal structure across all cultures; my perspective, instead, is a poststructuralist one in the sense that each social or cultural structure is different, and some are radically different. In addition, my archaeological way of thinking or perspective is itself the production of a particular archaeology, a Western one; I doubt that a Hindu monk in the 900s, even if he were contemplating other cultures and cultural differences, would think archaeologically or, for that matter, sociologically or anthropologically. He would think (act, talk, and be) according to his time and place, his context.

There is a fundamental problem (a problem that Foucault would label as humanism), though, with the conventional sociological or anthropological view that members of a culture think and act in the terms of their cultural context. Because of deep Western assumptions about the nature of an individual and an individual mind, it is assumed that individuals and their minds are somehow a different kind of category and that this category is somehow universal, that the nature of an individual and her/his mind is universally the same in all cultures. It is as if the culture is writing on a slate (the individual mind), blank or not, but the slate itself is the same across different cultures. This, I would suggest, is a crucial contradiction within sociology and anthropology. Why should we think that the nature of an individual self or an individual subjectivity is universal, while leaving all else contextual? My (posthumanist) position, in contrast, is that the nature of an individual mind or an individual subjectivity (and, thus, individual agency) is also deeply and fundamentally contextual, cultural, or, in my view, archaeological.

However, in the West and especially in the US, we cherish individualism. We are all romantic individualists; our whole civilization is. We think that the private conversations we have with our selves, our 'I's', are the most precious thing. We typically assume that this self, our individuality, our subjectivity, our agency, exists outside of the cultural array, that the individual is an autonomous self largely in control of her/his actions, thoughts, etc. In fact, this is inscribed in our legal system: in that system each person is autonomously, except in some extreme conditions, in control of and responsible for one's own actions and, even, in many cases, attitudes and thoughts.

In the archaeological view, individuality is not outside the array; it is but one more category or node within the array. It is just one more enactment of the array, as is any other category. The 'I', the self, is itself a enactment of the array. The culture constantly, not just in childhood but continually, teaches us and reinforces what an 'I' is and how to properly have one. Other cultures similarly produce different kinds of 'I's' or selves, some of which are more group oriented, such as the Japanese, and some of which, like Zen Buddhism, teach its members not to have an 'I' in the Western sense. Each culture, then, according to its array (or archaeology), teaches its members the nature of a self and the correct way to have one. But even this way of speaking is still too realist.

To say that an individual, a single self, thinks is, if you want to speak archaeologically, to say that the archaeology is calling forth or enacting an event that we think of as an 'individual thinking'. When I think, the 'I' that thinks is that which I have learned to have as an 'I' in my particular culture. When I think, the categories I use to think with are the categories of my culture, categories that derive their meaning from the linked web or array of other categories. When I think, what I understand as thinking has been taught to me by my culture, by my archaeology. It would be as if the nodes (including the individuality node, the autonomy node, the thinking node, the nodes for that what is being thought, etc.) were lights and the meaning linkages between the nodes were electric wires connecting the lights/ nodes (not in a linear sequence, but each connected to multiple others). At the same time as the 'individual' node lights up, the other nodes that this node is interdependent with when the event called thinking is occurring would also light up, though maybe less brightly, depending on their 'distance' from the node labeled 'individuality'. To some extent all of the nodes in the array would light up, though those more distant would barely light up. It is important, archaeologically, to understand, though, that the node labeled individuality is not some autonomous, independent source of light. The source of light is the archaeology itself. It is also important, archaeologically, to understand that the individuality node, along with its linkages to other nodes, does not initiate the lighting up; the lighting up is an event, an activity, an enactment of the archaeology.[3]

What I am trying to do here, then, is to construct a mode of thinking that works out of a different set of assumptions. How do we think, if we remove the actor, the self, from the privileged center of the drama? While it may be difficult to consider, an autonomous, self-directed subjectivity is not, I would suggest, necessary to the continuance of human life or society (additionally, I will later suggest that this privileged individualized subjectivity is only actualized by the elite and is actually a liability in the creation of an equitable society). For instance, a decentered self or decentered subjectivity could be seen as much more contextual, influenced by or immersed within its context. A mind or consciousness could be seen not as an atomistic singularity but as interwoven within a broader social or cultural or contextual field that includes others. In such a case, an 'I' would be more fuzzy and diffused, less coterminous with the body, more intermeshed within its context, more interdependent. We would talk about selves, actions, and, even, thoughts as less exclusively individual and more inclusively relational, webbed, arrayed, archaeological. We would not think so much of an individual person thinking alone but of a context or a field thinking or, more broadly, of a culture or an archaeology thinking. So, too, we would have a different kind of experience of being a subjectivity; I would not think I was the sole author of my thoughts (including these here), nor would I think of my self as a singular, separate 'I'.[4]

The key to this sort of reconceptualization is that all aspects of a culture are events, activities, enactments of the archaeology, including the 'I'. I do not mean, though, as discussed above, that an archaeology literally produces gross material reality, like rocks or bodies or trees. Instead, the archaeology produces the categories labeled 'material reality', 'rocks', 'bodies', or 'trees' and their meaning linkages to other categories (for example, these things are not just things; they have complex meanings that differ across various cultures). The archaeological array provides the assumptions, the rules, the names, the meanings, and different archaeologies, to a lesser or greater degree, provide different arrays, creating in the process very different assumptions, rules, names, and meanings. For example, for many Native American civilizations, plants, animals, and the human animal are all co-equal parts of interdependent life, while the dominant Western view is that humans are the privileged species and that they can use plants and animals, which are lesser, in any way they choose. These are two radically different archaeologies with radically different assumptions, rules, names, and meanings — thus, radically different ways of life.[5]

At this point, I will assume that there is some understanding of what I mean by an archaeology and of what I mean when I say that everything is within and of the archaeology.[6] But now I need to complicate the picture I have drawn. Within most civilizations, there are almost always multiple cultures or sub-cultures. Whether we are discussing civilizations of Africa, Central and South America, Asia, or the West, they almost always are not a monoculture. I will use the US as my example. There is a dominant Anglo culture. There are also an African-American culture, a Mexican-American culture, a Comanche culture, a Puerto Rican-American culture, a Hopi culture, a Vietnamese-American culture, and so on. Each of these, to a lesser or greater degree, has a different culture than the Anglo one. This does not mean, given that these cultures of color have coexisted within the dominant Anglo culture for some time, that there is no interactional overlap. Indeed, the US experience from the beginning has been, as Ronald Takaki so well shows in *A Different Mirror: A History of Multicultural American* (1993), one of multiple, interacting cultures, with the Anglo one dominating (sometimes horrifically as in slavery, in the genocide of Native Americans, and, currently, in the apartheid-like relegation of some racial groups to extreme poverty). However, the dominance of the Anglo culture has not meant that the other cultures have not had or do not have some counter influence on the dominant culture.

This point of interactional overlap is an important one. For example, the Chicago blues of Muddy Waters are a complex interactional overlap of two archaeologies (i.e., influences of African cultures or archaeologies continue in this music). The Native American Christian church is a complex interactional overlap (the influences of different tribal archaeologies continue to survive within the Native American Christian church). An interactional overlap, then, is a hybridic space in which two different archaeologies have intersected, creating something that is a complex combination of both, a combination which may be mainly positive for the non-dominant culture or mainly negative or a complex mix. However, it is a mistake to conclude that the US has evolved into an interracial archaeology, as if it were one large interactional overlap. The Anglo archaeology still maintains its racial dominance of archaeologies of color (for an extended discussion of racism seen archaeologically, see the seventh chapter, 'Coloring epistemology'), while, at the same time, archaeologies of color, with considerable difficulty, because of the Anglo dominance, work to sustain themselves as separate and different archaeologies (I would suggest that this archaeological perspective helps to better understand the nature of racial relations in the US, but, again, see chapter 7).

My more complex picture, then, is that the US as an archaeology is one in which there is one culture (archaeology) that has dominated and continues to dominate, significantly though not completely, several other cultures (archaeologies), which in their attempts to survive both work to maintain their own archaeological integrity *and* create hybridic spaces of interactional overlap. However, it seems unnecessarily awkward to say that in the US there is one archaeology dominating several others. Instead, I will propose that we think of the US as a single archaeology, within which there are several of what I will hereafter call 'formations'. Formations, then, are relatively coherent ways of life or cultures (some of which have once been separate archaeologies, like the Comanche, Cherokee, or African ones) that to some degree continue to survive (because they are forced to by the racism of the dominant formation and/or because their members seek to continue their way of life or culture) within the larger archaeology. In addition, the culture that is the dominant one I will also call a formation, though it is critically important to understand that the fundamental rules, assumptions, etc. of the overall multi-formational archaeology are almost exclusively those of the dominant formation, which is, in my opinion, the key source of its dominance.[7] That is, the deep rules, assumptions, etc. of the dominant culture or formation, because of its dominance, become the deep rules, assumptions, etc. of the overall archaeology, thus reinforcing its dominance at the deepest level. However, this does not mean that the non-dominant cultures or formations and their deep rules, assumptions, etc. disappear; they survive to a greater or lesser degree as formations within the overall archaeology.

For instance, African-Americans in their religion, their music, their beliefs, their use of language, etc., dynamically maintain a formation that is partially African and partially hybridic — African-American. Mexican-Americans, Comanche-Americans, Hopi-Americans, Navaho-Americans, Objibwe-Americans, Hawaiian-Americans, etc. do the same. These latter formations continue to 'exist', to various degrees, within the larger archaeology of the US.[8] In addition, like archaeologies, these formations play a significant role in constituting their own arrays of categories and meaning linkages, though this constitutional activity intersects in complex ways with the dominant formation and its constitutional activity. In addition, within multi-formation archaeologies, many members of non-dominant formations have to exist dynamically at the intersection of two formations, their own and the dominant one.

For example, a person of a non-dominant formation may have to learn the ways of the dominant formation to succeed in dominant formation-controlled areas, like in public schools or the corporate world, though some individuals from non-dominant formations may exist within areas where such biformational existence is unnecessary, like within some population areas almost totally dominated by non-dominant groups; an example of these are some sections in major cities and on Native American reservations. Whatever the circumstances, however, subjectivity (and all the rest that makes up what life is) is constituted by an individual's formational positionality within a multi-formational archaeology. For example, how identity is formationally constituted for an African-American is different than how it is formationally constituted for an Anglo.

But this added complexity of a multi-formational archaeology does not stop with racial cultures. Any group that for whatever reason is socialized or enculturated in a different way over a long period of time begins to develop, to a greater or lessor degree, a formation (again, an array of categories, assumptions, rules).[9] The less the difference in socialization or enculturation, the less the difference in the formation, the greater the difference, the greater the difference in the formation. Consequently, since Anglo women have been persistently socialized, over thousands of years in Anglo civilization, for instance, in different ways from Anglo men, these women live, to a greater or lessor degree, within a different formation than Anglo men, which is what books like those of Tannen (1990) are about. There are, thus, gendered formations just as there are raced formations, and both of these are constitutive of the nature of subjectivity, of appropriate ways to think, and of reality itself, so that in general the subjectivity of Anglo women (drawn from their formation) is different than the subjectivity of Anglo men (drawn from their formation).

Furthermore, in archaeologies, like those of the US or the UK, that have socioeconomic classes that have existed over many generations, a class-based formation emerges. The same could be said of sexual orientation, though the latter as a formation requires a more extended discussion, as does an SES-based class, because people do sometimes change their class, just as some few change their sexual orientation. This proliferation of formations, then, leads to a final complexity: in multiformational archaeologies, each 'individual' is constituted as a node or category at the intersection of several formations, including, for example, in the US, race, gender, class, sexual orientation-based ones. Thus, if I am an Anglo, upper-middle-class male, born and raised working class, I have been and continue to be constituted by the dominant Anglo formation, the dominant male formation, the influential upper-middle-class formation, and the non-dominant and not influential working class formation — what it is, then, to be this individual, to think/reason, to act, to know reality, all of these are constituted by this formational positionality and not by my romanticized individual choices. However, I do not mean to imply that all individuals who would claim this particular set of formations are exactly the same in all aspects of their life, but I am saying that they are in a broad, general sense constituted by the same formational set.[10]

However, subjectivity as archaeologically conceived should not be thought of as if the individual is at the intersection of multiple formations, all of which are influencing the individual. As discussed earlier, individualization and that which the individual does or thinks is an activity or an event or an enactment of an archaeological array or, in this case, of a multiformational archaeological array. Archaeologically, an individual IS an activity or event or enactment of an interactive intersection of multiple formations.[11] Thus, each individual within the US is being multiply constituted by race, gender, class, and sexual orientation formations and, given the particular circumstance, may be more constituted by one formation rather than others. For example, within a particular event, like a conflict between a male and a female, one's gender formation may be more at play, more constitutional, than one's race formation. That one formation may be more operative within a particular situation does not mean, though, that the individual is choosing which formation is in play; instead this is all an enactment of the particular set of multiple formations. Returning to the previous example, archaeologically, the gender identity/subjectivity of the male and female and the conflict are enactments of the particular formational *sets*; within a different archaeology, gender identity/subjectivity of the male and female and the nature of conflict between males and females would be constituted differently and so would be enacted differently.

Moreover, it needs to be understood that even the most privileged upper-class, heterosexual Anglo male is multiply constituted, both because the civilization that constitutes him is a multiformational archaeology (rather than simply a monoformational archaeology) and because exclusions (of formations of color, women, the middle and lower classes, homosexuals) are as constitutive as are inclusions (his own race, gender, class, and sexual orientation) — that which is excluded is as constitutive of what is as that which is included, a point both Derrida (1981) and Toni Morrison (1992) have made. Thus, while the archaeology of the dominant group is the most influential one, the most privileged one, such that all of the other formations exist in relation to and 'within' it, all people, both those of the dominant formations and those of the non-dominant ones, are constituted by their multiformational positionality. This means that the elite — the wealthy, the CEOs of corporations, the political leadership — are no more free and independent than anyone else; all individuals are equally enactments of the multiformational archaeology.

To recapitulate, human life occurs within and in the terms of archaeologies. These archaeologies are arrays of interlinked categories, with more foundational (and, thus, less changing) categories (i.e., social regularities) metaphorically near the 'bottom'. In addition, each category only exists interdependently with other categories within the array, and, thus, no categories are outside the array, all of which applies equally to the category of individual subjectivity. Further, many archaeologies encompass multiple formations, though one formation or one set of formations typically has historically dominated the range of other formational sets.[12] In these cases of multi-formation archaeologies with one set dominant, subjectivities, along with many other categories, exist as intersectional multiformational events or enactments; that is, subjectivities, along with other categories, are multiply constituted by more than one formation, though in any particular event one or more formations may be more constitutive than another or others. Consequently, the node labeled an individual is a shifting intersectional space or node of multiple formations. In these civilizations, to think archaeologically, then, is not to think of individuals acting or interacting, but to think of an array of multiple formations being in play, a play that constitutes everything within that array.[13]

Given this archaeological view, what would happen to the three analytic categories of research I stated earlier — the subjectivity of the researcher, a reasonable mind enacting the practices of reason (research methodology), and valid or trustworthy representations or interpretations of the real or, at least, of real stories. First, the subjectivity of the researcher: most individuals are raised and live their entire lives within a single intersectional space/node of gender, race, class, and sexual orientation formations, though some very few change one or more of these. It is these formations, changed or not, that constitute the nature of the individual subjectivity — how to have one, what it means to have one, how one thinks when one has one, etc. No individual, then, operates like an autonomous singularity who pursues through free choice whatever that individual wants, desires, etc. Each individual subjectivity (and its wants and desires), rather, operates according to, in the terms or categories of one's intersectional formations as those exist in relation to the overall archaeology, which, remember, is dominated by a particular set of formations — Anglo, male, elite, heterosexual. Instead of talking as if individuals autonomously think, feel, do, etc., we could, archaeologically, talk as if subjectivity and its thoughts, feelings, actions, etc. were complex interformational enactments or events. Consequently, from an archaeological point of view, the subjectivity of a researcher is a space or node within which multiple formations intersect as events or enactments we label thinking, feeling, doing. What a subjectivity is, then, is a kind of production of the multiformational array rather than an autonomous singularity that possesses free choice.

However, since what is being addressed is the subjectivity of researchers, this adds some other ingredients. Research is not an activity that many individuals do; in fact, while it may not be the most elite activity, it is a relatively elite one. Virtually all researchers are trained at the doctoral level at research universities. At this level within these universities, few are involved, and, notwithstanding the small increases of women, people of color, and those of other non-dominant formations, the formation that dominates this level of the university is close to that of the dominant formational set. Consequently, those who work at this level or are trained at this level are, to a substantial degree, being constituted as researcher subjectivities by the dominant formational set — i.e., to become a major research university-trained researcher is to be constituted as a researcher subjectivity by the dominant formational set.

Even when members of non-dominant formational sets become university researchers or are trained in these settings, to become a researcher means that they must be substantially constituted by the dominant formational set. To be a researcher, then, is to be an enactment of the dominant formational set. However, for those from non-dominant formations, like female scholars or scholars of color, these enactments are an interactional space that includes both the dominant formational set and the non-dominant formational set that they, in a sense, bring with them. The result is an interactional hybrid of the two sets, such that, for example, African-American researchers often turn research to issues of importance to the African-American formation. However, because of the unconscious but powerful influence of the dominant formational set on the deepest rules of the overall archaeology, rarely do professors of non-dominant formational sets question the deep rules of the archaeology, a questioning that might undermine research itself. That this type of questioning, though, has begun to occur within feminism, race-based perspectives, and queer theory is a hopeful sign of deeper changes in the relative power of the dominant and the non-dominant formations.[14]

Nonetheless, for all but a few researchers, the deep rules, assumptions, etc. of the dominant formational set continue to constitute the nature of researcher subjectivity. For this vast majority of researchers, being a researcher, being seen as a researcher, being able to continue to do research (like getting tenure or grants), being legitimated by one's researcher colleagues as a researcher, all of which are key aspects of being a researcher, require that certain activities are done in certain ways, like developing lines of research; like collecting, coding, and analyzing data; and, like publishing research articles. In other words, there are ways of thinking and kinds of acting that are defined as what a researcher does, and if these are not done, tenure, promotion, grants, collegial legitimation — those things that are necessary to be a researcher — do not occur. But this description is not an archaeological one.

To redo this description as an archaeological one requires, first, that the differences between the subjectivity of the researcher and the practices of research be erased. A particular subjectivity and its practices, that which a subjectivity does, thinks, feels, etc., are the same. A subjectivity is not some special something that is different from its internal practices (what Foucault has called the practices of the self) and external practices. Second, all of these activities or practices are nodes or categories of interlinked meaning constituted by the archaeology. That which a researcher is, her/his subjectivity as a researcher, is not, then, some autonomous, atomistic singularity, capable of creating whatever she/he thinks a research is; a researcher, to be a researcher, acts out a particular array or, to turn the tables, is enacted by a particular archaeological array. In contrast, other archaeological arrays, like Hopi or Tibetan ones, have not enacted researchers; these latter, instead, enact medicine people or Buddhist monks, respectively, among other subjectivities. To be a researcher is not, then, to be a free, self-defining entity. It is like being an aspect of an ecology in which no single aspect of the ecology moves freely and independently or can be said to have an independent existence; instead, any aspect is part of an interdependency, and, thus, it is the whole interwoven ecology that lives and moves, not just some individual part. The subjectivity of researchers is the same. This subjectivity has no free and independent existence. It is but one aspect of an interwoven archaeology. The researcher does not speak the archaeology; the archaeology speaks the researcher.

Second, a reasonable mind enacting the practices of reason (research methodology): as I have mentioned previously, all of the systematic procedures of research, whether qualitative or quantitative, are the applications of what the modernists mean by reason, and reason has been modernism's royal road to Truth about the really real. However, while even those philosophers who continue to defend reason, from Popper to Dennis Phillips, no longer see truth as the goal, the practices drawn from reason continue to thoroughly dominate how research is defined. For example, even radical researchers, who have questioned the deep rules and assumptions in education, still audiotape, systematically code, and do pattern or thematic analysis of data. These latter practices are the practices of reason, and they are assumed to accord with a researcher-trained mind.

In contrast, from an archaeological view, reason, research practices, and a researcher-trained mind are all the enactments of a particular archaeology. It is like the practices of a Tibetan buddhist monk — his praying, meditating, chanting, etc. are the enactments of a particular archaeological array. He does not do these things; his array enacts all of this, including him and his subjectivity. This is equally true of reason and its practices. Reason, especially that weak version of reason practiced in the social sciences, is not universal and ahistorical. Reason is a set of archaeologically produced and enacted practices, events, or activities, and it is certainly not the supreme universal development of humankind any more than meditation is the supreme universal development of humankind. The practices of reason, i.e., research, cannot just be lifted out of one archaeological context and put down in another. For example, research practices would have little meaning to the Hopi of the 800s, just as the spiritual practices of the latter would have little meaning for contemporary Westerners. Not only, then, does a particular set of practices have meaning solely within a particular archaeological context or fabric, but also such practices cannot be said to be carried out independently by the members of a particular archaeology. It is the archaeology that is so extensively giving meaning to all that it contains, both at more superficial levels and at the level of the deepest rules and assumptions, that it becomes necessary to give up an atomistic view of separated categories, such as reason and its practices or subjectivity, and to begin to see both the subjectivity of the researcher and the research practices of reason as archaeological enactments, as the complex play of the larger social, cultural, civilizational fabric.

Third: valid or trustworthy representations or interpretations of the real or, at least, real stories. It is in this third area of representational practices that there have been numerous efforts to develop postrealist representational practices. Some of Derrida's (for example, 1990) more recent works are some of the more radical examples of this, both in terms of composition and textual structures, though his works are not explicitly seen as research. Lather and Smithies' (1995) recent work on women living with HIV/AIDS is an example in research, though there are others, such as those of Laurel Richardson (for example, 1995) in sociology. Since there are already numerous examples of this, I will not focus on it. I will say, though, as I said previously, that to controvert realism by offering alternatives in only this aspect is substantially inadequate. To question or subvert only representational practices is to miss the larger crisis, the crisis of realism itself.

Instead of addressing specific representational alternatives to those of realism, I will focus here on representational practices in general and on the real itself. As has been argued throughout this chapter, all aspects of an archaeology are enactments of the archaeology. Thus, representational practices, realist or postrealist ones, are enactments of the archaeology. They are not acts researchers choose to do; they are enactments of the archaeology, and only those that are circulated by a particular archaeology are the ones that get enacted. For example, stories told by the Apache, which use specific geographical sites to signal specific life lessons, are a representational practice, from a Western point of view, but they as representational practices appropriately fit the Apache archaeology and not a Western one. Representational practices are, again, just another enactment of the whole fabric, the particular archaeology.

The same is true of the real itself. Reality is archaeological. I do not mean, though, as per my prior discussion of gross material reality, that an archaeology literally creates, in the fashion of idealism, materially reality. Instead, I mean that the archaeology categorizes, gives meaning to, takes up and uses material reality in its own way. For example, to a Christian of the Middle Ages, material reality was not true reality; true reality was heaven. Hindu archaeology is similar: the material world is the illusion; it is enlightenment that is real. To the Zen Buddhists, though, material reality (the many) and enlightenment (the one), according to the Heart Sutra, one of the most respected Buddhist treatises, are simultaneously different and not different. Thus, reality itself, what it means, how it is parceled out into categories, how it is to be used and understood — all of these are the enactments of a particular archaeology.

Of course, Westerners, because of science, tend to say that their version of reality, especially material reality, is superior to all others. But to me this is just another civilizational or archaeological imperialism. Other civilizations have 'mapped' reality, and those maps worked for those civilizations, often for much longer than science has existed. For example, the traditional Hopi way is essentially over 20,000 years old, which is a very long time for a reality map to work. I know, though, that the Hopi did not cure diseases like Western medicine or build rocket-ships like Western engineering, but they also did not kill millions through wars and exterminations, did not enslave people because of their race, or build weapons that could literally destroy life on the earth. To cure disease and prolong life, like has been done by the West, are the goals of an archaeology that assumes life ends with the death of the body. For other archaeologies, the pain of disease is not necessarily negative and the death of the body is not real death, the death of the spirit. In fact, in many of these latter archaeologies direct communication with those whose bodies have died is a common occurrence; to regularly have this experience would mean one had little fear of the death of the body. The different archaeologies simply create different ways to live. The West is, thus, not the best; it is just one more archaeology. To judge the Hopi as best would be to use Hopi evaluative criteria; to judge the West as best would be to use Western evaluative criteria.

If, however, it is the archaeology that enacts all three aspects of research, including the subjectivity of the researcher, where does this leave research? Research within the archaeology becomes the study of the archaeology or, in the case of the US, the study of a multiformational archaeology within the terms of itself.[15] Research becomes the reflexivity of the archaeology itself. While this might initially seem surprising, this is also what realist research is. The lens constructs the world according to the nature of the lens, and, in the archaeological view, the archaeology constructs the lens. In this regard, the difference between archaeology and realism is that archaeology knows this, while realism imperially thinks its lens is a window onto the really real. Another difference is that realism assumes it is able to achieve a purchase above or outside its historicized context, while archaeology assumes it is an enactment wholly within and of the archaeology. While Foucault seemed to have some ambiguity about the latter, his archaeological and genealogical works are examples of archaeological research. Derrida's deconstructions of the Western archaeology are also examples of archaeological research. Chapters 5 and 7 of this book are archaeological research, though none of these examples are directly based on the archaeological view I have developed and extended in this chapter.

Clearly, archaeological research could be conducted on any aspect of the archaeology. For example, in chapter seven, by implication, I have suggested that most fundamentally racism exists at the deepest level of the Western archaeology, at the level that the nature of reality is constituted. Because of this, white supremacy is embedded in primary or deep categories like property, as Harris (1993) has shown. As a result, efforts to address racism at a more superficial level, like as individual choices or values or even institutional choices or values, are continually reundermined by the fact that racism is more deeply embedded than this. As I argued in chapter 5, white supremacy is one of the social regularities of the modernist West, which means, given the discussion above, that white supremacy is a social regularity for the dominant formational set, the set that both dominates the other sets and dominates the overall archaeology. In like fashion, it would be possible to conduct archaeological research on other facets of social life.

Conclusion

As I said at the beginning of this book, it can be taken as an evolving theoretical development, a set of contradictions, a collection, or all of these. My conscious intention has been to explore postmodernism as it applies to research and research methods. While many of the chapters are chiefly critiques of modernist research and research methods, I have also tried to suggest what postmodernist research and research methodology could look like. In this regard, I have suggested that the deconstruction of Derrida, the archaeology and genealogy of Foucault, and chapters 5 and 7 are examples of postmodernist research and research methods. I have also tried to extend my own thinking about archaeology in this chapter, for which there is yet no research example, though I would argue that, in a significant sense, this chapter is itself research from an archaeological perspective.

I imagine, though, that especially my archaeological decentering of individual subjectivity, particularly given the abstract terminology I have used, may give serious pause to many researchers. I have, however, tried to use ecological and fabric metaphors to allude to a subjectivity that is interwoven within its context in contrast to my contention that the individualized subjectivity that dominates the Western archaeology is the problematic subjectivity of the master. I would suggest that this concept, as those of us who are not masters try to apply it to ourselves, is mainly the source of considerable personal pain, as most of us do not have the resources, social support, and archaeological fit to carry it off successfully. Accordingly, I would argue that for those who are not and never will be masters and for those seeking an archaeology that will support an equitable society, a decentered, interdependent, communal subjectivity may be a necessity; in short, romantic individualism and an equitable society may be an impossible contradiction. Further, I would argue, to understand ourselves not as singularities but as mobile, dynamic facets of complex archaeological ecologies or fabrics is a more appropriate, useful perspective for an equitable society in a postmodernist era. Of course, from an archaeological perspective, none of this is a choice, and it is arguable as to whether theoretical insight into archaeological changes will have any effect on those changes.

If my reading of the postmodernist changes in process are useful, substantial changes lie ahead for realist research due to its deeply modernist moorings. My prediction is that realist research will not survive postmodernism, not the philosophy but the era. The attacks on higher education and, thus, research itself from the right (politically, economically, and theoretically); from identity politics (politically and theoretically), especially through the development and spread of postrealist research epistemologies, like Afrocentrism or critical race theory (though these hybridically incorporate some realism); and from postmodernists (theoretically) are all equally enactments, in my view, of the shift from a fragmenting Enlightenment-based modernism to a multi-voiced, more relativist, global capitalist postmodernism, though to call it postmodernism is a Euro-American parochialism.

If intellectual reflectivity or theory is of any value at all, it may be helpful for researchers to realize that faculty accountability discussions, attacks against tenure, the proliferation of multiple paradigms, the resurgence of the right, identity politics, and postmodernism may all be part of larger archaeological changes. What does that mean, then, for that mobile metaphor we call research? What it means is that the critiques of realist research, by feminists, by race-based perspectives, by postmodernists, and, even, by the right, are not just critiques to be ignored, resisted, or repressed. They are the archaeological future. Research and research method in the postmodern is already fragmenting into a multi-voiced, multi-hued, clamorous circus, while the monological conversation of modernism, carried on by a relatively restricted group, is dying, an occurrence Bakhtin and I both would applaud. Poetically, the time of the one god, one path is passing, and the time of the multiplicity of goddesses and gods, many paths is returning.

This means that research is morphing, archaeologically being morphed. What it is to be a researcher is not what it was twenty years ago when there was one right way, and it will not be in another twenty years what it is today. Those who hold onto the old ways or the current ways, while both will continue to exist to some extent, will be increasingly ignored, as if they spoke Rorty's dead 'languages', by new researchers speaking new languages. What I have tried to offer here is a critique of the old language (realism), a description of a possible alternative language, and a frame for understanding the archaeological changes creating this historical moment. I have thus, offered a social theory and a methodology, a postmodernist social theory and a postmodernist methodology that accords with a postmodernist era. Nonetheless, this theory and its related predictions may be wrong, infused with too much realism, or simply ignored. If so, this theory and all of its implications will pass silently and invisibly as if it never existed, like most theories do. However, even if my predictions occur and the theory turns out to be useful, these, too, will pass because they have no special critical purchase, like all theories or methods, that places them outside of history. Most fundamentally, however, I, the theory, the critiques, the research methods suggested, and the predictions are enactments of the archaeological fabric. It is all intertextual; it is all archaeological, including research and its method, especially in the postmodern.

Notes

1 Simply saying at the beginning of a research report that one is doing interpretive, phenomeological, criticalist, feminist, or constructivist research does not mean that one is still not enacting a realist perspective. Some researchers, for example, will establish their paradigmatic claim by stating that they are focusing on interviewees' interpretations or constructions, but making this claim does not mean that the research is not realist. In other words, naming your research by a different label does not mean that you are still not enacting a realist perspective. Not being a realist requires a much greater shift in philosophical perspective than this, and this shift is not easy or simple because realism is so endemic to the way researchers 'naturally' think and especially to the way they think about research.

2 Tinker toys for those unfamiliar with them are a toy for children. The most important pieces are long and short wooden sticks and circular wooden pieces with multiple holes into which the sticks can be inserted. Consequently, it is possible to construct a three-dimensional structure of almost any shape, however odd. In my use of this toy as a metaphor for a culture or archaeology, the circular pieces are the categories or nodes (the names or labels of concepts or things) and the sticks are the meaning linkages connecting all of the nodes.

3 Freedom and determinism, that old conundrum of Western thought, is a useless categorical binary. Archaeology needs neither. There is no individual yearning to be free or resisting determination. Both the yearning and the resisting are plays within or productions of a game that assumes individualism as the primary locus. That is, the freedom-determinism conflict is a problem created by a particular set of assumptions or rules. In addition, the resolution of the freedom-determinism problem by Giddens (for example, 1984) and others is insufficient. They argue that individuals make or produce the society, the culture, while the society simultaneously makes or produces the individuals. To me, they have partially realized archaeology, but wish, because of the influence the realist game still has on them, to preserve some space for the individual, as if all meaning and joy would die with the demise of the individual (the Zen Buddhists, along with some mystics in other spiritual traditions, argue that true joy or the experience of the oneness is birthed by the demise of the 'I', a conclusion that Foucault, also came to about Zen: 'In Zen, it seems to me that all the techniques connected to spirituality tend . . . to obliterate the individual' [quoted in Eribon, 1991, p. 310]).

4 If all of this sounds like something close to the kind of subjectivity claimed by some feminists or persons of color, that is the point I am making. The subjectivity of the autonomous individual, the humanist subject, the one that supposedly lives within but not of history and the one that is, in my view, the basis for what we think commonly a researcher is, is a kind of imperial subjectivity. It is a rather arrogant subjectivity that

thinks that it is its own master and that it can name, know, and communicate the really real.

5   Some philosophers have raised the commensurability/incommensurability issue, and it would certainly apply to archaeologies. Here is how this issue would go: if there are many different archaeologies, how can there ever be any communication among them? Fortunately, this is not really that difficult of a problem as it is applied to archaeologies. Some archaeologies have more similarities among them than others, for various complex reasons, like the US and France have much in common historically, creating significant overlap upon which communication can be built, though anyone who has translated across French and English knows that there are many incommensurabilities. For archaeologies that are more radically different from each other, communication is a greater problem. However, two things help. First, all archaeologies are sufficiently complex that there are invariably some overlaps that tend to come out in interactions because those interacting are trying to make connections that they can 'see' based on their own archaeologies. Second, and more important, is the fact that as two archaeologies interact, they create a hybridic space composed of the results of the interactions; that is, the interactions build bridges, and the longer they interact, the more bridges the members of each archaeology have to use in communication. Consequently, it is not necessary to pose an underlying human universality to account for cross-archaeological communication. If there is such a universality, it is so deeply mediated by each archaeology such that each archaeology, if it tries to define universality, which all of them do not necessarily do, will define that universality according to its own archaeology. Therefore, such universalist stories like those of Joseph Campbell (for example, 1968) are Western archaeological-based stories — and, when taken as true, have a flavor of archaeological imperialism to them. Hopi stories, understood from within the Hopi archaeology, are very different stories. As many Native Americans say in their explanations of what holds the earth up, it is a turtle. When asked about what holds the turtle up, they reply that it is turtles all the way down. What this means in my archaeology is that it is interpretations or archaeologies all the way down.

6   One interesting question that I will not cover in any depth is that of where do archaeologies come from and how to they originate. I agree with poststructuralists, like Foucault, who argue that there are no origins. Archaeologies are coterminous with the existence of human societies, and all human societies evolve from other human societies, though some die out. There is also no teleology to any archaeology, though there are certainly tendencies based, especially, on the deepest assumptions, rules, etc. For example, if an archaeology is deeply materialistic, it will likely be that it will continue in that direction, though there is no guarantee. In addition, the interactions of the innumerable enactments of an archaeology are endlessly generative, particularly the interactions of formations, a concept I will define later. Randomness and complexity, in terms of interactions, then play a key role; all of this occurs within the boundaries of the deep rules and assumptions, though even those can change over long periods of time due to the random and complex play of interactions. A good example of this is that I recently read in the newspaper that some historians have suggested that the broad support the revolutionists achieved among the colonist in the US was significantly influenced by a series of poor harvests due to bad weather. As I remember it, these scholars suggested that the US revolution might not have come to fruition without this bad weather, thus, significantly changing the subsequent history of the US, including possibly its spread across the continent. It is like a rich ecological setting, randomness and the complex interactions within and across species of plants and animals, and

changes in physical conditions, like weather changes or movements of tectonic plates or the crash of huge asteroids into the earth, are sufficient to propel that ecology down through the pathway of its history. However, origins and teleologies or autonomous intentional subjectivities are not necessary to that propulsion.

7   While in discourses on politics, economics, or sociology, it is typically thought that power most fundamentally is vested in politics, wealth, or social influence, it is the naming of reality, the creation of the archaeological category array and the meaning linkages, that is the most powerful. Even though no individual consciously creates such arrays, since individuality itself is constituted by archaeologies, the individuals who are members of the dominant formation will receive the greatest benefits of the archaeology. For instance, in the US, elite, Anglo, heterosexual males are constituted in a way that most fits the fundamental assumptions, rules, etc. of the overall archaeology, and, thus, they become successful more easily, i.e., do well in school, go to the best schools where they connect with other members of the elite, get the better jobs, are more apt to start life with ample resources, etc. Those constituted by other formations — those of color, women, lower classes, homosexuals — either do not try to succeed or are not able to succeed in the terms of the overall archaeology, or, if they choose to try to succeed, must work harder, be better, and become bi-formational. Archaeologically, this suggests why upper middleclass children and the schools populated by these children, on average, do so well in public schools. These children are born into an archaeological positionality that is closely congruent with the dominant formation, the formation whose assumptions, rules, etc. constitute the overall archaeology. In contrast, children constituted by other formations do not fit, archaeologically speaking, the ruling formation and, thus, have a more difficult experience succeeding well in public schools, an institution, like all public institutions, that is primarily constituted by the dominant formation. This perspective also explains why the positive valuing and educational use of the culture and language of children from non-dominant formations in public schools is associated with improved school success for those children (see, for example, Au and Kawakami, 1994; Garcia, 1994; Hollins and Spencer, 1990; Ladson-Billings, 1995; Trueba, 1991).

8   Individual members of non-dominant formations may be more or less constituted by their own group formations or by the dominant formation. For example, a Comanche-American or a Mexican-American may, because of individual circumstances, have almost completely converted to the dominant formation. It is also possible that a member of the dominant formation may almost completely ally themselves with one of the non-dominant formations, through, for instance, living on a Hopi reservation for decades and adopting that way of life. While such conversions will probably never equal being raised within a formation, a significant transformation over many years of time is possible.

9   I not suggesting that a formation is somehow totally or even significantly separate from the overall archaeology (and, thus, the dominant formation). A particular formation might only exist in the upper portions of an archaeology, thus completely adopting the lower portions of the archaeology, the deep categories, assumptions, rules, etc. In addition, the extent to which an archaeology overlaps portions of the overall archaeology may vary among different formations. For example, traditional Sioux living on a Sioux reservation may be only minimally constituted by the dominant formation.

10   This may initially be difficult to recognize, but it should be remembered that the type of subjectivity we have in the west teaches us to focus strongly on individual differentiation — i.e., seeing differences rather than seeing similarities among individuals. In fact,

our type of subjectivity teaches us to believe our differences, especially our 'superior' differences, are what makes us special. I would suggest, however, that this is another aspect of our subjectivity that is highly problematic in terms of developing a more equitable and loving society.

11   I would argue that the fact that US society is an multi-formational archaeology is, rather than a threat to unity, a source of considerable creativity and is of consistently underestimated value. Those who worry about disunity or lack of civility, whether they realize it or not, are worried about the increasing voice or influence of the non-dominant formations and about losing Anglo male heterosexual dominance, which is the only 'unity' or 'civility' the US has historically ever known. (What, for instance, would unity of civility mean in a multi-formational archaeology with no formation dominant?) Within archaeological theory, I would suggest that an open, multifarious system, while sloppier and noisier, is superior to a closed, more unified system, in the long run, though probably not the short.

12   There are Native American civilizations in which men and women are constituted by different formations, but neither gender is superior to or dominates or excludes the other.

13   There have been some complaints about postmodernist subversions of autonomous subjectivity because it is seen as a conspiratorial decentering of the master individual just as women and people of color have begun to appropriate this individuality. However, I would suggest something like the opposite. The way that subjectivity has been defined within the Western archaeology is in the terms of the dominant formational set — Anglo, male, heterosexual, and elite. Because it is a subjectivity that emerges from a formational set that rules the archaeology, it is a set designed for those who rule both people and the natural world, masters of the universe. Consequently, I would suggest that a decentered subjectivity, an archaeologically enacted subjectivity, is actually closer to the kind of subjectivity enacted by many non-dominant formational sets. For instance, among African-Americans there has long been a de-emphasis of atomistic individuality and an emphasis on a more group-based individuality. There is also some similarity between what I am urging here and the more de-centered self of the Anglo female formational set. In addition, I would argue that an autonomous, atomistic individual subjectivity is one of the barriers to the possibility of a more communal society. A society that sees all of its members as interwoven enactments of a larger fabric is less apt to mistreat or use some of those members for the benefit of others.

14   In fact, I would say that this book in its entirety, like the questioning of the deep rules and assumptions of feminism, race-based perspectives, and queer theory, is an indication that an archaeological shift is underway. I say this because any perspective, including this one, is an enactment of the multi-formational archaeology and is not privileged as some sort of critique that is able to rise above its own historical horizon. This indication is, however, no guarantee that this particular shift will continue; it may reverse, disappear, or catalyze into something very different. History is simply not teleological and certainly not teleological progressive as modernism assumes.

15   What I am describing is a researcher doing research within her/his own archaeology, whereas a researcher from one archaeology researching a different archaeology raises some additional issues. As I have argued, the subjectivity of the researcher, her or his trained mind, the practices of reason/research, and the real are archaeological enactments. When, say, an anthropologist goes to study another culture, she/he is an enactment of one archaeology interacting with the enactments of another archaeology. There is, then, no discovery; there is an interaction. The anthropologist cannot discover in some intra-archaeological way how that other archaeology works because literally who the

researcher is, how she thinks, and how she does research are enactments of her own archaeology. Further, that which is interacted with are the enactments of a different archaeology. If the anthropologist assumes that her/his representation of the other archaeology is real or true, this is archaeological imperialism. Researching across archaeologies is interactional, which, when seen this way rather than seen imperially, can be positive or useful because it is generative of new possibilities. My suggestion to cross-archaeology researchers, then, is that they think archaeologically, that they think of the outcomes of the 'study' of another culture or society not as discovery but as creative, generative archaeological interactions in which neither archaeology is superior. This perspective needs also to be applied to cross-formational research, as when Anglos study Mexican-Americans. What such research has produced in the past, often with destructive consequences, is an Anglo formational view of non-dominant formations, which as I have said above is a kind of imperialism. In contrast, what ought to occur from an archaeological perspective is that cross-formational research should be seen as producing not a view of one formation from the point of view of another but as producing a creative, generative interaction of two equally important formations.

References

AU, K.H. and KAWAKAMI, A.J. (1994) 'Cultural congruence in instruction' in HOLLINS, E.R., KING, J.E. and HAYMAN, W.C. (Eds) *Teaching Diverse Populations: Formulating a Knowledge Base*, Albany, NY, State University of New York Press, pp. 5–24.

BHABHA, H.K. (1985) 'Signs taken for wonders: Questions of ambivalence and authority under a tree outside Delhi, May 1817', *Critical Inquiry*, 12, pp. 144–65.

CAMPBELL, J. (1968) *The Hero with a Thousand Faces* (2nd Ed) Princeton, NJ, Princeton University Press.

DERRIDA, J. (1981) *Positions* (A. Bass, trans) Chicago, IR, Chicago University Press.

DERRIDA, J. (1990) *Glas* (J.P. Leavey, J. and R. Rand, trans) Lincoln, NE, University of Nebraska Press.

ERIBON, D. (1991) *Michel Foucault* (B. Wing, trans) Cambridge, MA, Harvard University Press.

GARCIA, E. (1994) 'Attributes of effective schools for language minority students' in HOLLINS, E.R., KING, J.E. and HAYMAN, W.C. (Eds) *Teaching Diverse Populations: Formulating a Knowledge Base*, Albany, NY, State University of New York Press, pp. 93–104.

GIDDENS, A. (1984) *The Constitution of Society*, Berkeley, CA, University of California Press.

HARRIS, C. (1993) 'Whiteness as property', *Harvard Law Review*, 106, 8, pp. 1707–91.

HOLLINS, E.R. and SPENCER, K. (1990) 'Restructuring schools for cultural inclusion: Changing the schooling process for African American youngsters', *Journal of Education*, 172, 2, pp. 89–100.

JENSEN, R. (1995a) 'Men's lives and feminist theory', *Race, Gender and Class*, 2, 2, pp. 16–25.

LADSON-BILLINGS, G. (1994) *The Dreamkeepers: Successful Teachers of African American Children*, San Francisco, CA, Jossey-Bass.

LADSON-BILLINGS, G. (1995) 'Toward a theory of culturally relevant pedagogy', *American Educational Research Journal*, 32, 3, pp. 465–91.

LATHER, P. and SMITHIES, C. (1995) *Troubling Angels: Women Living with HIV/AIDS*, Columbus, OH, Greyden Press.

MORRISON, T. (1992) *Playing in the Dark: Whiteness and the Literary Imagination*, Cambridge, MA, Harvard University Press.

RICHARDSON, L. (1995) 'Writing-stories: Co-authoring "The Sea Moster", a writing-story', *Qualitative Inquiry*, **1**, 2, pp. 189–203.

TAKAKI, R. (1993) *A Different Mirror: A History of Multicultural America*, Boston, MA, Little, Brown and Co.

TANNEN, D. (1990) *You Just Don't Understand: Women and Men in Conversation*, New York, Ballentine.

TRUEBA, H.T. (1991) 'From failure to success: The roles of culture and cultural conflict in the academic achievement of Chicano students' in VALENCIA, R.R. (Ed) *Chicano School Failure and Success: Research and Policy Agendas for the 1990s*, London, Falmer Press, pp. 151–63.

Index